John Gay
SOCIAL CRITIC

John Gay

SOCIAL CRITIC

By SVEN M. ARMENS

KING'S CROWN PRESS

COLUMBIA UNIVERSITY, NEW YORK

1954

KING'S CROWN PRESS

is an imprint established by Columbia
University Press for the purpose of making certain scholarly material available at
minimum cost. Toward that end, the pub-
lishers have used standardized formats in-
corporating every reasonable economy that
does not interfere with legibility. The author has assumed complete responsibility
for editorial style and for proofreading.

PUBLISHED IN GREAT BRITAIN, CANADA, INDIA, AND PAKISTAN
BY GEOFFREY CUMBERLEGE, OXFORD UNIVERSITY PRESS
LONDON, TORONTO, BOMBAY, AND KARACHI

MANUFACTURED IN THE UNITED STATES OF AMERICA

DEDICATED WITH GRATITUDE

TO MY WIFE

AND MY FATHER

Preface

THE INTENTIONS of this study of John Gay are stated in the Introduction; the impulses which led to it are somewhat harder to elucidate. My interest in Gay was first stimulated by Professor James Sutherland's course in eighteenth-century poetry given at Harvard University in the summer of 1947 and reinforced by my reading of Professor William Henry Irving's biography, *John Gay, Favorite of the Wits*. In its earliest form this study served as a doctoral dissertation at Harvard University, and whatever value it may have is due largely to the expert guidance of Professor George Sherburn who shared his vast knowledge of the Augustan age with me most willingly as he has with so many other neophytes. I should like to take this opportunity to acknowledge also my debt to Professor Sherburn for his many personal kindnesses to me. His encouragement lent a warmth and pleasantness to my graduate study which would otherwise have been sorely missed.

I should also like to offer my special thanks to my colleague Professor W. R. Irwin for his assistance in the preparation of this study and for the many hours which he has devoted to the revising and editing of the manuscript. My appreciation is due also to the other readers of various intermediate forms of the manuscript for their encouragement and helpful criticism—Professors Harry Levin and Walter Jackson Bate of Harvard University and Professors Rhodes Dunlap and Charles B. Woods of the University of Iowa.

I am grateful to Dean Walter F. Loehwing of the Graduate

College of the State University of Iowa, and to Professors Baldwin Maxwell and Bartholow V. Crawford, Head and Acting Head respectively of the Department of English of the State University of Iowa for their assistance in obtaining grants toward the publication of this book; and my thanks must be given to Mr. Henry Wiggins, Dr. William Bridgwater, and Miss Elizabeth Adams of the Columbia University Press for their share in the formulation of this volume.

Finally I should like to acknowledge the kindnesses of the staffs of the Houghton and Widener libraries of Harvard University and of the library of the State University of Iowa.

SVEN M. ARMENS

State University of Iowa
December 20, 1953

Contents

Introduction

But he who studys nature's laws
From certain truth his maxims draws,
And those, without our schools, suffice
To make men moral, good and wise.

DESPITE the excellent biographical study by William Henry Irving,[1] the critical tendency still persists to regard John Gay as either the author of one successful, but trivial, play, *The Beggar's Opera*, or as the minor member of the Scriblerus Club who was the sycophantic friend of Swift and Pope. Perhaps this extended critical analysis of Gay's works is the result of a personal irritation at the injustice of such an estimate. But irritations do have a way of growing to quite sizable proportions, and it seems as if the best means to relieve this particular one would be to analyze the validity of these two common responses through a more complete explication of his poetry than has hitherto been attempted.

To examine the poetry of John Gay properly, the critical tenet of the late seventeenth century which insisted that the pastoral was a minor form of poetry must be somewhat discounted. This categorizing of genres, which perhaps justifiably exalts the epic and the tragic drama, failed to recognize that the pastoral lyric, and most certainly the satiric and burlesque eclogue, also possessed the capacity of transmitting serious moral values. The rules for a correct pastoral, as promulgated by Rapin and Fontenelle, and adapted for English poetry by translators like Creech and theorists like Walsh, needed great modifications for an artist such as Gay, who wished to satirize the perversions of his own social milieu. The too strict application of rules reflects not only a general critical limitation but also, with regard to bucolic literature, the over-all debasement of the pastoral tradition into a court vogue at both Versailles and St. James's. By the early eighteenth century this once meaningful tradition had lost almost all contact with men who had known and preserved in their memories warm feelings for the soil. The pastoral as a means of vital expression was now embodied in the art of Watteau and Fragonard, the romances of D'Urfé and Mlle de Scudéry, and the criticism of the group of sophisticates previously mentioned. The adaptation of the pastoral to the esoteric tastes of an urban court, ignorant in the main of a real rural environment, caused severe degeneration in a literary form which previously had often been employed to communicate intense moral and ethical preoccupations. Lycidas had shed his pastoral robes and cares for a courtier's resplendent silk stockings and carefree existence.

Such was the state of the pastoral at the time Gay was writing. It would be wrong to say that Gay fully intended to rehabilitate the pastoral as a genre, but he did revitalize various types of the eclogue as vehicles for his own conscious ideas and unconscious longings. Through his burlesque he encouraged, perhaps unwittingly, the return of a pastoral based on actual knowledge of [2] and sympathy with inanimate nature and simple rustic people. The *Golden Age* for Gay is not Arcadia, but his youth in Devonshire, fleetingly recaptured by moments spent in the countryside about London. Gay describes no fantastic age of innocence. His shepherds and shepherdesses do not recline on ancient Sicilian hillsides, nor do they gambol about terraced gardens amid artificial fountains and canals. They are, without doubt, grotesque at times, but they are real; as fairly faithful representations of the English peasantry, their customs and superstitions are still verifiable, and their habitat still exists for our inspection.

In this study the term "pastoral" is meant to embody the broadest possible range of connotation. Implied in this usage is the inevitable contrast between town and country which marks the basis of all pastoral writing, and which, as we shall see, particularly characterizes the work of Gay. In many of Gay's poems, the two chief subdivisions of pastoral, the eclogue and the georgic, are explicit in the form, while in the other compositions the pastoral is implicit in the content and feeling. To clarify our concept of Gay as a primarily pastoral poet, an application of the three subsidiary pastoral types embodied in the town and country contrast may be of assistance. W. W. Greg's fine book on *Pastoral Poetry and Pastoral Drama* outlines these types for us as

the ideal where [the contrast] breeds desire for a return to simplicity . . . the realistic where the humour of [the contrast] touches the imagination, and . . . the allegorical where [the contrast] suggests satire on the corruption of an artificial civilization.[3]

In the area of the "ideal," *Polly, Rural Sports, A Contemplation on Night, A Thought on Eternity,* certain parts of *The Shepherd's Week,* and a frequent use of favorable figures of speech and thought relating to the country, all indicate most clearly Gay's nostalgia for his Devonshire youth, his love for the natural beauties of landscape, and his admiration for the noble simplicity of the lives and philosophy of country people. The false idealizations of the debased pastoral of the late seventeenth century, as contrasted with the sincere idealism of Gay's best country poetry, appear in such plays and poems of his as *Dione, Acis and Galatea, The Captives, Panthea, The Story of Cephisa,* and some of his less accomplished pastoral lyrics.

The What D'Ye Call It, the greater part of *The Shepherd's Week*, *The Birth of the Squire*, *Molly Mog*, and portions of *The Epistle to Burlington* present with warmth and humor the actual life of the peasantry, their loves and their labors, in the light of a realistic social context. With the artificial idyll of the court pastoral as a touchstone, the real doings of Bumkinet and Cloddipole acquire additional zest and significance.

A slight idealization on Gay's part may be noted in the fulsome, and perhaps not entirely sincere, epistles written to flatter influential court ladies. These poems are in the Horatian tradition of letters from the country, although by the time of Queen Anne this tradition in England reflects only a request for necessary financial patronage. The idealization through poetic hyperbole is only a customary device. Among these poems is that strange mixture of deep and false feeling, *Mr. Pope's Welcome from Greece*, the *Epistle to a Lady* (her royal highness, Princess Caroline), and the *Epistle to Her Grace, Henrietta, Dutchess of Marlborough*. Fortunately, these poems are very few, and usually serve to satisfy the demands of decorum rather than those of base expediency. The georgic *Trivia*, supported by a few passages in other poems, gives evidence that Gay was absorbed by certain aspects of urban life. However, these aspects are usually presented directly with no idealization.

The tradition of an allegorical pastoral, so suited to the moral and social satire of Virgil, Mantuan, Spenser, and Milton, is modified by Gay's burlesque, which, with its admixture of humor and farce, is represented by *The Beggar's Opera*, *The Mohocks*, *Achilles*, *The Fan*, and parts of *Trivia* and *Newgate's Garland*. This group, which must include those gentler *Fables* based on burlesque by distortion rather than burlesque by satire, is never really vindictive, although these works do satirize mildly in the fashion of *The Tatler* the foibles and corruptions of an artificial urban civilization. In contrast, the more vehement of Gay's town pastorals partake heavily of verse-satire and the Swiftian mood, although never with the intensity of *A Modest Proposal.* In this category we may place parts of *Polly, The Beggar's Opera,* and *Newgate's Garland;* the remainder of the *Fables,* especially those of the second series; *Araminta;* the three town eclogues; and the four *Epistles*—to Pulteney on town evils, represented by those of Paris; to Methuen on patronage and taste; to William Lowndes on the Land Tax Bill; and to Thomas Snow, the goldsmith, on his profiteering from the South Sea Bubble.

It must be noted that certain other songs and ballads of Gay's such as *Daphnis and Chloe* and *The Despairing Shepherd,* and frequently the airs of *The Beggar's Opera, Polly,* and *Achilles,* also contain pastoral elements. Gay's *Tales,* ribald anecdotal verses, similar to the *Fables* in structure, but entirely lacking in their moral purpose, comprise the only significant class of poems that does not express the pastoral contrast between town and country.

If the structural scope and variety of Gay's usage of pastoral forms indicate the existence of suitable molds, we must then inquire as to the worth of the content poured into them. In the late seventeenth century the peripheral elements of life, superficial love relationships, a continual pursuit of banal amusements, and an overemphasis on luxury, formed the chief subject matter of the distorted version of the pastoral then prevalent. Gay must receive more credit than has hitherto been accorded him for his part in the revival and subsequent development of bucolic literature in the eighteenth and nineteenth centuries. Without Gay's re-examination of the rural environment, it is possible that an insufficient impetus would have been provided for the neo-georgic poems of Thomson and Cowper which culminated in the pastoral preoccupations of Wordsworth and the pastoral elegies of Shelley and Arnold. If this chain of development is valid, it becomes apparent that Gay's concern with moral and social problems caused a new interest in the elucidation of the values to be derived from either a town or country existence, and that his examinations reflect the continuance of an older tradition associated with the names of those more famous pastoralists, Virgil, Spenser, and Milton. Any comparison of the pastorals of this triumvirate with passages in their other works provides sufficient evidence that their concern with morals and ethics was not confined to their epics alone. It is the sagacity and wisdom expressed in their pastorals that convince us that the character of the author and his moral views are of more importance than the form in which he chooses to work. A poor pastoral is no more to be condemned than a poor epic; we should not judge the possibilities of the eclogue by the works of Philips any more than we would judge the possibilities of the epic by the deplorable pomposities of Blackmore.

The decline of the epic since Milton's time has forced poets to propound their ethical interests through other genres. Since the time of Gay, the nontraditional use of the pastoral has been valid for the propagation of serious thought, serious thought which Gay himself often attempted. The "ancient" rule that a poet wrote pastorals only in his youth or period of apprenticeship became applicable no longer. Gay failed in his own attempts to write in the style of the outworn pastoral of tradition, but he succeeded admirably when he distorted this genre for his own purposes. Communication of enduring truths is as possible within the pastoral as within any other form; the value and felt meaning which the truth has for the basically competent artist determines its significance in poetry, not the mold in which it is expressed.

We may ask then by what methods does Gay communicate

these positive values? With much ingenuity, he employs a most precise use of still valid forms, such as the modified georgic or the fable, distortion of degenerate forms such as the traditional eclogue, or invention of an original form such as the ballad opera. For direct expression of values, Gay relies on straightforward description, and very detailed statement. For the indirect elucidation of values, he relies on burlesque and satire. His burlesque methods, being fundamentally good-humored, partake of the same gentle spirit of Horatian satire which characterizes the essays of Addison and Steele, although a generous admixture of farce often results in the belly laugh rather than the quiet appreciative smile. Many of his works may be analyzed in terms of the following burlesque categories: the mock-heroic, or irony by magnification; travesty, or irony by diminution; and parody, which Gay employs almost exclusively as a farcical device.[4] Gay's satire, confined mostly to his later works, is Juvenalian in tone, and Juvenalian also in the sense that it attacks the particular vices of flattery, ambition, greed, and lust instead of being more general in its condemnation. Moreover, Juvenalian characteristics appear in the centering of his vehemence on one man, such as Snow or Lowndes in the *Epistles*, or on Sir Robert Walpole in the ballad operas and fables. In its pleasantry, the genial, milder form of mockery inherent in much of Gay's poetry hardly fulfills the tone of savage indignation which Juvenal and Swift have taught us to expect in the cauterizing satirist, preoccupied in his aim of moral improvement. But a further investigation of Gay's themes proves quite conclusively that he desired men in general, as well as Walpole and the Court Party in particular, to acquire much more honesty in their mutual affairs by changing the ethical bases of their actions.

Since the irony of both Gay's burlesque and his satire is based on distortion, it is necessary to be always on the alert when reading him. His ironic subtleties, like those of *Gulliver's Travels,* demand acute attention. Various devices are employed. Direct distortion twists the use of an established form or method to convey Gay's personal meanings. Perversions often illustrate the misuse of man or woman in society, or the misuse of a virtue such as love for evil ends. Debasements lower a satirized subject through analogy to beast or to something ludicrous. Degenerations indicate the decay of the pastoral as a genre, the decay of the nobility as a class, or the decay of love as an impulse toward good. And finally, idealizations, which are actually forms of distortion, are employed, probably unconsciously, to sentimentalize some deep-rooted feeling or attitude, often connected with his love for the country. Of course, to use these terms for the clarification of literary methods, it is obviously quite necessary to remove all derogatory connotations which may cling to them from their ordinary meanings.

An organistic critical method has seemed occasionally helpful in testing each poem for its structure, and in deciding whether the thematic content and development have determined the fused form. But since Gay is a neoclassicist, and therefore thoroughly imbued with mechanistic critical standards of the best sort, we must be constantly alert to place his poems in the Augustan tradition. However, rather than base criticism of Gay's poems on the precepts of one or two specific systems and attempt to squeeze all of them into Procrustean twin beds, it seemed more just to utilize, if only slightly, any critical approach which served to illuminate hitherto unnoticed excellencies of content or technique.[5]

The chief portion of this study is to be devoted to an investigation of the serious elements in John Gay's poetry as they are made explicit in the form of major reiterated themes in both the dramas and the poetry. Neoclassical concepts presuppose many of the same moral, ethical, and artistic beliefs that characterize the sanity, lucidity, and idealism of the true classics of Greece and Rome. A poet, such as John Gay, considered too long to be a "mere elegant trifler," may also be explored for the indirect manifestations of this classic idealism, because, as a satirist, we may assume that he holds to certain standards which are being violated. Men like Aristophanes, Horace, Juvenal, and Rabelais do not present coarse vignettes simply to appeal to the risible and ribald in our natures; they are men, who, like Swift and Pope, in a period of false values reaffirm positive, universal values. It is possible that John Gay was another such man.

Since he is primarily a pastoral poet, the chief unifying theme in our conception of the thoughtful Gay must be the town and country contrast. The categories employed to indicate the structural variety of Gay's works are also useful for indicating the thematic scope of this continually explored contrast. Under the category of "the ideal," Gay examines certain concepts which he associates with the country. Among these themes are primitivism and the character of the noble savage; nostalgia for a personally conceived Golden Age; and a belief that the country affords a means of escape from the frustrations of an urban milieu. These rural associations often represent for Gay the branch of illusion in the illusion-reality dichotomy which is found in almost all serious satiric writing.

The presentation of "realistic" themes reflects Gay's interest in the amusements of country life, the coarse but healthful duties of country toil, the superstitions of country folklore, and the egalitarianism of country society. These exemplifications of rustic reality, softened by humor and warmth, are all meant to serve as pertinent contrasts to the illusions embodied in the courtly pastoral and urban civilization. The detailed realism of *Trivia*, with its pictures of city labors and city crime, is a further attempt to present an en-

vironment directly; in its three sections, we see the life of
the town as it is, not as the court and the fashionable urban
mimics of the court fancy it to be.

To be complete, this category of the "realistic" must be
broadened to include further themes, otherwise we too shall
make the critical error of regarding Gay's poems as mere
records of perceptions. Descriptive realism is occasionally
employed by Gay to vivify his commentaries on the moral
issues contained in his illustrative vignettes. These commentaries are mostly concerned with Gay's conception of
the great chain of being, his hints of philosophical Stoicism,
his antimilitarism, and his attempts to define true liberty.
In this grouping we must also include the conceptual basis
for most of Gay's value judgments, the theme of functionalism, and its corollary, health. Functionalism involves subsidiary themes chiefly concerned with the acquisition, characteristics, and purpose of wisdom; health involves the
problems of humanitarianism, and the approbation or dis-
approbation of natural or unnatural human impulses.

Those themes most associated with the urban milieu frequently elucidate the illusions which town society cherishes
as realities. Gay's burlesque and satire point out the actual
social and moral motives which impel society to delude itself; his purpose is to hold these improper motives up to
rightful scorn and to advocate the necessity of a transforma-
tion of values. The works exposing these illusions must be
assigned to an "allegorical" category, because, although the
illusions are real in the sense of their being actually performed
perversions of the Augustan period, they are false or illusory
in the light of positive, universal values which are not clouded
over by the shades of a provincial and particular civilization.
Attacks on such illusions form the basis for Gay's allegory
both in the *Fables* and in his other works. His satire on the
corruption of urban life points out clearly that the desire to

be "in vogue," the greed for money or power, or the thrill of illicit love, are all shadows in the pool, and the longer we lust for these false meats, the more beastlike our features become. It is only when we have lost the real meats of contentment that we realize what foolish dogs we are. Gay has Jupiter advise the malcontent Countryman in Fable II:vii (so pertinently inscribed, "To Myself"),

> If you true happiness prefer,
> 'Tis to no rank of life confin'd,
> But dwells in ev'ry honest mind.
> Be justice then your sole pursuit,
> Plant virtue, and content's the fruit.[6]

These phrases, which at a hurried glance may appear to be mere abstractions, possess a heartfelt significance for Gay. "True happiness" was a shadow pursued and lost amid his frustration, confusion of desire, and aimlessness of purpose. The problem of "rank in life" frequently perturbed him, caught as he was in a conflict between indolence and a need for personal liberty. His admiration for "the honest mind" is reflected in one of his major themes, *Know Thyself*, and in his love for that most honest of minds, Jonathan Swift; and it is very much to Gay's own credit that Professor Irving can say,

This adjective *honest* is applied to him more frequently than any other. Just as the contemporaries of Shakespeare always spoke of him as gentle Shakespeare, so men of Gay's time were continually recalling honest John Gay, the honest speech of Gay, the inflexible honesty of Gay.[7]

One of Gay's foremost concerns, and probably the source of that bitterness which occasionally discomposed his last years, was a growing preoccupation with the terrifying abstraction, "justice," always the greatest illusion of all, and yet so real, so concrete, that it continually impinges on every man's personal life. Justice, both social and moral, both public and personal, was increasingly Gay's "pursuit," and its usual frustration added to his own sense of discontent. When faced with the actual problems of how to accomplish justice, and how to "plant virtue," Gay retreated, like most of us, into aesthetic speculation. However, it has always been, and still should be, the province of literature to point out the problems of human experience rather than to solve them immediately. Gay must be praised for so preserving the individual integrity of his art that he merited the epithet, "honest," from the greatest of his contemporaries. It is but fair then that we also acknowledge Gay's contribution toward making his era aware of injustice; that we give him due credit for recognizing the vitality of the moral issues at stake in the Augustan age; and that we fully apprehend his attempt to indicate that sin and virtue can never be considered as mere abstractions when the artist has a genuine concern for the welfare of his society.

Gay's elucidations of the true motives underlying the announced aims of human beings show him to be an acute amateur psychologist. In certain of his works, he plays the role of the exposer, and what he exposes of corruption and hypocrisy often leads to a severe depression on his own part. There are moments when Gay cannot merely burlesque or laugh off the sordidness and treachery inherent in many aspects of the town and court milieu. There are moments when even the thought of rural refuge, the comforting philosophy of Leibniz, or the stony virtuousness of Stoicism fail him. Then for a split second we see on the page a cynical and bitter Gay, a disillusioned and frustrated man who recognizes that the human countenance in the mirror could be that of a beast—or worse, that of one who saw no difference between man and beast. Gay may have been smiling in 1720 when he wrote in his ambiguous epitaph,

> Life is a jest; and all things show it.
> I thought so once; but now I know it.

But in 1729, when, sick in body and depressed in mind, he
quotes it again in a letter to Pope (speaking of his death, and
the making of his will, he says, "this is . . . my present sentiment in life."),[8] there was only a terrible mockery left in the
"jest." If illusions of any sort, even good ones, have a moral
reality, they must be expressed in terms of the strength which
they give us in times of distress. In these last years of his life,
it seemed as if Gay's illusions had ceased to give him any
comfort at all. With what a tone of hopelessness he writes to
Swift in 1732, "I find myself dispirited for want of having
some pursuit. Indolence and idleness are the most tiresome
things in the world, and I begin to find a dislike to society." [9]
This from a man to whom good company and laughter and
wit had once been everything.

Lest this depiction of Gay in his least Gay-like moments
confuse the issue of this study, let us restate its aim. Of Gay,
we may say with Prufrock, "I am not Hamlet, nor was I
meant to be"; but we must also say, as a corrective, that he
was not meant to be an eighteenth-century Prufrock. The
chief purpose of this investigation is to look upon Gay as a
serious figure, to try to determine what he thought about in
his serious moments and what he was genuinely serious about.
In elucidating these moral issues or values, as they appear in
individual poems or plays, it was necessary to separate them
momentarily from their interaction within the human matrix
for purposes of analysis. Particular issues have been investi-
gated in what seemed to be their most pertinent contexts
within the scope of Gay's works. Because mere multiplicity
of reference is helpful supporting evidence in this type of
study, references have been made to both themes and poems
outside the specific chapters in which they are treated most

fully as the chief topics of consideration. This is an inevitable consequence when one attempts to explain the dramatic presentations of a poet whose mirroring of our natural and unnatural impulses is as subtle and complex as the impulses themselves. Mephistopheles showed Marlowe's Faustus cardboard figures of allegory, a masque of sins which entertained statically but which did not instruct or terrify. Gay attempts to dramatize these sins or impulses dynamically by picturing general types reacting to particularized exemplary circumstances. The amount of his success can usually be measured by the intensity of his hatred for the vice or his love for its opposite virtue.

CHAPTER I

Implications of an Age of Innocence

> Ye happy fields, unknown to noise and strife,
> The kind rewarders of industrious life;
> Ye shady woods, where once I us'd to rove;
> Alike indulgent to the muse and love;
> Ye murm'ring streams that in *Maeanders* roll,
> The sweet composers of the pensive soul.

WITH THE INTRUSION of countesses and court ministers into
the sacred confines of Arcadia, any respecter of the simple
morality of virtuous shepherds realized that it was time for
these shepherds to move elsewhere. Under the literary aegis
of Aphra Behn, and with the differing philosophical sanctions
of Locke and Shaftesbury, the poets and dramatists of the
eighteenth century substituted a spatial for a temporal distance and moved their Golden Age of Innocence to far-off
exotic realms which actually existed in their own time. One
of the most popular pseudo-Arcadias was the West Indies,
one of the possessions where British criminals were transported and where slaves were sold from British ships. The
Indies furnished a perfect social atmosphere for the town
and country contrast of the pastoral. The evils of civilization, represented by the practices of the plantation owners,
traders, and London criminals, existed side by side with the
virtues of happy and honorable primitivism, as exemplified
by the natives and the African slaves. Thus, Virgil's Menalcas
becomes Aphra Behn's Oroonoko or John Gay's Cawwawkee,
and the "fine sentiments" of Virgil's shepherds are echoed in

Gay's noble savages. To say that Gay actually believed that
the values he respected were part and parcel of this primitive
society would be a misstatement. Gay was too much of a
cynic to believe in the actual existence of Arcadian Utopias
of any sort, but he did see the expediency of using this type
of a society in *Polly* for the propagation of those moral concepts which he found more prevalent in simpler societies like
that of England's countryside. Gay's work constantly involves a contrast between the utopia of innocence and the
corruptions of civilization as known in his day. One can see
this fully exemplified in his *Polly* and, perhaps more naturally,
in *Rural Sports*.

The Preface to *Polly* (1729), which is certainly the defense
of an honorable man genuinely concerned about his personal
integrity, declares Gay's principles and disavows certain
slanderous implications of sedition which had arisen because
of the suppression of *Polly* by the Lord Chamberlain. In this
preface Gay asserts that "my only intention was to lash in
general the reigning and fashionable vices, and to recommend
and set virtue in as amiable a light as I could." "The reigning
and fashionable vices" are primarily those of the town, and
by extension, civilization; "the amiable light" in which virtue
is to be set is the primitive environment of the West Indies,
and, as we shall see, by indirect idealization, the remembered
environment of Devonshire.

The core of Gay's benevolent idealizations or illusions,
those which sustain human dignity in terrifying or debasing
situations, is stated immediately in the first air (XL) of the
opera sung by the hero, Cawwawkee:

> The body of the brave may be taken,
>   If chance bring on our adverse hour;
> But the noble soul is unshaken,
>   For that still is in our power. (p. 569)

Such sentiments embody the essence of what has been called the cult of independence in Gay.[1] In Cawwawkee's aria we recognize that for Gay true liberty lies in a sense of personal honesty, the ability to face one's own conscience. Although it may be difficult to imagine the corpulent and comfortable body of Gay swinging at the end of Macheath's (Morano) gibbet, we do know that his body had been prey to the tortures of gout and severe inflammations.[2] Regardless of the complaints which he, like all of us, confided in his letters to his closest friends, we can see in this passage and throughout his works that "in adverse hours" nobility of soul is constantly advocated as the basis for a consoling stoic courage.

The ingredients of this nobility are further defined in *Polly* as honesty, friendship, gratitude, a sense of honor, and a sense of justice. Cawwawkee, early in the play, states his ethical position to Polly, "You may do as you please. But whatever you promise for me, contrary to the *European* custom, I will perform. For tho' a knave may break his word with a knave, an honest tongue knows no such distinctions" (p. 574). It is clear then that though certain sections of *Polly* are meant only to burlesque the perversions of the drama of sensibility, Gay's insistence on the value of certain ethical concepts must not be disregarded. In *Polly* it is much more often the stock characters who are being mocked rather than the sentiments which they express, for these same sentiments are reiterated with all possible seriousness in the *Fables* which Gay was writing at approximately the same time. The primitivism of human relationships in the West Indies then brings daily living down to a matter of basic integrity. The simplest and least complex impulses are the right ones, the virtuous ones. The man who will not break his word with a knave will naturally be honest with everyone.

The second ingredient of nobility is friendship, exalted

in true classical fashion above the inferior concept of romantic love:

> Love with beauty is flying,
> At once 'tis blooming and dying,
> But all seasons defying,
> Friendship lasts on the year. (p. 577)

After the pirates have been properly disposed of, Pohetohee,
the prototype of the noble ruler, honors Polly with his gratitude, which, with social love and friendship, form the chief
components of eighteenth-century benevolence:

How shall I return the obligations I owe you? Every thing in
my power you may command. In making a request, you confer
on me another benefit. For gratitude is oblig'd by occasions of
making a return: And every occasion must be agreeable, for a
grateful mind hath more pleasure in paying than receiving.
(p. 585)

Polly, with an air of virtue being its own reward, reciprocates,
"The pleasure of having serv'd an honourable man is a sufficient return."

It is apparent that to Gay the inner sense of honor so extolled by Stoic philosophers (*Polly*, p. 569) should be sufficient grounds for enduring all of life's misfortunes, and
even for gaining that happiness which comes with virtuous
self-approbation. When Morano first captures Cawwawkee
and attempts to bribe or torture him into betraying the num-
ber and location of his troops, Cawwawkee firmly refuses,
knowing that "[his] virtue is [his] own," even though his
life may be at the mercy of this ruthless town pirate. Jenny
and the other members of the gang comment superciliously
upon his ignorance in preferring pain to profit.[3] But the noble
heroine, Polly, penetrates to the center of Gay's regard for
this type of virtue with the aside: "How happy are these

savages! Who would not wish to be in such ignorance." Since Gay relies heavily on irony in his dramas to bring out his positive values by negative implication, this ignorance is in reality one of the purest uses of man's natural reason. Although the tones of Cawwawkee and Pohetohee bespeak passionate conviction of ideal moral principles, their passion is based on a Swiftian common-sense sort of reason which is the equivalent of the natural impulse toward good found in Shaftesbury's natural man. On the other hand, the clever reasoning, constantly employed by the pirates to justify their criminal methods, is actually based on an overwhelming passion for money. Common sense tells Gay that honor, with all its ramifications, is the only reality both ideally and practically; money and power are the phantoms fools pursue.[4]

Indicative of Gay's attitude toward justice and the divergent moral codes of town and country is the caustic irony implied in Pohetohee's denunciation of Morano, the town-bred pirate:

Shall robbers and plunderers prescribe rules to right and equity? Insolent madman! Composition with knaves is base and ignominious. Tremble at the sword of justice, rapacious brute. (p. 581)

Such remarks suggest the abyss between the town as Gay knows it and the country as he nostalgically remembers it. In London and at Court (with special innuendoes cast at Walpole and political life), robbers and plunderers *do* prescribe the rules. The inference is that those rapacious brutes who nourish themselves on money, swollen as they are with the fat of power and the sweat of lechery, have buried the sword of justice in Fleet Ditch—and human dignity with it. Pohetohee, again speaking for Gay's most sincere beliefs, condemns the plea of human frailty by Ducat, the utterly base plantation owner, with this humanistic outburst:

How different are your notions from ours! We think virtue, honour, and courage as essential to man as his limbs, or senses; and in every man we suppose the qualities of a man, till we have found the contrary. But then we regard him only as a brute in disguise. How custom can degrade nature! (p. 576)

The natural man then is the only true *man* in Gay's particular version of the neoclassical humanistic tradition; those who have succumbed to the corruptions and customs of civilization embodied in the town have forfeited their right to the title. The basis of the natural man's dignity is of course his belief in justice, that final ingredient of nobility. It is really the justice and virtue of the Stoic Cicero's *De Officiis* which eventually forms the sentiment expressed in Cawwawkee's battle cry (Air LIV):

> We the sword of justice drawing,
>   Terror cast in guilty eyes;
>   In its beam false courage dies. (p. 580)

And when the resolution of the dramatic action occurs, sure enough, Morano flies "with all the cowardice of guilt upon him." Because he is evil, because he cannot face the accusation of "his own conscience," all his bravado and bluff desert him. Justice triumphs because only the good are truly brave. Polly sums up Gay's Stoic view of human character with this prose epigram:

Thousands have false courage enough to be vicious; true fortitude is founded upon honour and virtue. (p. 583)

When Pohetohee, not realizing that the loss of her beloved Macheath is the cause of Polly's sorrow, asks her, "Can my treasures make you happy?" she replies, "Those who have them not think they can; those who have them know they cannot." We think immediately of the younger Gay who in 1720 refused to sell his South Sea stock with a modest return on his investment in the hopes that he could accumulate an income sufficient for absolute independence. We know that he lost everything on this risk and spent the next few years trying vainly to attain a place at Court that could give him adequate financial security. Now in 1729 with the economic independence he so desired guaranteed by the phenomenal runs of *The Beggar's Opera* and the lucrative subscription list from his edition of *Polly*, he realized with full force that his moral principle of condemning money was even more pertinent to his own daily life. He had his independence and his liberty to do as he wished, but he found that mere financial independence was not enough. The amusements of society palled; [5] he could not buy genuine satisfaction, let alone complete happiness. He discovered that independence was one of the greatest illusions of all, that the mutual dependence of friends was the only real liberty for a man without a family. The Duke and Duchess of Queensberry were good and true friends, but something really stimulating was lacking in Gay's relationship with them; he did not see Pope enough; he did not see Swift at all.

Where then was happiness to be found? For Gay the sad answer was—in a realm of illusion or idealization—in childhood where there can be dreams without responsibilities—in the surroundings of childhood which for so many English authors before the twentieth century meant pleasant fields and a healthful environment. The emotional combination of childhood and natural beauty which we find in poets such as Vaughan, Traherne, Shenstone, and Wordsworth is also to be found in Gay, and the means of its expression need not necessarily be "romantic" at all. But in the cloudy realm of nostalgia, strange associations often take place, and an important one for Gay was the connection of the noble virtues which he respected and elucidated in *Polly* with poverty as well as with the country environment. When Cawwawkee and Polly discover their mutual virtuousness, the scene (II, xi) is *A room of a poor cottage;* and when Polly assures the pirates of Cawwawkee's honesty, the best analogy she can think of is "You may rely on the prince's word as much as if he was a poor man." Gay seems to associate poverty with nobility and honesty, honesty with peace of mind, and peace of mind with the country life. Perhaps only the fairly well-to-do sons of country gentlemen or respected Barnstaple families can afford to indulge in this type of nostalgia; perhaps the dream country of Gay's vague yearnings is really peopleless; his peasants of *The Shepherd's Week* are certainly not portrayed as "noble"; and the pleasures of *Rural Sports* are those which a busy freeholder or tenant farmer would not have too much time for; but the general atmosphere of both of these poems and of the majority of his references to the country emphasize rosy cheeks and good simple hearts as opposed to the pallor of the town which sets its gray stamp on the languid faces and diseased hearts of city people.

Only wasted effort would result from any attempt to prove that Gay's love of simple country folk and country places is expressed in mystical or transcendental terms. He observes closely the decorum associated with the topographical poem, and *Rural Sports*, probably Gay's most detailed examination of the country environment, is formulated according to the most proper eighteenth-century manner. *Rural Sports* is an Augustan georgic in the Virgilian tradition, and, like all georgics, it deals with the occupations of the country and the beauties of landscape and wild life, with some philosophical concepts injected for nobility of tone. The georgic may be distinguished from the simpler and more dramatic eclogue by its descriptive qualities and its more technical subject matter. It is associated with certain works of the classical authors, Hesiod, Lucretius, Horace, Ovid, and particularly Virgil.

Medieval allegories in verse form occasionally contained passages on specific skills. Didactic poems on science and pseudo science were popular in the Renaissance, and pamphlets similar to the *Farmer's Almanac* included parts of Thomas Tusser's *Five Hundred Points of Good Husbandry* even into the nineteenth century.

The growth of didactic verse after the Middle Ages was due to Petrarch's confusion of the scholar and the poet. This confusion led to the principle that all knowledge belonged to the province of poetry and that fine Latin versification enhanced the appeal of practical knowledge. "The common ideal among theorists of the Renaissance was eclectic: poetry may deal with any subject so long as it be transmuted with beauties of invention and ornament." [6] This familiar Horatian precept of mingling delight with instruction served to combat three powerful opposing precepts: namely, Plato's censure of overexciting the emotions as detrimental to order; the Christian's disapproval of poetry as pagan, despite his own use of it for allegorical didactic purposes; and the new science's distrust of imagination and the passions. Nevertheless, theorists who partially adopted these three points of view forced certain types of poetry to emphasize instruction above delight. Simultaneously, these theorists also encouraged the adoption of that precision in style which we connect with Ciceronianism in prose. This tradition of meticulous craftsmanship was best exemplified in poetry by the *Georgics* of Virgil, and thus their subject matter and fine Latin style set the pattern for the didactic poem. [7]

The English poets of the sixteenth century did not follow the classical didactic models as closely as the Italian poets of the time did, but in the seventeenth century, under the influence of the Royal Society, the critical leadership of Rapin, and the many new translations of classical poets and neo-Latin didactic writers such as Vida and Fracastoro, Eng-

lish poets began to recognize didactic verse as a traditional
genre. In the eighteenth century, under the guidance of
Dryden's third theory of *imitation,* a method which involves
variation within the confines of some other accepted literary
model, at least two important types of didactic literary
imitation may be distinguished; the Horatian tradition, exemplified by Pope's *Essay on Criticism,* and the Virgilian,
exemplified by Gay's *Rural Sports.* In addition to serious
imitations, we also have satirical or burlesque adaptations of
these two traditions which rely heavily on English scenes
and conditions; the Horatian being represented by poems
such as William King's *Art of Cookery,* and the Virgilian
by Gay's *Trivia.* The first statement in English of the principles of Virgilian didactic poetry is often credited to Addison, who felt that the form of the georgic could be best
adapted to analyzing nature. Addison considered practical
precepts important, but he thought they should be concealed
in detailed description and a casual tone. Moralizing and
exemplary digressions should be couched in noble and dignified terms.[8] Later imitators of Virgil agreed that it was proper
to use the figures of extended simile and metaphor, invoca-
tions, moral parallels, episodic variations, and mythological
allusions. Additional georgic elements which might be included were passages on the origin and development of something, such as Virgil's care of bees, or Gay's tracing of the
rise of the patten; discussions of the necessary physical and
mental qualities suitable to the practice of certain skills; and
variations of the concept which asserts that deity is revealed
through natural phenomena.

    Rural Sports, like most of the georgic poems of the eight-
eenth century, is more a direct imitation of Virgil himself
than of his neoclassical imitators. But it is hardly as strict an
imitation as John Philips' *Cyder* which actually determined
the form of the English georgic. It is more of a preceptive

poem on the field sports of fishing, fowling, and hunting. The didactic content is less than in either Virgil's or Philips' georgics, and some of the conventions, such as the episodic variation, which Gay uses so frequently in *Trivia*, are omitted entirely. Like *The Shepherd's Week*, *Rural Sports* gives us information on country labors and amusements, and precise descriptions of natural beauty, communicating and evoking keen emotional responses.

It is the theme of functionalism, operating as it does on many levels, which sounds most frequently the didactic note in Gay's poetry. We may distinguish the direct practical lesson which gives advice on how to accomplish some particular task or skill; the social lesson with benevolence as its standard criterion which condemns abuses through satire; and the moral lesson which is pointed up through the *Fables* or through fabulistic passages in other works. The direct practical lesson is the kind we encounter most readily in a georgic such as *Rural Sports*. This poem deals with its problems in the same manner as do the more technical georgics, but it has more of the tone of a friend writing of some heartfelt event to another friend who has shared such precious moments with him before. And, of course, this is precisely the case. The inscription to Pope, the references in the first eight lines to Pope's *Pastorals* and to *Windsor Forest*, and the line, "Friendship, for sylvan shades, the palace flies," introduce a personal element quite unusual in Gay's poems, and a tonal background of mutual regard for the life enjoyed in rural retreats. Alexander Pope was probably much more interested in the construction of the ideal rural home at Twickenham, in swelling the terrace or sinking the Grot with Nature never to be forgot, yet he too would be charmed by the details of the much simpler construction of "the curious fly," and the advice on how to angle correctly for the finny brood. The importance of eternal order, as estab-

lished by God in the original "state of Nature," is reflected
strongly in the following didactic passage:

> To frame the little animal, provide
> All the gay hues that wait on female pride,
> Let nature guide thee; sometimes golden wire
> The shining bellies of the fly require;
> The peacock's plumes thy tackle must not fail,
> Nor the dear purchase of the sable's tail.
> Each gaudy bird some slender tribute brings,
> And lends the growing insect proper wings:
> Silks of all colours must their aid impart,
> And ev'ry fur promote the fisher's art.
> So the gay lady, with expensive care,
> Borrows the pride of land, of sea, and air;
> Furs, pearls, and plumes, the glittering thing displays,
> Dazles our eyes, and easie hearts betrays. (ll. 177–190)

We see above that Gay also recommends that we hearken
to the "voice of Nature" which spake thus to us in Pope's
Essay on Man:

> Go, from the Creatures thy instructions take:
>
> . . . .
>
> Thy arts of building from the bee receive;
> Learn of the mole to plough, the worm to weave;
> (ll. 172–176)

The natural man, celebrated in Epistle III of Pope's poem
(ll. 147–160), could rely on his Instinct as did Cawwawkee
and be sure that "Reason's part" was being correctly exer-
cised. By close observation of his friends, the beasts and in-
sects, he could learn "laws as wise as Nature," and methods
of constructive art. But when he becomes a "foe to Nature"
and the victim of his own pride, he subjects art to artifice.
This is also the underlying contrast in Gay's passage—the
precision of the fisherman's art serves a functional purpose;

the plumes and scarfs and furs and silks serve to catch the unwary fish who provides necessary relaxation for the country gentleman, or, better still, food for the family of a hungry freeholder. But the misuse of natural life, the exploitation of man's divinely created friends for the luxury and satisfaction of a town woman's false pride, results in a social, if not a moral evil, whereby the gulled lover is caught by the gay lady (who may be either a marital prospector, a gold digger, or a prostitute).

It is against the background of this frequently employed opposition of town and country that we gain our insight into Gay's principles and his use of Augustan social and intellectual ideas. The countryman, being closer to nature and thus better able to observe and absorb natural laws and skills at their source, is assumed to partake of Pope's natural reason and so be less corrupt. He is also assumed to be more purposeful in his daily life and less given to indulgence in useless luxuries. We must note, however, that in this form of sentimentalism Gay and the eighteenth century often fail to ascribe his "favored" lot to the hardships of practical necessity. Nevertheless, it was probably no severe aberration of taste on Gay's part to prefer the warm cosy thatch-roofed cottages of Devonshire to the cold palaces of Vanbrugh.

In addition to the lessons on how to do something, the functionalism of the georgic also extends to a discussion of rural occupations, such as Virgil's descriptions in his first two georgics of preparing soils and cultivating trees. In *Rural Sports* the discussion centers primarily on rural amusements rather than on rural duties. The joys and skills of fishing, fowling, and hunting are substituted for the cares and processes of crop rotation, planting, and breeding, but the emphasis is still on the healthfulness and social value of the life of the husbandman in contrast to the diseased and worthless life of the citizen of the town. The injection of a moralistic

apostrophe or encomium of country life is part of the tradition and yet it also reflects Gay's deepest feelings. Virgil
pictures his Roman peasant in this manner:

> O fortunatos nimium, sua si bona norint,
> Agricolas, quibus ipsa procul discordibus armis
> Fundit homo facilem victum iustissima Tellus!
> Si non ingentem foribus domus alto superbis
> Mane salutantum Totis vomit aedibus undam.[9]

And Gay, who regrets having been "long in the noisie town
. . . immur'd," where "faction embroils the world," finally
chooses like Pomfret a calm retreat where he can rest his
fatigued mind from the dishonesty and calumny of the court:

> 'Tis not that rural sports alone invite,
> But all the grateful country breaths delight;
> Here blooming health exerts her gentle reign,
> And strings the sinews of th' industrious swain.
>
> (ll. 31–34)

Rural Sports presents a very pleasant picture of Gay
spending a day in the environment he loved so well, wandering about, observing, and speculating, even lying on a "mossy
couch" by a brook rereading Virgil's georgics. He gives us
(ll. 71–90) a compact summary in twenty lines of his Mantuan master's four poems, bringing out the full flavor of
Virgil's descriptions of "the various rural toil," as comparisons for his own genre sketches of the occupations he has
noted during his day in the fields. Gay employs the usual
georgic division of the day into time elements, and lines 31
to 120 may be considered another *L'Allegro* describing vignettes of a day in the country with a similar tone of pastoral
speculation. This small poem within a poem begins with an
evocative picture of a spring harvest. It is a harvest redolent
with the fresh sweet smell of hay, newly cut, and it seems to

contain the very essence of that nostalgic purity which Gay
associated with the country:

> When the fresh spring in all her state is crown'd,
> And high luxuriant grass o'erspreads the ground,
> The lab'rer with the bending scythe is seen,
> Shaving the surface of the waving green,
> Of all her native pride disrobes the land,
> And meads lays waste before his sweeping hand:
> While with the mounting sun the meadow glows,
> The fading herbage round he loosely throws;
> But if some sign portend a lasting show'r,
> Th' experienc'd swain foresees the coming hour,
> His sun-burnit hands the scatt'ring fork forsake,
> And ruddy damsels ply the saving rake;
> In rising hills the fragrant harvest grows,
> And spreads along the field in equal rows. (ll. 39–52)

The ultimate healthiness of these sunburnt swains and ruddy
damsels is meant to picture what the ideal country life in
accord with nature can be. This life is ordered, it has an
innate decorum of its own which is violated by the intrusion
of town influences; for example, the country-bred girl returning home to vaunt the foibles and airs of the town over
her friends; or the country people being driven to the town
by enclosure where they must endure the distressing social
evils of factory and slum life. In our examination of Gay's
rural milieu, we must disregard momentarily the excitements
and advantages of the pursuit of knowledge. This disregard
is a necessary concomitant of the pastoral ideal because the
shepherd, as in Gay's *Introduction to the Fables*, possesses
natural wisdom drawn from the divine source of Nature herself; he is not the Miltonic university-trained man browsing
for a day at Horton. The philosopher of Gay's *Introduction*
recognizes the superior wisdom of the shepherd, because the

shepherd truly knows himself which is the aim of all philosophy and art. Study and human experience must be translated into terms of self-betterment so that we can be freed
from ourselves to exert whatever divine understanding and
sympathy may reside in us for the betterment of others. The
implication of all pastoral forms of poetry, including *Rural
Sports*, is that this country life is the ideal for all mankind;
the illusions of power, vast armies, and subtle gradations in
bombs; of money, vast houses, and subtle distinctions in rank;
of love, vast varieties of sexual partners, and subtle modifications of pursuit are meant to crumble before the idyllic pastoral picture of physical and mental health which Augustan
reason, based on natural instinct, immediately recognizes as
true. Gay, like Thomson and most of the preromantic poets
of the century, does not investigate the spiritual relations of
the peasant to his environment with really painstaking care.
He and the others lack, and perhaps it is a good thing, the
mystical tool of a transcendental philosophy; but most of
them do apprehend the connection of the two types of health
with environment. Gay speculates, with the almost inevitable
analogy:

> What happiness the rural maid attends,
> In chearful labour while each day she spends!
> She gratefully receives what heav'n has sent,
> And, rich in poverty, enjoys content:
> (Such happiness, and such unblemish'd fame
> Ne'er glad the bosom of the courtly dame. (ll. 410–415)

Gay reaffirms what the classic and neoclassic traditions had
discovered to be basic to man; physical health to give him
the strength to subsist by his own hands; and mental health,
gained by worthwhile labor close to the soil, to prevent him
from becoming the victim of those frustrations and anxieties

which the needlessly complex civilization of the town imposes upon him.

The popularity of georgic poems in the eighteenth century reflects the traditionally English taste for the country and its folk, which we find so obvious in such diverse authors as Thomson, Dyer, Fielding, Goldsmith, and Crabbe, as well as Gay, who shares some traits with each of them. These poems also reflect a growing interest in the precise details of landscape as contrasted with the vaguer, more generalized pictures that characterize the work of Milton and other earlier English poets. It is in this increasingly keen perception of landscape, in the more acute observation and notation of the variance of the seasons and their moods, and in a growing affinity for the animate and inanimate objects of nature that we must look for the seedlings and shoots of preromanticism in Gay. It is obvious that the use of the term *preromanticism* to indicate the development of a rather dubious green stem into the gorgeous flower of romanticism is a bit extreme. The feeling for nature in the eighteenth century is fully as genuine as that which we attribute somewhat too exclusively to Wordsworth or Byron, but the expression of this feeling and the connotations of ordered country life which it implies are different.[10] Because of the degeneration of the eclogue, the georgic had become the main instrument for the sketching of realistic scenes of country life and natural beauty. Small sketches such as that of Gay's harvest morning were expanded into the full-size portraiture of Thomson's *Seasons;* the modification of the georgic into the descriptive-didactic poem provided a genre which could assimilate on a large scale the increased knowledge of natural science and the theories of benevolence and primitivism which arose during the first half of the eighteenth century. Wordsworth, as we know, only incorporated these already existing theories into his poetry, especially the georgic devices of moral digression, topographical setting, and seasonal structure, and then amplified them with doctrines from Rousseau, Godwin, and other philosophers whose tenets sanctioned the French Revolution. If we accept the critical belief that Wordsworth's poetry contains the essence of the romantic attitude toward nature, that attitude which posits a close affinity between man, animals, landscape, and the phenomena of sun, wind, and rain, it may be profitable to examine Gay's poetry in the light of his pre-Wordsworthian (preromantic) use of similar georgic attitudes and devices.

We have already noticed Gay's eulogizing of friendship and the rural retreat; in the following passage, we notice an example of his sensitivity to the particular nuances which seem to be inherent in each part of the day:

> Now when the height of heav'n bright *Phoebus* gains,
> And level rays cleave wide the thirsty plains,
> When heifers seek the shade and cooling lake,
> And in the middle pathway basks the snake;
> O lead me, guard me from the sultry hours,
> Hide me, ye forests, in your closest bowers:
> Where the tall oak his spreading arms entwines,
> And with the beech a mutual shade combines;
> Where flows the murm'ring brook, inviting dreams,
> Where bord'ring hazel overhangs the streams
> Whose rolling current winding round and round,
> With frequent falls makes all the wood resound;
> Upon the mossy couch my limbs I cast,
> And ev'n at noon the sweets of ev'ning taste. (ll. 53–66)

The constant interpenetration of man, beast, and nature is fully apparent here; the use of the heifer seeking shade, and the snake basking in the middle pathway serve as symbolic realizations of the intense heat of the sultry midday hours. The sincere plea to the forests to hide him in their cathedral-

like coolness, where the brook sounds are like quiet organ
music, is similar to the apostrophes of Wordsworth to daffo-
dils, or nightingales, or favorite sites in the Lake Country.
It is no mere conventional address; behind it lies a genuine
feeling of shared existence. The climax of Gay's sensitivity in
this passage appears in the concluding lines where, though
he knows it is noon, the emotion which suffuses him is associated with the peacefulness and sense of refuge characteristic
of twilight.

The contemplative resigned melancholy of dusk, most apparent in the tones of Gray's *Elegy*, seems to be the traditional literary time for speculation on life's grander mysteries. At the close of his day in the country, Gay catches the
mood of this moment perfectly:

> Or when the ploughman leaves the task of day,
> And trudging homeward whistles on the way;
> When the big-udder'd cows with patience stand,
> Waiting the strokings of the damsel's hand;
> No warbling chears the woods; the feather'd choir
> To court kind slumbers to their sprays retire;
> When no rude gale disturbs the sleeping trees,
> Nor aspen leaves confess the gentlest breeze; (ll. 91–98)

and caught in the midst of this meaningful silence, he tells us

> Engag'd in thought, to *Neptune's* bounds I stray,
> To take my farewel of the parting day;
> For in the deep the sun his glory hides,
> A streak of gold the sea and sky divides;
> The purple clouds their amber linings show,
> And edg'd with flame rolls ev'ry wave below:
> Here pensive I behold the fading light,
> And o'er the distant billow lose my sight. (ll. 99–106)

The tone here is one which anticipates the emotional response
which Burke associated with the *sublime* (although the influ-

ence of Longinus's theory is possible), especially in its sense
of infinity as the eyesight follows the successive flame-edged
waves onward and onward into the gold and purple sunset.
Gay, for a moment, is overwhelmed by an impression of
eternality, evoked by the natural majesty of sea and sun.

Another tone in Gay anticipating preromanticism is one
similar to Richard Payne Knight's *pathetic*,[11] the definition
of which was based on the associative theory that our greatest
sympathies are invoked by those objects or situations which
we like best. Such an object or situation possesses an actual
force whereby its inclusion in a descriptive passage can make
this passage a real instrument for evoking certain responses
in the reader. Knight's study concentrated on the pathetic,
and we shall discover that this sense of pathos is very active
in Gay, probably because of his regard for the Latin poetry
of the Silver Age which also emphasized the pathos of human
situations. Thackeray found this tone manifested especially
in the ballads of *The Beggar's Opera* and *Polly*, but he
realized that it is basic to all of Gay's poetry.

What used to be said about Rubini, *qu'il avait des larmes dans
la voix*, may be said of Gay . . . there is a peculiar, hinted, pathetic sweetness and melody. It charms and melts you. It's in-
definable, but it exists; and is the property of John Gay's and
Oliver Goldsmith's best verse, as fragrance is of a violet, or
freshness of a rose.[12]

This "pathetic sweetness" permeates all of *Rural Sports*,
probably because it is the poem of Gay's which most reflects
his nostalgia for the country and its virtues. But the poem
does more than merely reflect a type of homesickness. For
example, let us look at a very specific use of the pathetic
which illustrates that affinity for animals and their feelings
which is characteristic of such poets as Cowper, Burns, and
Wordsworth. At the end of the stirring description of the
chase, enlivened by the "jocund thunder" and "smoking

nostrils" of the hounds, the hare is tiring badly; Gay sympathizes with his plight, and meditates on death, the relentless pursuer:

> Where shall the trembling hare a shelter find?
> Hark! death advances in each gust of wind!
> New stratagems and doubling wiles she tries,
> Now circling turns, and now at large she flies;
> Till spent at last, she pants, and heaves for breath,
> Then lays her down, and waits devouring death.
>
> (ll. 382–387)

For though the chase is "a pleasant task," it implies an evident departure from the golden age voiced by Pope in the *Essay on Man* when

> Man walked with beast, joint tenant of the shade;
> The same his table, and the same his bed;
> No murder clothed him, and no murder fed.
>
> (III, 152–154)

This humanitarian sentiment, echoed also in *Windsor Forest* (ll. 93–134), lies at the root of Gay's attitude toward animals. The personal note, rare in Augustan poetry because it reflects the particular or the nonuniversal (aberrations of order or individual passions), emerges seldom in Gay's work, but when it does it usually indicates a very genuine belief. The sentiment of benevolence toward animals, most obvious in Gay's protest against the lashing of horses by draymen in *Trivia* (II, 231–242), is to be noted again in *Rural Sports* when Gay avows that he will not trap his finny victims at night with nets, nor drain the ponds for carp, nor use such unfair means of capture as the "barbed spear." He will not even stoop to torture the worm by twining him around his steel hook (ll. 261–267). Gay's attitude of pity never becomes completely romantic in the dangerously maudlin sense, because as a neoclassicist, he values mankind above all other life, and

because the smooth operation of the great chain of being demands the use and occasional subjection of the lesser elements in the scale for the welfare of the higher elements.[13] This concept of ordered preservation serves as the basis for the pursuit of the "rav'nous otter" by fierce dogs, because the otter is apt to destroy "the num'rous finny race" who provide food and relaxation for man. Thus, the dogs, who often "tear with goary mouths the screaming prey," are really the divine instruments for the upholding of the natural balance of this particular situation. Possibly part of Gay's cynicism and bitterness and ineffective stoicism come from such recognitions of evil as inevitable necessity; Gay was not a man to reconcile such necessity with his deepest feelings of error in the scheme of things.

Additional indications of preromanticism in *Rural Sports* may be found in the associational effects of the seasons on the moods of men. Gay notes that "As in successive course the seasons roll,/So circling pleasures recreate the soul." It is this similar regeneration within both nature and man which has prompted Gay to flee the city and indulge his wish for at least a partial participation in the beauty of a spring harvest. The coldness and artifice of town life are doubly repugnant in the spring to Gay and all mankind; that apathy within living creatures which characterizes the end of winter is only really banished by a return to the more primitive relationship with nature that man was meant to possess and that animals are still believed to possess.

In "Friday" of *The Shepherd's Week*, the approach of winter mirrors the psychological state of Grubbinol over the death of Blouzelinda; Bumkinet asks,

> Why, Grubbinol, dost thou so wistful seem?
> There's sorrow in thy look, if right I deem.
> 'Tis true, yon oaks with yellow tops appear,
> And chilly blasts begin to nip the year;

> From the tall elm a show'r of leaves is born,
> And their lost beauty riven beeches mourn. (ll. 1–6)

Not knowing of Blouzelinda's death, Bumkinet, the simple shepherd of the country environment, immediately attributes Grubbinol's sorrowful mood to the onslaught of winter and its barrenness.[14] The intimacy of the man-nature relationship is almost that of the primitive tribes of the anthropological past, with their fertility rites mourning the death of the deity in winter, and celebrating his resurrection in spring, only in Gay's poem the similar concomitant moods or religious feelings are expressed in words instead of actual ceremonies. We can see evidence in the above quotation of the notion that external nature can by association cause the upsurge of the most elemental feelings in man; and that the great function of poetry is to reveal the interaction of mind and nature. Particular objects, such as oaks with yellow tops, or riven beeches, arouse the imaginative will to regrasp its affinity with nature. And it is this perception of unity through vivid and immediate experience which shines through Gay's extremely sensitive pictures of nature and reflects his yearning for country quiet and country health.[15]

Gay's use of the pathetic fallacy represents a much less subtle method of indicating this problem, how nature mirrors man's sorrow at his own mutability. When Bumkinet is finally informed of Blouzelinda's demise, he bewails her fate in thoroughly stock personifications:

> The rolling streams with watry grief shall flow,
> And winds shall moan aloud—when loud they blow.
>
> (ll. 35–36)

In the following passage, where the fields are commanded to cease their natural course of bearing flowers, and bear only weeds and hemlock as "symptoms" (or symbols) of Blouzelinda's death, the use of apostrophe is hardly superior to the direct use of the pathetic fallacy. A possible advance may lie in the connotative echo of Spenser's "November" of *The Shepherd's Calendar*, and of Milton's depiction of the mourning fields of Eden in *Paradise Lost* when Eve, like Ceres, has been gathered in by the forces of the Under-World:

> Lament, ye fields, and rueful symptoms show,
> Henceforth let not the smelling primrose grow;
> Let weeds instead of butter-flow'rs appear,
> And meads, instead of daisies, hemlock bear;
> For cowslips sweet let dandelions spread,
> For *Blouzelinda*, blithesome maid, is dead!
> Lament ye swains, and o'er her grave bemoan,
> And spell ye right this verse upon her stone.
> *Here* Blouzelinda *lyes— Alas, alas!*
> *Weep shepherds—and remember flesh is grass.*
>
> (ll. 83–92)

The metaphysical chord of *flesh is grass* contains another key to the closeness of the man-nature affinity where all flesh is resolved to dust, and from the dust grow the grasses which nurture living man, who all too soon will again be food to nurture grass. This cycle whereby the king passes through the stomach of the beggar is but another facet of the ancient primitive concept which mingles the tragedy of human dignity with the joy of human regeneration—and, as always, the variance of the human state embodies and reflects the variance of the seasons.

A more complex device to bring out the man-beast affinity is the combination of distortion and the pathetic fallacy, where the contrast of vulgar realism with the rather idealized memories of Blouzelinda bring out the full pathos of her loss. (Although, when their amatory hungers are fed by *Susan*, the shepherds forget Blouzelinda as soon as do the animals when another swineherdess satisfies their actual hunger.) Men and animals come closer in their mutual grief; a bond is created between them; and the dirge of the shepherds finally gives intelligible voice to the grunting laments of the swine, just as it gave intelligibility to the moan of the wind. Desolate and hungry, the pigs and poultry wander aimlessly about waiting in vain for Blouzelinda's "charitable hand"; their suffering is voiced by Bumkinet's wistful howl:

No more her care shall fill the hollow tray,
To fat the guzzling hogs with floods of whey.
Lament, ye swine, in grunting spend your grief,
For you, like me, have lost your sole relief.
(ll. 65–68)

However, we must keep in mind that any preromantic anticipations which appear in Gay are not meant to celebrate the triple alliance of man, beast, and nature for the sole sake of the alliance alone, as sometimes happens in certain romantic poetry. All of Gay's rural poems are firmly supported by the Virgilian tradition of including themes of benevolence and humanitarianism in the georgic. The themes of benevolence in Gay, illustrated by the incident of his refusal to trap fishes unfairly by the use of nets, are meant to serve the definite purpose of direct lessons in social feeling. To Gay, like Thomson, these feelings, so well elucidated by Locke and Shaftesbury, were the bases of all virtue; and thus, we have Gay, as well as Pope, condemning the chase, showing interest in the lives of country people, and emphasizing the ethical value of the harmony of virtue. This virtue is not based on a supernatural ethic; it springs from the social feelings of kindliness and friendship which we have seen Gay eulogize. Such feelings are ultimately human, and beyond any but the most instinctive sort of realization in animals. Thus, it is that only the human mind and voice can express the pain of the dying hare, or the death struggle of the caught salmon (ll. 225–252). And because man is man, and not merely superbeast (except in some of the *Fables*), he can create and cope with far more complex problems. He can cause the violence of war with its waste of fields and men and its shattering of family life; but he can also protest strongly against it as Gay does in *Rural Sports* (ll. 396–409), and he can celebrate the security and prosperity of peace as the normal human state, especially in the "naturally good" primitive country environment.

In a more specific instance of social irresponsibility, Gay urges the keen hunter to refrain from the chase lest he "render all the plowman's labour vain," by riding through his fields and trampling down his corn. Just a small example, such as this of squirearchical tyranny, points out once more how Gay is interested in the recurrent social problems of the period, and how the eighteenth century attempted to re-educate modes of thinking by bringing social evil to light. In the final analysis, even in a poem on rural sports, Gay advocates the superior rights of the whole, and the subjection of sport or amusement to social necessity. Such an attitude indicates little real egocentricity in Gay; it shows a regard for others and a preoccupation with the realm of social order which is entirely admirable. It is this preoccupation which is even more fully amplified in Gay's satires on the town where the disruption of the social norm constitutes the basis of his social protest.

A superficial glance at *Rural Sports*, which is all that seems to have been accorded it in the past, might well deceive one into considering it merely a georgic poem of pure description, lacking that modification of a predominant passion which Coleridge in his *Biographia Literaria* (Chapter XIV) insists gives a poem its innate truth. But a closer examination of the text and its tone, with the supporting evidence from Gay's other works kept constantly in mind, clearly indicates that the predominant passion of *Rural Sports* is that of nostalgic regret. This emotion is rather difficult to define in its subtlety, but it is one which continually recurs as a basic tone in Gay's poems, and which perhaps reflects for his life the "ruling passion" described by Pope in *An Essay on Man*. The mood of nostalgic regret is connected both with the Golden Age of the traditional pastoral and with the concept of primitive society's natural goodness. It is a mood which also reflects the theme of escape to a rural retreat, apparent in much of eighteenth-century poetry, and even apparent in the poems of that renowned and formidable battler, Pope, who much preferred Twickenham to the clamor of Grub Street. But, as we have noted, most important for our study of Gay is the reflection in *Rural Sports* of Gay's memories of his youth, and his desire to recapture the health and peace of mind which he once possessed in Devonshire. The rural maid, whom we have seen portrayed "in chearful labour," "rich in poverty," and blooming with health, lives the life which Gay remembers and cherishes:

> If love's soft passion in her bosom reign,
> An equal passion warms her happy swain;
> No homebred jars her quiet state controul,
> Nor watchful jealousie torments her soul;
> With secret joy she sees her little race
> Hang on her breast, and her small cottage grace;
> The fleecy ball their busy fingers cull,
> Or from the spindle draw the length'ning wool:
> Thus flow her hours with constant peace of mind,
> Till Age the latest thread of life unwind.
>
> (ll. 426–435)

There is more than the mimicry of an old stock convention in the above lines; the occasionally homesick boy of 1713, and the hopeful poet of 1720 [16] both possess an ominous feeling that the life of the town with its dishonesty and nonfunctionalism may be only waste. Beyond the actual denotation of what Gay describes in *Rural Sports*, there lies a joy and enthusiasm in his scenes of angling for the wary trout or springing the woodcock which we do not find in any of the town poems, except those parts of *Trivia* which describe the activity of the natural elements. It is these more joyous, more healthy aspects of life which Gay associates with the peace of mind that comes as a reward for a life of industry devoted to really purposeful duties, such as the swain's tilling of the fields, or the rural maid's raising of a loyal and virtuous family. And this for Gay seems to be the ultimate, and in this world, unique justice—that the poor country peasant can attain a fulfillment and content far beyond all the strivings of the rich and powerful. The assumption of almost all of Gay's works is that this content is only to be found in the country life. And thus, it is with redoubled pathos that *Rural Sports* concludes on the following note:

> Farewel.—The city calls me from your bow'rs:
> Farewel amusing thoughts and peaceful hours.
>
> (ll. 442–443)

The pathos lies in the sense of physical farewell, the loss of the actual scene which can momentarily give him the unity of perspective (and thus, peace of mind) which he somehow loses the minute he returns to town, "where news and politicks divide mankind" and the individual. Conflicting desires seem to have continually irritated Gay, and modern psychiatry has suggested that indolence is one of the most obvious symptoms of this state of mind. It is easy to observe Gay's behavior patterns through his letters; a sudden spurt of energy, an attempt to get a place, or, better still, to complete a poem, and then a renewal of the old indolence, an onslaught of the old frustrations, anxieties, and laments. These moments of depression are not too long lasting, but they are periodic, and the waters of Bath do not seem to cure them.

Gay could work, and as a result we have many excellent poems for which to be grateful; but he could also become hopelessly immersed in his dejection, seemingly unable to escape the pressures of money and ambition, and the knowledge that they both were only the means to the attainment of barren and futile ends. Gay seeks escape from these pressures in quiet or boisterous cameraderie, in sleep, or in dreams.[17] But the most comforting escape is an actual day in the country; and the most regretful moments of Gay's existence are often those he experiences when he awakens from the illusion or daydream of the country with its fulfilled wishes to discover that, unfortunately, he is still immersed in the reality of the town. It is when these moods control the dominant tone of a passage in a poem or play that we can recognize most clearly the two chief anticipations of preromanticism in Gay's poetry, a sense of the pathetic, and a concomitant sense of nostalgia.

One of the georgic themes most elaborated upon in the eighteenth century was the concept that nature revealed the immanence of divinity in itself. These theories of natural revelation disguise themselves in many forms from the rationalism of Pope's *Essay on Man* to the mysticism of Wordsworth, although the majority of statements reflect Thomson's Newtonian belief that God is a supporting and guiding principle of law, exerting an influence analogous to that of the sun on nature. It is difficult to ascertain Gay's precise beliefs on this topic, because he offers us little direct information in his poetry and letters, and what does exist is often alloyed with other somewhat inconsistent subject matter. In *Rural Sports,* when Gay is overwhelmed by the sublimity and eternality of the sunset dropping its flame on every wave, he falls into a "pensive mood" which continues to prevail over him as he surveys:

> Millions of worlds hang in the spacious air,
> Which round their suns their annual circles steer.
>
> (ll. 111–112)

This "sweet contemplation elevates [his] sense,/while [he] surveys the works of providence." Gay obviously employs here the georgic reverence of immanent Deity, and these lines also reflect the departure of *An Essay on Man* from a more personal God to "the great directing Mind" which is to Gay,

> The glorious author of the universe,
> Who reins the winds, gives the vast ocean bounds,
> And circumscribes the floating worlds their rounds.
>
> (ll. 116–118)

The principle of plenitude serves as a basis not only for Gay's social philosophy, but also for the rare expressions of his religious philosophy. The amazing diversity of nature, and the assumption, gained from Newton, that all creation reflects a universal order and harmony, seem almost to paralyze Gay's rationality. He seems to possess only an emotional reaction to the majestic "traces of th'almighty hand," which he has rather generally (in contrast to his usual precision) evoked in *A Contemplation on Night*. Gay hardly holds the deistic position of Shaftesbury that man can form an adequate notion of God by the mere exercise of unaided human reason. His moody speculation reflects a rational paralysis, or refusal to struggle with the physicotheological arguments of the age. In this poem Gay avows that God by his "Word" created all these stars out of "nothing," and can repeat this act of creation whenever he so desires; but, despite the Newtonian optimism of his age, Gay says,

> Whether those stars that twinkling lustre send,
> Are suns, and rolling worlds those suns attend,
> Man may conjecture, and new schemes declare,
> Yet all his systems but conjectures are.
>
> (ll. 27–30)

Man can but *conjecture* about the laws of creation, he cannot *know*. The rationalistic anti-intellectualism [18] prevalent in the early eighteenth century seems particularly applicable to Gay and what we know of his methods of trying to reduce all intellectual complexities down to their simplest terms. The members of the Scriblerus Club were certainly among those who believed that all the knowledge necessary for men to live wisely and happily was already available to them. Gulliver's experiences in the Grand Academy of Lagado are a sufficient proof that Swift and his friends felt that the application of logic to needlessly complex and relatively unimportant problems was a futile task. The pedants so mercilessly satirized in *The Tale of a Tub* had a propensity to amplify all moral and theological questions to overelaborate systems incapable of substantial proof, and thus it was deemed safe to ridicule or ignore their absurd problems rather than deal with them seriously.

Since the Scriblerians felt that the normal man actually possessed enough basic common sense to cope with his problems if he were not hoodwinked by the propagation of vicious and distorted values, a concept of rationalistic primitivism arose which implied that those universal truths of reason learned by following nature could probably best be found in relatively primitive environments where the chances of civilized perversion were minimized. The noble savages of *Polly* as well as the Houyhnhnms were thus felt to be morally superior because they were uncorrupted by perverted standards of social action and the traditions of diseased civilizations. It is quite obvious how neatly these concepts parallel Gay's belief in country goodness and town degeneration; and according to these prevalent concepts of rationalistic anti-intellectualism and primitivism, Gay could even be momentarily considered a deist (as far as the ambiguity of the term allows for reality).

However, although Gay was probably not a very religious

person, the attitude shown in *A Contemplation on Night* and in *A Thought on Eternity*, both on the whole quite conventional Christian poems, indicates that he was more of a rational theist than a strict deist. The denial by certain deists of the orthodox attributes of mercy, kindness, and justice to God in his dealings with men would conflict entirely with those theories of benevolence which Gay supports. The tenor of Gay's poems is philosophical rather than theological, but there is nothing in any of his utterances that would be inconsistent with Christian tradition. The principle of uniformitarianism, also based on the similarity of reason in all men, is probably the most central tenet of Gay's rational theism. As we have seen in our discussion of *Polly*, Gay's presentation of rationalistic primitivism in the noble savages presupposes certain standards which the savages (so close to nature and thus to divinity) uphold, and which the town-bred pirates and planters violate. It is the self-aggrandizement of the latter which rational theism finds so contrary to a divine and reasonable view of life. The town and its people embody peculiarities of warped desire which run counter to the universal natural order and destroy the esteemed decorum or uniformity of the Enlightenment.

Nature, as used in the above philosophical sense, means, of course, the actual operative laws of the universe, not the general phenomena of harvest or sea described by Gay in *Rural Sports*. Yet, nature as scenery, or phenomena, is an important factor in determining the order and harmony of natural law, and of natural religion. In *A Contemplation on Night*, Gay feels that the variance of the seasons, and the contrasts of dawn and dusk in opposite latitudes should enable every man, through the identical reasoning capacity which he shares with every other man, to arrive at the general truth that there is a deity. Of course, this is nothing but the old Socratic proof by analogy that the complicated, yet ordered, mechanisms of the watch presuppose a watchmaker. Any doctrine that attacked the narrow, particularized sectarianism of the numerous Christian creeds was bound to appeal to Gay. The antagonistic diversities of sometimes fanatic sects, whose tenets lacked universal verification, could only further confuse a man who sought to avoid philosophical complexities of any sort. A very basic Christianity was most suitable for Gay in the sense that fundamental teachings usually strive to find and elucidate the basic denominator of life, the scientific laws (also an accepted theme of the georgic) which will enable a man to see the construction of the "watch" on the simplest level. However, Gay himself never really investigates these laws with much thoroughness. In *A Contemplation on Night* he ascribes the creative act, Christian-wise, to the symbolic *Word*, which contains an overtone of the Scriptural Revelation so subordinated in this age. Like Thomson, Gay draws an analogy with the sun; God is like the sun, yet greater; God is boundless, immutable, and eternal. "When the pure soul is from the body flown," when night and day decay and merge, Gay, with a full sense of life's limitations, pleads:

> Oh, may some nobler thought my soul employ,
> Than empty, transient, sublunary joy!
> The stars shall drop, the sun shall lose his flame,
> But Thou, O God, forever shine the same.
>
> (ll. 51–54)

Most of the images which Gay employs to designate the deity involve a sense of limitless boundaries. *A Thought on Eternity* is a complete poem on this theme. Gay refers to the soul this time as a part of eternity and therefore immortal. He also refers to the origin of man's body in terms of the Christian creation, "when the warm dust shot up in breathing man." Here again he echoes the Platonism of the Gospel according to St. John, as the agent of this act is also the *Logos,* "th' Almighty word." We must conclude that, in reality, this poem exists to contrast the grandeur of eternity with the misery of man's life on earth. Although the first version was published as early as 1714, the tone of the poem anticipates the cynicism of his epitaph, and the bitterness of the last *Fables:*

> Ah! what is life? with ills encompass'd round,
> Amidst our hopes, Fate strikes the sudden wound:
> To-day the statesman of new honour dreams,
> To-morrow death destroys his airy schemes;
> Is mouldy treasure in thy chest confin'd?
> Think all that treasure thou must leave behind;
> Thy heir with smiles shall view thy blazon'd herse,
> And all thy hoards with lavish hand disperse.
> Should certain fate th'impending blow delay,
> Thy mirth will sicken and thy bloom decay;
> Then feeble age will all thy nerves disarm,
> No more thy blood its narrow channels warm.
> Who then would wish to stretch this narrow span,
> To suffer life beyond the date of man? (ll. 13–26)

The echoes in this passage of Pope's *Moral Essay,* Epistle III, combine with the references to Fate to support a contention that Gay could never have trusted that facile optimism which Voltaire and Dr. Johnson destroyed so thoroughly in *Candide* and *Rasselas.* The refuge in virtue for its own sake, which we have noticed as a theme in *Polly,* is again illustrated by the conclusion of this poem:

> The virtuous soul pursues a nobler aim,
> And life regards but as a fleeting dream:
> She longs to wake, and wishes to get free,
> To launch from earth into eternity.
> For while the boundless theme extends our thought,
> Ten thousand thousand rolling years are nought.
>   (ll. 27–32)

This paradox is very pertinent to our understanding of Gay and his search for escape—the dream of the virtuous soul regards reality (life) as illusion (dream). The distortion of values, and the lack of uniformitarian standards, make reality simply a series of particularized illusions, such as the statesman's dream of "new honour," or the miser's dream that the "mouldy treasure" in his chest is really his. The virtuous soul feels that the only reality is to become part of eternity, where the illusions of this earth, or more precisely, of society, are seen for what they are; and to Gay, they are *illusions,* nebulous wraiths that cannot possibly bring universal good out of their partial evil.

The rationality of Gay's basic theism, appearing in *Rural Sports, A Contemplation on Night,* and *A Thought on Eternity,* in addition to hinting at his principles of natural philosophy, also supports his views on international and intellectual egalitarianism. Under the aspect of eternity, local or national beliefs in politics, religion, society, and morality seem peculiar and limited. Outside of an occasional stock patriotic panegyric, Gay is usually universal in his humanistic and humanitarian outlook, and thoroughly democratic in the rationalistic anti-intellectualism which holds that the simple shepherd can apprehend the divine laws of the universe as well as the philosopher.[19] The *Introduction to the Fables* is his most explicit poem on this connection of natural theology with natural wisdom; the uneducated "Swain" claims that:

> ev'ry object of creation
> Can furnish hints to contemplation,
> And from the most minute and mean
> A virtuous mind can morals glean. (ll. 69–72)

The "Sage" compliments the shepherd on his fundamental common sense, and sums up for us the few philosophical implications of Gay's attitude toward the pastoral:

> Thy fame is just, the Sage replys,
> Thy virtue proves thee truly wise;
> Pride often guides the author's pen,
> Books as affected are as men,
> But he who studys nature's laws
> From certain truth his maxims draws,
> And those, without our schools, suffice
> To make men moral, good and wise. (ll. 73–80)

However, a complete investigation of Gay's interest in natural theology or philosophy would indicate quite conclusively that he is rarely concerned with these problems. As a poet and dramatist, he is primarily interested in the social aspects of moral philosophy, a realm where man can supposedly know himself at least. Gay does little else but accept (in *A Contemplation on Night*) that

> Nature's various face informs my sense,
> Of an all-wise, all pow'rful Providence. (ll. 3–4)

And although Pope says practically the same thing in *An Essay on Man* (I, 267–280), a real distinction may be drawn between the two friends. In his philosophical epistles, Pope actually tried to fully poetize these tenets, whereas Gay was satisfied to make only a few scattered references to them.

CHAPTER II

The Beggar's Milieu:
THE BEGGAR'S OPERA

Knaves of old, to hide Guilt by their cunning Inventions,
Call'd Briberies Grants, and plain Robberies Pensions;
Physicians and Lawyers (who take their Degrees
To be Learned Rogues) call'd their Pilfering, Fees

. . . .

Some cheat in the Customs, some rob the Excise,
But he who robs both is esteemed most wise.

WHEN the pastoral coin is reversed, we find that the town
image reflects realism in contrast to country idealism,
cynicism in contrast to country sentimentalism, and vice
in contrast to country virtue. Yet, the coin still maintains
its pastoral unity. It has been remarked that the realistic
pastoral, which is often embodied in the mock-pastoral
of Gay's town eclogues and town georgic, often gives
a natural expression for a sense of social injustice. The
consciousness of poverty isolates a person; and because such
a person is too poor for the benefits of society, he is independent of it, and thus, like the "artist," can criticize it with
some degree of honesty and moral objectivity.[1] Such is the
role the Beggar plays in the introductory frame to *The Beggar's Opera;* but we are all aware that the part is actually
John Gay's, especially since the frame to *Polly,* the sequel of
The Beggar's Opera, substitutes the Poet for the Beggar in
the introductory discourse with the Player. The artist, Gay,
is the beggar, a commissioner of state lotteries, searching for

a better place, but unwilling to stoop to insincere flattery. The beggar ekes out his meager income by the publishing of poems, or the production of a minor dramatic success like *The Captives* (January, 1724), but he is always on the verge of financial disaster in the years before the record-breaking run of *The Beggar's Opera*. It is not that Gay was a bad manager of his money, as Pope is quoted as asserting,[2] but that having been deceived, with many others, by the South Sea Bubble, he had no money to manage. When the profits from *The Beggar's Opera* and *Polly* finally gave him his much desired financial independence amounting to at least £3000, he managed his money with competence and even managed to increase his estate.[3] But this sense of security came only in his last years; the anxiety over his lack of money, with the resultant curbing of his liberty, caused feelings of injustice which haunted most of his life and formed the main themes of much of his poetry. This divided attitude of contempt for and need of money is prevalent both in the days before his success, when anxiety was a part of most of his waking minutes, and also in the days after his success, when it was a depressing memory.[4]

   The Beggar's Opera, in addition to being aesthetic criticism in its burlesque of the fashionable Italian opera, is also the social criticism of the poor man as artist. The attitude expressed by Gay in this play toward the human components of his society is quite similar to that of Dr. Harrison in Fielding's *Amelia;* "The nature of man is far from being in itself evil; it abounds with benevolence, charity, and pity, coveting praise and honour, and shunning shame and disgrace. Bad education, bad habits, and bad customs debauch our nature, and drive it headlong as it were into vice." Man is not basically vicious; he is the victim of vicious social forces. It might be more accurate to say that Swift, Pope, and Gay, although

they never mention him, actually shared the belief promoted
by the Earl of Shaftesbury that there was essential good in
human nature. Believers in such a God faithfully observed
the ritual of *following Nature*, and in accord with the contemporary emphasis on the study of mankind, devoted the
bulk of their consideration to the moral and social aspects
of this ordered plan. Man was thought to have an innate
moral sense [5] which distinguished good from evil and taught
its possessor that his affections, to be virtuous, must be consistent with public as well as private good. The many popular
ethical concepts which united to form Gay's practical humanitarianism all insist on the identity of the moral law with
natural law, and the subjection of the individual welfare to
that of society.

Aberrations of Reason however may distort the individual
moral sense; man is to a certain extent malleable by his environment.[6] A certain philosophical skepticism or common-
sense intellectualism in the members of the Scriblerus group
prevent them from subscribing too wholeheartedly to Locke's
theory that a wise education imprinted upon the *tabula rasa*
of the mind will produce a virtuous man. Although they had
no use for the cynical materialism of Hobbes and Mandeville,
they knew that the Yahoo was not to be fully trusted even
at his best. Nowhere did he seem to approach the ideal state
as expressed by Pope:

> Such is the World's great harmony, that springs
> From Order, Union, full Consent of things:
> Where small and great, where weak and mighty, made
> To serve, not suffer, strengthen, not invade; . . .
> (*An Essay on Man*, III, 295–298)

Gulliver and Cawwawkee are to be exhibited as freaks in
Brobdingnag and London; Yahoos use one another malevo-

lently to satisfy their own selfish ends with no thought of the
social well-being and utilitarian precepts which Scriblerians
seek to inculcate.

Perhaps the fault lies in the attempt of the Scriblerus
group, Gay among them, to reduce the actions of the Yahoo
to a system of logic. That this group was subject to the confusion of philosophies prevalent among the purely literary
figures of the early eighteenth century is most evident in
Pope's *Essay on Man*. The neostoicism which is the only
escape from the determinism implicit in Pope's poem also
constitutes Gay's answer to the threats of Chaos and Dark
Night; yet Gay too has found the chain of being compatible
with his over-all view of human nature.[7] Although he has
sympathetically absorbed benevolist ethical theories and has
a firm belief in the duties of philanthropy, especially as they
involve the lower classes, still Gay can say in one of his last
works (Fable II: xv),

> Consider man in ev'ry sphere;
> Then tell me, is your lot severe?
> 'Tis murmur, discontent, distrust,
> That makes you wretched. God is just.
>   I grant that hunger must be fed,
> That toil too earns thy daily bread.
> What then! thy wants are seen and known;
> But ev'ry mortal feels his own.
> We're born a restless needy crew:
> Show me the happier man than you. (ll. 1–10)

The reiteration of attacks on the pride and vanity of man
during the eighteenth century indicates that the moralists
of this period feel that it is these vices which cause this "rest-
less needy crew" to commit its worst ethical crime, the attempt to rise above a destined place on the scale.[8] The core
of Gay's social philosophy, accepted by both shepherd and

beggar, may be found again in the *Introduction to the Fables* where the pastoral contrast expresses clearly that the countryman has usually *kept his place,* and that the townsman is usually *aspiring for a place.* The countryman, in Gay's adaptation of Shaftesbury's identification of the beautiful with the good, can almost absorb honesty, healthfulness, and virtue by being functional in the wholesome, life-giving, countryside. The townsman, on the other hand, is subject to the greeds which civilization has developed and centered in the town. He is almost forced to step out of line or out of his proper position on the chain to succeed, otherwise he is very apt to be trampled upon and have his natural rights abrogated by those who must use him as a stepping stone to a "place"—a place on an illusory social chain of being based on false values.

The Beggar's Opera is probably the most complete statement of Gay's attitude toward the town and its evils. Beneath the laughing irony and jocular airs lies the spirit of the Tory satirists.[9] This spirit has been defined as a gloom, a gloom which "is not an indulgence in lyrical melancholia, but the astringent and penetrating observation of the realist." It may be a pessimistic spirit, but it is pessimism "of a variety both tonic and exhilarating." [10] In *The Beggar's Opera* much of this gloom can be traced to a sense that a severe economic injustice is being perpetrated against the poor man, both as artist and beggar, a feeling on Gay's part, as expressed by Macheath, that "money well tim'd, and properly apply'd, will do anything." Money is equated with reason and serves the purpose of logic in Macheath's statement that "of all the arguments in the way of business, the perquisite is the most prevailing." And Peachum, in calming Mrs. Peachum's passion over Polly's mismarriage to Macheath, reasons that money can buy a good character as well as affluence and success:

But money, wife, is the true fuller's earth for reputations, there is not a spot or a stain but what it can take out. (p. 496)

An examination of almost any part of this play shows conclusively that money has become the standard by which town society judges all values. The rich man is good because he is wealthy and can buy people, their love, their friendship, and their services. The poor man is somehow contemptible, if not downright evil, because his poverty forces him to love (flatter) and serve (cringe). Money thus forms the basis of social liberty and moral independence; its constant misuse in the town results in the distressing separation of human beings into economic abstracts of "Haves" and "Have-Nots." There is a somewhat socialistic tone to the proposed remedies of Macheath's robber gang who, for the most part, are portrayed as possessing concepts of honor similar to those of the earlier rural heroes of Sherwood Forest:

Ben. We are for a just partition of the world, for every man hath a right to enjoy life.
Matt. We retrench the superfluities of mankind. The world is avaritious, and I hate avarice. A covetous fellow, like a Jack-daw, steals what he was never made to enjoy, for the sake of hiding it. These are the robbers of mankind, for money was made for the free-hearted and generous, and where is the injury of taking from another, what he hath not the heart to make use of? (p. 502)

Gay's utilitarianism is revealed again in this passage; money should be a fluid item of exchange; it should be apportioned with some measure of equality so that all mankind can benefit from the necessities, and even the luxuries, that "the perquisite" can buy. The hoarding of money, or the perversion of its use by usury are directly contrary to the customary precepts of this commonly held theory of eighteenth-century utilitarianism, expressed most often in terms of a cycle of change whereby excessive luxury leads to poverty which leads to ambition and the accumulation of further wealth which leads again to luxury and the renewal of the cycle. Thus, the natural passions of mankind compel him to act in a manner which is best for the economic good of the whole social structure.[11]

However, these natural passions no longer operate without hindrance from the unnatural passions of greed and avarice. Gay's great objection in both his poetry and dramas is that money is being constantly misused and overesteemed. This misuse causes false class distinctions based on the illusory sociofinancial chain of being instead of on the real chain which has its links ordered according to merit and virtue. Though there are anticipations in the above words of Ben Budge of that feeling for democratic equality which arises in later eighteenth-century writers such as Rousseau, Godwin, and Tom Paine, Gay generally holds to the common Augustan principle of subordination. This subordination of one man to another should be based on universal distinctions such as merit, genius, general intelligence, and kindliness. The claims to superiority of nobility or powerful politicians are only to be allowed when the person in question has earned this superior respect by his good deeds (a rare case in the eyes of eighteenth-century satirists). Parochial distinctions due to wealth, to keeping in vogue with social foibles of dress and amusement, or to places acquired by flattery and bribery, build up this false social chain which Gay tries to expose and tear down by his ironic attacks.

The function of Gay's irony in *The Beggar's Opera* is to reverse the traditional concepts of class distinction. In reality, all of the characters in the ballad opera are of the lowest class of society—no one could pretend otherwise. But economic differences, based on the having or not having of money, combine with the varying ethical and moral sentiments of individuals to separate the characters into pseudo aristocrats and pseudo bourgeoisie for contrast with certain of the poorer classes who keep their social as well as their artistic integrity. At the end of the opera, after the Player has persuaded the Beggar to reprieve Macheath to satisfy the taste of the town (a satirical indication on Gay's part of the servility, hypocrisy, and lack of integrity in the artists of his age), the Beggar summarizes his dramatic purpose:

> Through the whole piece you may observe such a similitude of manners in high and low life, that it is difficult to determine whether (in the fashionable vices) the fine gentlemen imitate the gentlemen of the road, or the gentlemen of the road the fine gentlemen.— Had the Play remain'd, as I at first intended, it would have carried a most excellent moral. 'Twould have shown that the lower sort of people have their vices in a degree as well as the rich: And that they are punish'd for them. (p. 531)

With relation to the depiction of a pseudo aristocracy, there is a constant tendency throughout the play to regard Macheath, not as mere hero, but as chivalric knight-errant, the Robin Hood hero with his merry crew—only much more sophisticated. Macheath is one of the few characters in this play (outside of Polly) who shows any comprehension of honor or friendship in the true senses which Gay respects. Macheath always supports the members of his gang who have become destitute. Of course, giving away money is almost unthinkable in this town society, but Macheath wants to prove that he "is not a meer Court friend, who professes every thing and will do nothing." The gang, in turn, fully appreciate this attitude of *noblesse oblige* on the part of Macheath. Ben Budge says, "It grieves my heart that so generous a man should be involv'd in such difficulties, as oblige him to live with such ill company, and herd with gamesters." But Matt of the Mint, who voices most explicitly the Beggar's social protest, points out that these gamesters are aristocrats themselves, and that Macheath is really in his own element. Even the Peachums recognize the qualities of an aristocrat in their son-in-law:

Mrs. Peach. . . . Sure there is not a finer gentleman upon the road than the Captain! If he comes from *Bagshot* at any reasonable hour he hath promis'd to make one this evening with *Polly*, and me, and *Bob Booty*, at a party of Quadrille. Pray, my dear, is the Captain rich?
Peach. The Captain keeps too good company ever to grow rich. *Marybone* and the Chocolate-houses are his undoing. The man that proposes to get money by play should have the education of a fine gentleman, and be train'd up to it from his youth.
Mrs. Peach. Really, I am sorry upon Polly's account the Captain hath not more discretion. What business hath he to keep company with lords and gentlemen? He should leave them to prey upon one another.[12] (p. 491)

Gay also makes it quite clear that Macheath has the vices of the gentleman, and as he is most at home in the company of lords, it is implied that they are no better than he is in their actions. This then is the Beggar's first moral: that men of noble blood, good education, and good training, men who should be exemplars of virtue for the rest of society, really act (gamble and rob) like the basest highwaymen.

Peachum and Lockit, on the other hand, represent the rising bourgeoisie of the eighteenth century, the Whig mercantile class who were gaining more and more economic power in London because of their control over shops and manufacturing processes. Peachum's tactics are of course those of the recently deceased Jonathan Wild, a supposedly respected magistrate who was in reality a receiver of stolen goods, and Gay attempts to show us through their actions and motives how the Peachum and Lockit families represent the two prime bourgeois evils, hypocrisy and avarice. The middle class represents for Gay the true perverters of morals through their attitude toward money. They do not enjoy the uses of money as do the aristocrats or the lower classes; they are the hoarders and the usurers, their spirits are devoured by money because they love money as an end in itself and not as a purposeful means.[13] It is the utterly cold-hearted practicality of a father's willingness to sell his daughter's honor and chances of marital fulfillment for the sake of business deceptions which appalls us in these words of Peachum's:

> Look ye, wife. A handsome wench in our way of business, is as profitable as at the bar of a *Temple* coffee-house, who looks upon it as her livelihood to grant every liberty but one. . . . Married! If the wench does not know her own profit, sure she knows her own pleasure better than to make herself a property! My daughter to me should be, like a court lady to a minister of state, a key to the whole gang. (p. 491)

Yet, to make matters even worse, such base attitudes are generally cloaked by superficially snow-white motives. The very tone of both the Peachums and Lockit is always sentimentally hypocritical. Mrs. Peachum, enthusiastic about trifles and a typical middle-class club woman in her general appearance, is in reality as avaricious and hard as her husband. But she is constantly given to using such phrases as "I hope nothing bad," "how should we help her," "I am in the utmost concern," "I am as fond" and so forth, when we know only too well that she does not care for anything but her own self-interest.

The members of the gang, who are probably quite representative of the unskilled laboring class of early eighteenth-century London, workers by day and thieves by night, are described by Gay as dishonest but honorable. Except for the "imitators of high life," aristocratic whores like Jenny who practice the deceit of fine ladies, or bourgeois "peachers" like Jemmy Twitcher who will sell out their leader and their honor for money as courtiers and politicians do, most of the

prostitutes and thieves of the play at least make an effort
toward being virtuous in their own way. The contrast of
thief and courtier (poor man and aristocrat) is implicit in
the gang's own words of self praise:

Crook. Where shall we find such another set of practical phi-
losophers, who to a man are above the fear of Death?
Wat. Sound men, and true!
Robin. Of try'd courage, and indefatigable industry!
Ned. Who is there here that would not dye for his friend?
Harry. Who is there here that would betray him for his interest?
Matt. Show me a gang of Courtiers that can say as much. (p. 501)

Of course, this is all ironical to a certain extent. Perhaps, they
would perform none of these honorable acts when faced
squarely with the issue. The characters of the opera are all
people who have their vices to a degree, and the gang may
be loyal only from motives of fear and mutual security. Gay
has two segments of the scale of being in mind for purposes
of contrast: the ruling classes and the beggars. Put under his
spiritual microscope they are identical. The aim is not so
much a defense of the poor, but a criticism of the rich by
pointing out their close resemblance to those of the poorer
classes who have become criminals.

But there is a positive aspect to Gay's portrayal of honor
among thieves. What the Beggar is saying is that there are
remnants of respect for certain universal values, at least in the
realm of personal relationships, which the thieves (or poorer
classes) still preserve. The aim of presenting the thieves in a
better light than the aristocrats is to heighten the social injustice involved in having them punished for crimes, com-
mitted on a small scale, which the aristocracy (as courtiers)
and bourgeoisie (as politicians) commit on a grand scale and
from which they prosper rather than suffer. This is the Beggar's second moral: that the poor man, like the rich, may
believe in his own virtue, but, unlike the rich man, feel that if

he cannot *purchase* justice, he must suffer unfairly for his vices or indiscretions.

A further means on Gay's part of showing social injustice, i.e., favoritism toward the rich and powerful, and discrimination against the poor, is to equate the practices of various professions with those of the thieves. The problem is posed by Jemmy Twitcher at the beginning of Act II:

Why are the laws levell'd at us? are we more dishonest than the rest of mankind? what we win, gentlemen, is our own by the law of arms, and the right of conquest. (p. 501)

In other words, the thieves, though dishonest, exert some measure of valor to attain their money, money which is barely enough for the necessities of life, but "the rest of mankind" (the respectable portion) usually practice their kind of deceit to earn an enormous wealth which is usually wasted on the foibles of luxury. One of Gay's most severe condemnations of professional deceit and hypocrisy is voiced by Peachum in the famous first air of the opera:

> THROUGH all the employments of life
>> Each neighbour abuses his brother;
> Whore and Rogue they call Husband and Wife:
>> All professions be-rogue one another.
> The Priest calls the Lawyer a cheat,
>> The Lawyer be-knaves the Divine;
> And the Statesman, because he's so great,
>> Thinks his trade as honest as mine.[14] (p. 488)

What is singularly condemnatory about this passage is that the Priest, Lawyer, and Statesman are compared to Peachum, the most evil character in the play, a man whom even the thieves and whores despise, though they are forced to do his bidding because he (like Walpole and Wild) is "the great man." The receiver of stolen goods, or "fence," is thoroughly dishonorable because he is always playing a double game; he lives by lying and betrayal; and if he is as powerful as Peachum, he assumes the further guilt of playing the false god toward his fellowmen. This is naturally a severe displacement on the chain; and such action also involves the crime of using others for selfish or unsocial purposes, a crime which is attacked constantly by Gay.

In *Polly* (I, iv), Trapes, the bawd, gives a most explicit account of the slim line of demarcation, dependent only on favorable opportunity, which divides "pimp and politician":

> I wonder I am not more wealthy; for, o' my conscience, I have as few scruples as those that are ten thousand times as rich. But, alack-a-day! I am forc'd to play at small game. I now and then betray and ruine an innocent girl. And what of that? Can I in conscience expect to be equally rich with those who betray and ruine provinces and countries? Introth, all their great fortunes are owing to situation; as for genius and capacity I can match them to a hair: were they in my circumstance they would act like me; were I in theirs, I should be rewarded as a most profound penetrating politician. (p. 543)

Gay's satire on the professions is more concerned with the problems of honor and self-interest than the companion problems of justice and money. The point which Gay wishes to make is that just as the go-betweens, the bawd and the fence, should be the most reliable and dependable persons for their sort of business, so should professional men, such as lawyers responsible for justice, priests responsible for general morality, and statesmen responsible for the welfare of the whole society, be the most conscientious guardians of both the individual and the state entrusted to their care. But are they? By identifying these professions in motive and practice with Trapes, Peachum (the betrayer even by name), and Lockit, the trustee (as jailer) of public welfare who can be bought, Gay mirrors the deceptions, treachery, avarice, and selfishness of those influential men who lose their honor and betray their trust for similar motives of self-interest.

One of the most significant ironies in *The Beggar's Opera* may be discovered in the uses of the word *honor* by Peachum and his confederate, Lockit. Gay presents us with the case of poor Ned Clincher, a thief who has been hanged two sessions earlier than he had expected after paying Lockit for a reprieve. Lockit, of course, has received a second bribe from the justices to turn Ned over for immediate hanging so the Tyburn cart will be well filled, indicating the alertness and industry of these hypocritical judges. Peachum, angry because he did not receive his "cut" on this particular deal, objects vociferously on the grounds of honor:

Peach. Here's poor Ned Clincher's name, I see. Sure, brother *Lockit*, there was a little unfair proceeding in *Ned's* case: for he told me in the condemn'd hold, that for value receiv'd, you had promis'd him a Session or two longer without molestation.
Lock. Mr. *Peachum,*—this is the first time my honour was ever call'd in question.
Peach. Business is at an end—if once we act dishonourably.
Lock. Who accuses me?
Peach. You are warm, brother.
Lock. He that attacks my honour, attacks my livelyhood.—And this usage—Sir—is not to be born.
Peach. Since you provoke me to speak—I must tell you too, that Mrs. *Coaxer* charges you with defrauding her of her information-money, for the apprehending of curl-pated *Hugh*. Indeed, indeed, brother, we must punctually pay our Spies, or we shall have no Information.
Lock. Is this language to me, Sirrah—who have sav'd you from the gallows, Sirrah! [Collaring each other.
Peach. If I am hang'd, it shall be for ridding the world of an arrant rascal.
Lock. This hand shall do the office of the halter you deserve, and throttle you—you dog!—

Peach. Brother, brother,—we are both in the wrong—we shall
be both losers in the dispute—for you know we have it in our
power to hang each other. You should not be so passionate.
Lock. Nor you so provoking.
Peach. 'Tis our mutual interest; 'tis for the interest of the world
we should agree. (p. 511)

This burlesque epic argument between the pseudo Brutus
and pseudo Cassius reflects the urbanized methods of Lawyer
and Statesman as well as the hypocrisy and mode of betrayal
of two criminals. Lockit shows the touchiness of the guilty
judge who has taken a bribe and meted out injustice instead
of an impartial verdict (ll. 28–29). Peachum voices the code
of the honest merchant that good business depends on honorable dealings and a fair return for money invested (l. 30),
although we know that in his real business as fence, where he
should follow this code, he is engaged in cheating both the
thief and the purchaser of stolen goods. Lockit (as merchant
or newspaper publisher for instance) is only too aware that
the reputation for honorableness is a business asset, and so he
becomes outraged when this supposed reputation and his
"livelyhood" are endangered (ll. 33–34). Peachum immediately brings up another case of Lockit's dishonesty in betraying the betrayer, Mrs. Coaxer, of her "information-
money." The lawyer or the justices (since there was no
organized Police Department in London in Gay's lifetime)
must pay off their "stool pigeons," otherwise they cannot
obtain reward money for apprehending impoverished criminals or extort blackmail. In Peachum's conciliatory conclusion, we see finally the key to the continuance and increase of town evils; each evil person is dependent on the
next one (ll. 45–46), each can destroy the other, so they
compromise when they can not betray each other (ll. 48–49).
Without honor, they divide like amoebæ, they multiply like
termites until the whole structure of society is weakened.

Peachum's words voice the essence of duty perverted, trust neglected, and social morality corrupted, " 'tis for the interest of the world we should agree." This is the great hypocritical illusion of the responsible person debased—that his own petty self-interest is really in the best interests of society.

This self-obsession represents again the assumption of divinity which Gay dislikes so intensely. The person who puts his own particular welfare above the welfare of the general whole is really departing from his place on the social scale. To pretend to be something you are not by following fashionable foibles and being in vogue is a minor upset in the scale—an attempt at rising to where you probably do not belong. But to rise on the scale by cheating and betraying, to rise by putting your foot on the next man's head and shoving him down, that is to Gay real evil. By their control over other men's lives, Peachum, in his position as fence, and Lockit, in his position as jailer, actually do usurp the functions of divinity; and by their misuse of their "divine" power it is possible for them to destroy the very lives of others. In Act I, scene iii (p. 489) Peachum is introduced examining "A Register of the Gang"; he looks over the records of eight men. Why?—to find a "decent Execution against next Sessions." He weighs their usefulness to him very carefully; his standard of judgment is "to hate a lazy rogue, by whom one can get nothing 'till he is hanged." There are in *The Beggar's Opera* a succession of these Last Judgment scenes (I, iii; II, x; III, v) which actually reflect the divine power of the Justices of the Bench in the London districts, and the Justices of the Peace in the outlying districts. The literature of the age is full of instances of bribable judges whose justice can be bought for money because their own self-interest rules their verdicts.[15] And it is because these "gods," Peachum, Lockit, and the dishonest judges, are unlike the sacrificial

Gods, Christ or Apollo, who do sacrifice themselves for the welfare of man and the perpetuation of honor and justice, that the Gang or the innocent prisoner at the bar, being poor and unable to provide a burnt offering, must be damned. In the town, "gods" must not suffer:

> Our selves, like the Great, to secure a retreat,
> When matters require it, must give up our gang:
>   And good reason why,
>   Or, instead of the fry,
>   Ev'n Peachum and I,
> Like poor petty rascals, might hang, hang;
> Like poor petty rascals, might hang. (Air LVI, p. 527)

Although these men assume divine authority and feel that somehow they have risen in the scale, Gay knows that in reality they have sunk to the level of the beasts. There is justice operative when we view the problem in its broadest perspective, because evil men fall proportionately on the scale according to the distance they have tried to rise out of their place. Lockit really condemns himself and Peachum, as well as all the corrupt professional men of London, in this self-revealing soliloquy:

Peachum then intends to outwit me in this affair; but I'll be even with him.—The dog is leaky in his liquor, so I'll ply him that way, get the secret from him, and turn this affair to my own advantage.—Lions, Wolves, and Vulturs don't live together in herds, droves or flocks.—Of all animals of prey, man is the only sociable one. Every one of us preys upon his neighbour, and yet we herd together.—*Peachum* is my companion, my friend—According to the custom of the world, indeed, he may quote thousands of Precedents for cheating me—And shall not I make use of the privilege of friendship to make him a return? (p. 518)

The false animal god of certain primitive tribes, in having human sacrifices offered to his fangs, had his friends die for him; the true God dies for his friends.

The Beggar's Opera and *Polly* also provide satisfactory keys to what has been referred to as the endeavor to rise above one's place on the social scale by being "in vogue." The subject of the fashionable foibles of fine ladies and fops can be just a source of amusing comment on female pretensions and male vanity. But such matter can also have definite social implications, and such actions can have social and moral consequences which are genuinely deplorable. The Poet (obviously Gay) in the introduction to *Polly* states his artistic principles clearly in answer to the First Player's advice to comply with the taste of the town:

Poet. I know that I have been unjustly accus'd of having given up my moral for a joke, like a fine gentleman in conversation; but whatever be the event now, I will not so much as seem to give up my moral.

1st Player. Really, Sir, an author should comply with the customs and taste of the town.—I am indeed afraid too that your Satyr here and there is too free. A man should be cautious how he mentions any vice whatsoever before good company, lest somebody present should apply it to himself.

Poet. The Stage, Sir, hath the privilege of the pulpit to attack vice however dignified or distinguish'd, and preachers and poets should not be too well bred upon these occasions: Nobody can overdo it when he attacks the vice and not the person.

1st Player. But how can you hinder malicious applications?

Poet. Let those answer for 'em who make 'em. I aim at no particular persons; my strokes are at vice in general: but if any men particularly vicious are hurt, I make no apology, but leave them to the cure of their flatterers. If an author write in character, the lower people reflect on the follies and vices of the rich and great, and an *Indian* judges and talks of *Europeans* by those he hath seen and convers'd with, etc. And I will venture to own that I wish every man of power or riches were really and apparently virtuous, which would soon amend and reform the common people who act by imitation. (p. 537)

The poet as responsible artist, in the Platonic sense, is bound by his ethical principles to propound universal precepts of morality. If he refrains from letting his "Satyr" loose on the taste of the town and the "fashionable" vices, he contributes to the perpetuation of those vicious customs of the rich and powerful which the common people are only too prone to imitate. The power of the artist must be available to the social criticism of the beggar, the poor but wise man. As one of "the lower people," it is his duty to guide his fellow beggars by showing them what the envied rich, noble, and powerful are really like. The ostentation and exterior trappings of their position must not be allowed to conceal the moral evil which lies underneath. Claudius must be exposed, and the disease of Denmark bared to the populace before it can be excised.

It is natural that the town society which Gay pictures as founded on greed for money and self-interest, and utterly devoid of honor and justice, should be rampant with crime. *The Beggar's Opera* is one of the masterpieces of rogue literature, and it shares with Greene's pamphlets, Jonson's London plays, and the novels of Fielding, Smollett, and Dickens an intimate knowledge of the methods and practices of the London underworld. The opera is in many ways an elaboration of those parts of *Trivia* which warn against the tricks practiced on unwary gulls. Murder is not only common but justifiable in the eyes of slick syndicate bosses like Peachum (p. 490). Petty larceny is naturally the most frequently perpetrated criminal act, and an examination of Peachum's register shows how his business associates operate. The whores ransack the trousers of their clientele, while the thieves pick pockets, steal clothes and household articles at fires, and hold up coaches on the highway. But these overt criminal acts are nothing compared to the much more subtle methods of fleecing victims which Peachum has developed.

Like Wild, he is a genius at his trade of dealing with stolen goods. A few illustrations will suffice for evidence: he rips out the coronets and marks of cambric handkerchiefs, and makes slight changes in clothes, and then resells them; he lends expensive watches and swords to the gang so they can "make a figure" in some select gathering where the loot is apt to be more valuable; he lends stolen gowns to Mrs. Trapes, the bawd, who decks out her whores fashionably, because the rate of their payment is in proportion to the fine appearance of the individual prostitute; and he exports jewelry, fancy snuffboxes, and other too easily identifiable goods to "fences" in other countries. Out of all of these deals he reserves a tremendous share for himself, because he is the only one who has the influence to get the goods or to get rid of them, and in his role as god and judge, he has the power to hang either the thief or the purchaser by a little treachery. Lockit is no amateur either in his business, which concentrates on extortion and the selling of liberty or protection. Lockit and Peachum are the two faces of the Janus criminal god; as we noted (II, x), they cannot exist without one another. For the sake of mutual interest they share a Book of Doom, and this carefully kept register of the gang affords them a further great source of income. The ramifications are many, but the pattern is roughly this: with regard to the thief in the register, Peachum can force him to sell his loot at extremely low prices, because otherwise he can turn him over to the authorities and either get a reward or secure the good will of the authorities for some future evasion of justice; with regard to the purchaser, Peachum can make him pay to retrieve his own goods or else resell other stolen articles to him for a much higher price than he had given the thief previously—in addition, it is always possible later to blackmail the purchaser through someone else for buying illegal or "hot" merchandise. If Peachum finds it more profitable to turn a crook over to the police officials, then Lockit gets him at Newgate. There, the culprit, if he has any money left, must pay for all sorts of so-called privileges—does he want heavy or light chains?—does he want to have visitors, or not?—does he want a fairly clean comfortable cell with companions, or does he want a dirty, rat-infested dungeon and "solitary"? All these things cost money, and at Newgate one must pay Lockit or suffer. But these items merely constitute Lockit's small change; he gets his big "pay-offs" by preventing criminals from being sent up to the Sessions (for trial and sentence), or by letting them escape entirely through some clever ruse which does not damage his reputation as jailer.

The Beggar's Opera is almost like *Rural Sports* and *Trivia* in the sense that it is a dramatic georgic on how to evade justice and make a living through crime. But it is more than a georgic, because the implied moral commentary of its satire is so vehement. The poor man (as the beggar) resorts to art (as the poet) to describe and criticize those false values of society which have isolated man from his fellow man. Gay, like Fielding, uses irony in his attempt to show us that it is the education, habits, and customs which society has evolved that are bad, not the very basic nature of man. An evil environment like that of the town corrupts a nature which probably might be innocent, functional, unselfish, and virtuous in the country and "drives it headlong into vice." What better way then of curing this essentially healthy nature than by eradicating its vices by making them known; by exposing every little trick of the trade, and every cankerous, diseased attitude of a society with the "moral pox."

CHAPTER III

The Beggar's Milieu:

TRIVIA

Careful observers, studious of the town,
Shun the misfortunes that disgrace the clown

. . . .

Now venture, Muse, from home, to range the town,
And for the publick safety risque thy own.

IT WOULD BE entirely misleading for this study to give the
impression that Gay absolutely despised the town. After all,
whether by choice or not, he did spend most of his adult life
there, and throughout his dramas and poems we find many
indications that he shared to some extent Dr. Johnson's
genuine love of London. But it is London as a curious and
eternally fascinating study in human nature that he enjoys,
not London as a social structure. As representative of "the
town" and its distorted moral attitudes, London is a wicked
and corrupt place; but as purely objective scene, apart from
the inevitable human judgments we must make of it, London
is a remarkable place, full of all sorts of bustling, scurrying
people in the midst of infinitely varied actions, kind, cruel,
or merely foolish. There is an element of the country "clown"
in John Gay, and *Trivia* is a record of his experiences in the
big city, told with some remnant of earlier awe and enthusiasm to another clown newly arrived.[1]

This record, along with the practical wisdom which Gay
has acquired, is cast in the form of the mock georgic; the
tone is playful rather than vehemently satiric. *Trivia* is bas-

ically a pleasant poem of observation, and its burlesque qualities are not meant to attack either the model, Virgil's *Georgics,* or the London scene which it depicts. As a mock poem, it represents neoclassic imitation in its most engaging manner; it shows not only Gay's appreciation of the *Georgics* but also his knowledge of other classical models which are similarly "imitated" in the themes and structure of this poem. The influence of Juvenal's *Third Satire,* which served as a common model for poems on the town to such neoclassicists as Oldham, Dryden, and Dr. Johnson, may also be seen in *Trivia.* Structural similarities such as contrasting nocturnal and diurnal differences or describing varying street scenes combine with the study of problems common to both ancient Rome and modern London to give a genuinely Juvenalian touch to certain parts of Gay's poem. Gay's pictures of thieves, corrupt politicians, oppressed poor, and bullying rakes may all be found in the *Third Satire,* and what is particularly interesting is that, despite the primarily Horatian bent of Gay's early satire, the moral tone of the two poets is occasionally very similar. Juvenal is also a firm believer in judging a man by his moral character and his fulfillment of an ethically valuable role in society rather than by the wealth or power which he has accumulated. Juvenal, too, feels that environment partially determines the character of man, and he shares with Gay a sympathy with and understanding of the poor, as well as a comparable detestation of the injustice which money enables the rich to impose upon these poor. Any subtle indictments of society which appear in *Trivia* may probably have been given added impetus by the influence of this *Third Satire* of Juvenal, and the affinity which Gay felt for its themes.

Although Horace's *Journey to Brundisium* (*Satires,* I, v) is probably more analogous to Gay's *Epistle to Burlington,* subtitled *A Journey to Exeter,* certain elements of this type of progress poem also appear in *Trivia*. These verse travelogues combined with the old broadside ballads of journeys throughout London or England to establish a genre particularly suited to the precise detailed descriptions of scene or circumstance which Gay could do so well. The lack of any narrative in *Trivia* does give it a sort of newsreel quality, and like the newsreel its objectivity is limited by the particular choice of scene or vignette which the poet or cameraman chooses to focus upon. The oft-made comparison of Gay as the Hogarth of eighteenth-century poetry is especially applicable to *Trivia*, because its realism has both that seeming detachment of the artist as photographer, and that implied moral judgment which does come from the selection of scenes like *Gin Alley* to be depicted. And Gay, as well as Hogarth, truthfully portrays their very degradation in the faces of the town's inhabitants.

In our discussion of *Rural Sports*, we have outlined the georgic tradition and the growth of didactic verse in the eighteenth century. The structure of *Trivia* is quite similar to that of *Rural Sports*, but because *Trivia* is a mock poem instead of a more serious Virgilian imitation, Gay has attempted to follow (or parody) Virgil even more closely to point up the burlesque. Since the essence of successful burlesque depends upon the clarity of reminiscence with which the original model is called to mind, Gay has tried to adapt verbal echoes (ll. 149–150) and themes from the first three georgics of Virgil with great care in the three books of *Trivia*.[2] In addition to a detailed comparison of Virgil's arts of the fields with the arts of traversing London streets, Gay includes parodies of more subtle Virgilian devices such as mythmaking in his interspersed tale of how Vulcan created pattens to protect the feet of Patty, the milkmaid. Of course, such mock mythology is meant to burlesque Virgil's account of how Aristaeus received the divine gift of engendering bees by sending funeral gifts to Orpheus. Throughout the three books of *Trivia* the occupations of the husbandmen are mocked by the occupations of the city dwellers with their street cries and stalls, their coaches and sedan chairs, their duties, and their amusements. The net result is thus not only a vivid and picturesque newsreel of eighteenth-century London, but also a fond recollection of the lines of a beloved classical author, and above all a precisely outlined realization of how the pastoral contrast emerges in Gay's careful weighing of two kinds of life, the country as portrayed by Virgil, and the town as he himself experiences it in London.

The fact that the model for *Trivia* is a georgic about the country life, and that this environment represents for Gay so many of the virtuous aspects of existence, makes caution necessary in any investigation of Gay's poem on town life. Does *Trivia* represent only another side of Gay's nature, a love for the town as well as for the country? Or are the evil influences of town life which were so much more apparent in *The Beggar's Opera* also hinted at in this lighter and much less condemnatory work? And are the good aspects of town life, as seen in *Trivia*, really only reflections of country life still extant in the town? Elements of happiness, healthiness, healthfulness, functionalism, and honest poverty must be examined carefully to see if they are expressed through country images and figures, or whether they seem to be integral aspects peculiar to the town. The question is how impartial is the newsreel? Is the narrator of this *March of Time* of early Augustan London just an objective describer and commentator, or does he possess attitudes of admiration or detestation which are more characteristic of the omniscient novelist?

The didactic purpose of *Trivia* is immediately set forth in epic fashion: "How to walk clean by day, and safe by night, . . ./I sing" (I, 1–5). And although this is a mock poem, it does possess a benevolent, if jocose, social impetus which drives Gay to outline the necessary precautions for safe existence within the town:

> Yet shall I bless my labours, if mankind
> Their future safety from my dangers find.
>
> (III, 397–398)

This existence varies naturally according to diurnal and seasonal conditions, and Gay takes this variance into full account. The mere titles of Books II and III ("Of walking the Streets by Day," and "Of walking the Streets by Night") indicate the contrast in atmosphere, which is more fully realized in certain passages, evocative of two very different moods; the bustle and cries of crowds as the shops open in the morning to the sound of trundling carts (II, 21–24); and the sinister play of shadows about the "common-shores" at night when the street lantern has been blown out (III, 335–341). The perceptive observer can even distinguish the days of the week, not by an affinity with nature, as in *Rural Sports*, but by the logic of the constant repetition of social customs. The parade of "the muzled bear," and "the surly bull" through the town to the pits always occurs on either Monday or Thursday. When "the fishy stalls with double store are laid," one will know that it is a fast day of Wednesday or Friday. And one can always tell when it is Saturday by the dirty waters that drop from the balconies as the maids clean up the house for Sunday.

When we remember how in *Rural Sports* the aspects and moods of nature called up similar moods in man, the difference between town and country becomes immediately apparent. In the town, man does not share an affinity of mood with nature and the changing seasons or weather, instead he reacts to them only for the benefit of his own business or pleasure. In the "milder weather, and serener skies" of spring,

the fawns in the parks, who are still close to nature, frisk
and gambol with healthy love of life, while the town ladies
express spring only by dressing themselves in fine clothes
(I, 145–152). Other signs of town spring are equally artificial
and "unnatural"—coachmen snore on their boxes, and chair-
men crowd idly about tavern doors. Rainy weather does not
seem to be the primary cause of low spirits in *Trivia* as in
The Shepherd's Week; booksellers are too busy closing their
stalls, and the watermen are too busy tempting fares by
"Cloathing their tilts in blue" to be attacked by the spleen.
In town everyone is too preoccupied by his own self-interests;
in their egocentricity they are not even aware that nature is
gaining her revenge by turning their mechanical devices
against them. The stink of the common shores and the tor-
rents from the rainspouts cause discomforts and diseases un-
heard of in the country (I, 171–174). For the city dweller,
winter, which brings such clean beauty to the countryside,
brings only the added dangers of falling on the "slipp'ry
roads," or of being struck by snowballs (II, 323–334). Only
when the products of the countryside become a part of town
life by being sold and cried out in the streets do any elements of freshness, healthfulness, or seasonal change permeate
the town's businesslike monotony. The precise choice of a
summary seasonal symbol indicates that Gay, at least, re-
sponds to evidences of nature even in the town:

> Successive crys the seasons' change declare,
> And mark the monthly progress of the year.
> Hark, how the streets with treble voices ring,
> To sell the bounteous product of the spring!
> Sweet-smelling flow'rs, and elder's early bud,
> With nettle's tender shoots, to cleanse the blood:
> And when *June's* thunder cools the sultry skies,
> Ev'n *Sundays* are prophan'd by mackrell cries.
> Wallnuts the fruit'rer's hand, in autumn, stain,

Blue plumbs and juicy pears augment his gain;
Next oranges the longing boys entice,
To trust their copper fortunes to the dice.
  When rosemary, and bays, the Poet's crown,
Are bawl'd, in frequent cries, through all the town,
Then judge the festival of *Christmas* near,
Christmas, the joyous period of the year.
Now with bright holly all your temples strow,
With lawrel green, and sacred misletoe. (II, 425–442)

However, since *Trivia* aims at being primarily didactic
("the busy city asks instructive song," II, 220) in seeking to
give practical lessons rather than social or moral lessons,
logical relationships and newsreel description are more to be
expected than subtle affinities of tone. Advice on the *how* of
things governs much of the poem. When walking the streets,
"let firm, well hammer'd soles protect thy feet/Thro' freezing
snows, and rains, and soaking sleet." In other words, wear at-
tire that is practical, clothes that might even serve one in the
country.[3] The town being the town, i.e., very businesslike
and very dishonest, Gay feels that he must give his friend,
the country clown, a shopping guide:

Shall the large mutton smoak upon your boards?
Such, *Newgate's* copious market best affords.
Would'st thou with mighty beef augment thy meal?
Seek *Leaden-hall; St. James's* sends thee veal.
Thames-street gives cheeses; *Covent-garden* fruits;
Moor-fields old books; and *Monmouth-street* old suits.
Hence may'st thou well supply the wants of life,
Support thy family, and cloath thy wife. (II, 543–550)

And because the clown is so inexperienced in the ways and
wiles of the town, he must be taught how to avoid certain
dangers. If he gets lost while walking, he must "enquire the
way" only from the "sworn porter," or the "grave trades-

man" ("He ne'er deceives, but when he profits by't"); the idle 'prentice will misdirect him on purpose for a joke, or the "female guide" will steal his watch and lose him in a crowd. The unwary walker is apt to suffer a multitude of mishaps; if he loses his companion for a minute in the throng, he will seek him (or her) forever in vain as Aeneas sought Creusa or Nisus sought Euryalus; if he turns to look at a voluptuous "damsel," he will probably bump into a post, or get soaked with fishy water thrown out from a stall. He is in imminent danger of being spattered by dirt, slipping on beesom spread on the sidewalk by waggish boys, being hit by hogsheads rolled off carts by porters, knocked over by 'prentices in a football game, lashed in the eye by a coachman's whip, tripping over brewers' ropes, alehouse benches, and wheelbarrows, and falling into open cellars. The newsreel occasionally becomes a Chaplin comedy.

Trivia, as a georgic, naturally gives us a genre sketch of the occupations and amusements of the town. The Hogarthian newsreel centers on many of the varying businesses and professions of the age, gives us a side glance at the relaxations of the town away from its pursuit of money, and also a view of certain unique social types, such as the fop and the bully. In the gray morning before the streets are filled with hurrying crowds, Gay tells us we can "see a draggled damsel, here and there,/From *Billingsgate* her fishy traffick bear." How different from the jolly rustic fishermen of *Rural Sports* is Gay's implication; and his disparaging attitude is immediately voiced in another example;

> On doors the sallow milk-maid chalks her gains;
> Ah! how unlike the milk-maid of the plains! (II, 11–12)

The use of adjectives such as *draggled* and *sallow* show the state of the laboring class of London, as Gay sees it. Recall for an instant the picture of Blouzelinda in her dairy (*The Shepherd's Week*, "Friday," 57–58) as described by Bumkinet:

> For there her goodly countenance I've seen,
> Set off with kerchief starch'd and pinners clean.

The wasted bodies and the drawn faces of the town maids make us remember how often in eighteenth- and nineteenth-century London the poor purveyors of wholesome food never tasted it themselves—a fair business measure was meted out to the customer but not to the worker. Except under the peculiar circumstances of despotic squires or bad crops, the healthy buxom Blouzelindas of the country rarely suffered from undernourishment.

Other human beings were similarly starved and degraded because of the specialized needs of an urban society. The burlesque myth of Cloacina providing a livelihood for her bastard son by inventing the job of bootblack is told in humorous fashion, but the task of removing caked mud from boots was both difficult and unremunerative. The chimney sweep and the dustman fared no better; their jobs were the dirtiest imaginable, and they were equally underpaid and therefore undernourished. It is no wonder that these ignorant, starved creatures turned to petty crime to eke out their meager incomes. In sharp contrast we have Gay's references to typical country occupations in *The Shepherd's Week:*

> As with *Buxoma* once I work'd at hay,
> Ev'n noon-tide labour seem'd an holiday; (Monday, l. 65)
>
> · · · ·
>
> *Marian*, that soft could stroke the udder'd cow,
> Or lessen with her sieve the barley mow;
> Marbled with sage the hardn'ing cheese she press'd,
> And yellow butter *Marian's* skill confess'd.[4]
>
> (Tuesday, ll. 11–14)

The tone in which these country labors are described be-speaks a regard for the work that is healthful and clean in the most natural sense. The soil is good although it be dirt; but shoe blacking, soot, and dust are man-made, unclean, and very apt to lead to some such urban disease as tuberculosis or pneumonia.

Besides being healthful, country labor is extremely func-tional. Knitting, baking for one's family, growing fruit and vegetables, tending bees, shearing sheep, and caring in gen-eral for the barnyard and the farm serve immediately useful ends; a family eats, is clothed, grows strong, and becomes happy. But many city jobs just cater to vain and wealthy people who wish to be in vogue. The barber, the wigmaker, the perfumer, the baker of fancy pastries, all these exist only to satisfy a taste for luxurious living in the fop and fine lady. Gay questions whether these lives are actually worth per-petuating at the expense of the labor of so many tradesmen. In terms of his descriptions of the fop and bully (II, 53–64), the conclusion would seem to demand a negative answer. The fop, who minces about the streets in his "mantling peruke," will shower you with powder from his clothes if you mis-takenly bump into him. The bully, who is close kin to the rake, a Juvenalian character who also appears in Elizabethan satire as the "roarer," is even more of a menace. Though he is basically a coward at heart, when he moves in packs as Nicker, Scowrer, or Mohock, he will instigate riots, destroy property, and flout justice by maiming and wounding its pitiful custodians, the more than inadequate watchmen who fearfully patrolled the streets before Fielding's reorganiza-tion of the Police Department (III, 322–333).

The amusements of the town reflect the violence and dis-regard for the feelings and welfare of others which char-acterize the corruption of the town spirit. In "Monday" of *The Shepherd's Week* Gay describes the pleasant pastimes of the rural folk, singing matches, *Blindman's Buff*, *Hotcockles*, swinging, and seesawing. In contrast to these innocent communal games, *Trivia* pictures the football war with its dangers to the spectators, bear- and bullbaiting, the "game" of chasing the thief and ducking him "in the miry pond," and the penchant for throwing eggs and rotten vegetables at the "perjur'd head" locked fast in the pillory. In addition to these lower- and middle-class games, *The Mohocks* presents us with the refinements of the wealthier and more cultured classes of society. (It is obvious that the fop, bully, and rake were wealthy, and quite often of noble blood, otherwise they could not afford such extravagance in dress, or afford to purchase immunity from the chastisements of justice which they so much deserved.) On their nightly revels, they were supposedly given to slitting noses, cutting off ears and tongues, pricking people in the calves with their swords to make them dance, and ravishing unprotected women.[5] The general tenor of their "pranks" is best exemplified in *Trivia*, III, 329–333, where Gay describes a legendary incident of how they encased an innocent matron in a barrel and rolled it down a steep hill. In the town with its atmosphere of repression and tension, diseases of the mind break out in mass epidemics just like the London plagues of the seventeenth century. The country, according to Gay, shows men, properly tired after a truly functional day's work, sharing their moments of relaxation in a warm, communal manner—the affinity of man with nature operates to form an affinity of man with man, and man with beast. But the town separates man from man and beast. We see frequently how the city dweller, preoccupied with his own self-interest, gnaws away at his own frustrations, and builds up repressed violence to the breaking point. The enormous screaming crowd in the Roman amphitheater was a disintegrating social mass of unintegrated individuals; to the Christian in the pit they formed one howling bloodthirsty crowd, but each one of them to himself was the lion letting loose the frustrations and violence of his self-imposed spiritual imprisonment by tearing the Christian apart with his paws. Such, in a mild form, was the attitude of violence which Gay felt lay behind some of the amusements of the town in Augustan London.

Many of the aspects of *Trivia* which we have already considered must certainly be classified as moral episodes, episodes which in their contrast of the lives of the husbandman and the city dweller eulogize the former and disparage the latter with certain moral standards as criteria. However, the chief mode of expression of moral disapproval is embodied in Gay's references to crime, on both the grand and the minor scales represented in *The Beggar's Opera*. Besides the poverty and oppressed state of the laboring classes, and the extravagance and vanity of the wealthier classes, a further reason for the emergence of crime given in *Trivia* is the actual physical corruption of the town environment. The town inhabitant is not only subject to being run over by carmen and coachmen but he is also in imminent danger from unhealthy smells and diseases:

Who would of *Watling-street* the dangers share,
When the broad pavement of *Cheap-side* is near?
Or who that rugged street (Thames-street) would traverse o'er,
That stretches, O *Fleet-ditch*, from thy black shore
To the *Tow'r's* moated walls? Here steams ascend
That, in mix'd fumes, the wrinkled nose offend.
Where chandlers cauldrons boil; where fishy prey
Hide the wet stall, long absent from the sea;
And where the cleaver chops the heifer's spoil,
And where huge hogsheads sweat with trainy oil,
Thy breathing nostril hold. (II, 243–253)

This is the environment to which the country clown and rural squire come, healthy and ignorant, used to a life of some cleanliness and some honesty, a ready-made dupe for "the jugler's feats, . . . the thimble's cheats" (the old shell game), and the clever, syphilitic prostitute. Greene's cony-catchers and the cheats of Jonson's London have changed very little in a hundred years. Nightingale of *Bartholomew Fair* still practices his wiles:

> Let not the ballad-singer's shrilling strain
> Amid the swarm thy list'ning ear detain:
> Guard well thy pocket; for these *Syrens* stand
> To aid the labours of the diving hand. (III, 77–80)

The pickpocket and the cutpurse with "unfelt fingers" still steal the country lad's last shilling. Night brings additional menaces; Gay warns the clown:

> Where *Lincoln's-Inn*, wide space, is rail'd around,
> Cross not with vent'rous step; there oft' is found
> The lurking thief, who while the day-light shone,
> Made the walls echo with his begging tone:
> That crutch which late compassion mov'd, shall wound
> Thy bleeding head, and fell thee to the ground.
> Though thou art tempted by the link-man's call,
> Yet trust him not along the lonely wall;
> In the mid-way he'll quench the flaming brand,
> And share the booty with the pilf'ring band.
> Still keep the publick streets, where oily rays
> Shot from the crystal lamp, o'erspread the ways.
> (III, 133–144)

Occasionally, the theft is espied, the thief is chased through the streets by an ever-increasing mob of honest tradesmen, caught,

> And stretch'd beneath the pump's incessant spout:
> Or plung'd in miry ponds, he gasping lies,
> Mud choaks his mouth, and plaisters o'er his eyes.
> (III, 74–76)

The moral is pointed out clearly by Gay, "Ill-fated boy!
Why did not honest work thy youth employ?"
    It is also of the utmost importance for the clown "How to
know a Whore," and thus preserve his moral virtue and
bodily health when in the city. Gay cautions him:

> O! may thy virtue guard thee through the roads
> Of *Drury's* mazy courts, and dark abodes,
> The harlots guileful paths, who nightly stand,
> Where *Katherine-street* descends into the *Strand*.
> Say, vagrant Muse, their wiles and subtil arts,
> To lure the strangers unsuspecting hearts;
> So shall our youth on healthful sinews tread,
> And city cheeks grow warm with rural red. (III, 259–266)

Note again how the inevitable pastoral contrast is made; even
city youths who walk and who preserve their bodies from
venereal disease can change the color on their pallid cheeks
to a healthy rural red and become like the clown. When
health exists in the town, Gay implies, it reflects country
characteristics and associations. The converse is brought out
strongly in the following moral vignette which tells how the
yeoman (the clown) sells his herds for gain and then loses
his money to a prostitute, who robs him while he is drunk and
completes the bargain by giving him syphilis. When the
country becomes subject to the evils and diseases of the town,
it takes on town characteristics and associations.[6]
    Despite the dangers to which he is exposed, the life of the
walker, as representative of a remnant of country existence,
is much to be preferred over the life of the rider, more truly
representative of town life in its laziness, unhealthfulness,
and misuse of others. The walker is only liable to dangers
because he must thread his way through the complex maze
of civilized or artificial existence. We might almost sum up
Gay's attitude in *Trivia* by this important contrast; the walker
is only going through the city on his way to the country,

to the freedom outside of the maze; the rider never leaves the city, but goes about in circles under the illusion that he is free, whereas he never leaves the maze at all. To the townsman the maze is freedom. In Gay's mind although walking is associated with unforeseeable and disgusting dangers of being befouled, it is also associated with health, functionalism, poverty, honesty, and peace of mind. Gay praises Venice because of its gondolas, and then with characteristic nostalgia, he speaks of how "of old Brittania's city [was also] blessed,/ E'er pride and luxury her sons possess'd" (I, 101–108). Before coaches, chariots, and chairs were invented, "the proud lady" walked to visit her friends, and "Her rosie cheek with distant visits glow'd,/And exercise unartful charms bestow'd." But now, the rich, vain, proud, deceitful, and dishonest supplant the healthy and the virtuous, and their mode of travel is riding:

> But since in braided gold her foot is bound,
> And a long trailing manteau sweeps the ground,
> Her shoe disdains the street; the lazy fair
> With narrow step affects a limping air.
> Now gaudy pride corrupts the lavish age,
> And the streets flame with glaring equipage;
> The tricking gamester insolently rides,
> With *Loves* and *Graces* on his chariot's sides;
> In sawcy state the griping broker sits,
> And laughs at honesty, and trudging wits: (I, 109–118)

While the wealthy "in gilded chariots . . . loll at ease,/And lazily insure a life's disease" (I, 69–70), the walker maintains his health and sanity, safe from the physical disorders and accidents (jaundice, asthma, gout, broken arms and legs) to which the rider is liable (II, 501–522).

Gay, as always, is absorbed by humanity, the individual human beings who make up the town and its society. As he walks through the narrow alleys of London, he tries to read the professions and characters of the people he meets:

But sometimes let me leave the noisie roads,
And silent wander in the close abodes
Where wheels ne'er shake the ground; there pensive stray,
In studious thought, the long uncrouded way.
Here I remark each walker's diff'rent face,
And in their look their various bus'ness trace.
The broker here his spacious beaver wears,
Upon his brow sit jealousies and cares;
Bent on some mortgage (to avoid reproach)
He seeks bye streets, and saves th' expensive coach.
Soft, at low doors, old letchers tap their cane,
For fair recluse, who travels *Drury-lane;*
Here roams uncomb'd the lavish rake, to shun
His Fleet-street draper's everlasting dun. (II, 271–284)

Such townsmen as these, reminiscent of Pope's Japhet Crook, Otway's Antonio, and Congreve's Valentine, are pictured and caught by the newsreel in their typical poses. The impression left after the last flicker of film is one of creeping evil. The modern slang phrase of "being taken for a ride" is somehow the best way of expressing how this evil creeps in beneath the illusion of easy transportation with its concomitant illusions of the importance of money and power. Gay expresses the illusion thus as he points up the moral significance of the walker's life:

What walker shall his mean ambition fix
On the false lustre of a coach and six?
Let the vain virgin, lur'd by glaring show,
Sigh for the liv'ries of th' embroider'd beau.
  See yon bright chariot on its braces swing,
With *Flanders* mares, and on an arched spring;
That wretch, to gain an equipage and place,
Betray'd his sister to a lewd embrace.
This coach, that with the blazon'd 'scutcheon glows,
Vain of his unknown race, the coxcomb shows.
Here the brib'd lawyer, sunk in velvet, sleeps;
The starving orphan, as he passes, weeps;

> There flames a fool, begirt with tinsell'd slaves,
> Who wastes the wealth of a whole race of knaves.
> That other, with a clustring train behind,
> Owes his new honours to a sordid mind.
> This next in court-fidelity excells,
> The publick rifles, and his country sells.
> May the proud chariot never be my fate,
> If purchas'd at so mean, so dear a rate;
> O rather give me sweet content on foot,
> Wrapt in my virtue, and a good Surtout! (II, 569–590)

Certainly, the "vain virgin," the "embroider'd beau," the pimp for his own sister, the bastard-coxcomb, the dishonest lawyer, the foolish wastrel, the court favorite with the "sordid mind," and the treasonable statesman, all are "being taken for a ride" (i.e., tricked) in the sense that they have sold what is really valuable and virtuous—chastity, modesty, honor, integrity, self-respect, independence, and honesty—for empty riches, empty show, and empty power. These dubious rewards are in reality only things that constitute being in vogue for our own brief lifetimes and they are most often evanescent even then because circumstance can so quickly spin the wheel. Virtue, to Gay, as to the ancient Christians and Stoics, is the only permanent value—the one really general and universal object—and its basic expressions must be similar in all times and places. The wealth that is "purchased at [the] so mean, [and] so dear a rate" of the starving orphan's tear is to be rejected absolutely, because this purchase means "being taken for a ride" in a second sense (i.e., a ride to one's death); in this case, the trip leads to the spiritual and moral death which comes to all those who choke off their feelings of compassion and sympathy for the welfare of others.[7]

Gay's *contemptus mundi*, with its final proof of the frailty of life and the futility of wealth and power, appears in his direct description of man's last ride: [8]

> Contemplate, mortal, on thy fleeting years;
> See, with black train the funeral pomp appears!
> Whether some heir attends in sable state,
> And mourns with outward grief a parent's fate;
> Or the fair virgin, nipt in beauty's bloom,
> A croud of lovers follow to her tomb.
> Why is the herse with 'scutcheons blazon'd round,
> And with the nodding plume of Ostrich crown'd?
> No: The dead know it not, nor profit gain;
> It only serves to prove the living vain.
> How short is life! how frail is human trust!
> Is all this pomp for laying dust to dust? (III, 225–236)

Whether the grief be sincere or merely "outward," the event is inevitable. Death will come sooner or later, and in Gay's mood it makes little difference if he takes us in "the black train (with proper) funeral pomp" or in the hangman's cart. All the luxury and aspiration of the town must return again to mere country dust.

One of the admirable traits of the eighteenth century is the growth of an increased sympathy for the mistreated, the impoverished, and the helpless. Whether the object of compassion was the foundling or just the drayman's horse, the change in attitude from callousness to benevolence was everywhere apparent. The growth of such philanthropic concepts of humanitarian reform was partially due to the efforts of men like General Oglethorpe whose sensibilities were outraged by the vast injustices prevalent in their society, and partially to more subtle intellectual influences such as Steele's and Shaftesbury's praise of social feelings and benevolent emotions as evidence of the highest virtue in the possessor. But we must also attribute this growth partially to that innate human decency which men as sensitive and intellectual as most poets are usually endeavor to preserve. The contrast between the lives of rich and poor had become so obvious that exhortations to alleviate the miserable state of the poor were deemed almost necessary by many writers of the century. The georgic picture of the lives of humble folk took on added meaning when a sense of ethical responsibility for their diminished welfare was aroused. The symbolism of the rich as riders and the poor as walkers is intensified within *Trivia* by repeated associations of the rich with fair weather and the poor with bad weather. We noticed that the chief sign of Spring was the fine lady, "gayly dressed" (I, 145–148); but the chief signs of winter almost invariably involve socially conscious pictures of the poor and feeble (I, 134–142).

Gay is also very much concerned about the many pitiful cases of injustice toward the young and helpless of Augustan England. The question of what to do with little bastard children thrown upon an unfeeling community was one of the chief social problems of the entire century. The actual practices of ignorant, penniless young mothers is mirrored in the tale of Cloacina, the pregnant Goddess who, "cautious of disgrace, . . . sought no midwife's aid, . . . [but all] "Alone, beneath a bulk, she dropt the boy" (II, 135–140). With such a start in life, the boy has little choice but to harden himself through struggle for mere existence. Beggary and crime are likely to be his means of livelihood:

> The child through various risques in years improv'd,
> At first a beggar's brat, compassion mov'd;
> His infant tongue soon learnt the canting art,
> Knew all the pray'rs and whines to touch the heart.
>
> (II, 141–144)

The even more abominable crime of forcing the helpless part of one's society to beg is revealed in these lines; the child, whose emotions should be naturally felt and expressed, is forced to learn how to work upon the feelings of others. The real pity is that this pathetic creature "who whines to touch the heart" is not only homeless and hungry, but has also lost his capacity to feel naturally as a child should. In his earliest youth he has been forced to be a trickster, a cony-catcher of compassion because it means money to him. The penny we give to this child does not pay for our lack of social responsibility. Gay recognizes this false humanitarianism of the rich; and with Swiftian irony he draws the rich-poor contrast again as he apostrophizes:

> Oh happy unown'd youths, your limbs can bear
> The scorching dog-star, and the winter's air,
> While the rich infant, nurs'd with care and pain
> Thirsts with each heat, and coughs with ev'ry rain!
> (II, 145–148)

Gay's command of pathos, which we have already noticed in *Rural Sports*, is again very evident in this tale. But it is frequently mixed with that strange attitude of cynical jocularity which idealists often adopt to hide the overwhelming convictions of their deepest feelings. Gay avoids the maudlin expression of sentimental drama only by slightly burlesquing the loneliness, to which he, an orphan who had early lost his own father and mother, must often have been subject:

> Now dawns the morn, the sturdy lad awakes,
> Leaps from his stall, his tangled hair he shakes,
> Then leaning o'er the rails, he musing stood,
> And view'd below the black canal of mud,
> Where common-shores a lulling murmur keep,
> Whose torrents rush from *Holborn's* fatal steep:
> Pensive through idleness, tears flow'd apace,
> Which eas'd his loaded heart, and wash'd his face;
> At length he sighing cry'd; That boy was blest,
> Whose infant lips have drain'd a mother's breast;
> But happier far are those, (if such be known)
> Whom both a father and a mother own:
> But I, alas! hard fortune's utmost scorn,

Who ne'er knew parent, was an orphan born!
Some boys are rich by birth beyond all wants,
Belov'd by uncles, and kind good old aunts;
When time comes round, a Christmas-box they bear,
And one day makes them rich for all the year.
Had I the precepts of a Father learn'd,
Perhaps I then the coach-man's fare had earn'd,
For lesser boys can drive; I thirsty stand
And see the double flaggon charge their hand,
See them puff off the froth, and gulp amain,
While with dry tongue I lick my lips in vain. (II, 169–192)

Gay's humanitarianism partakes of a spirit of real concern and genuine pity for those less fortunate than he. In his instructions on to whom "to give the Wall," there is an attitude that transcends mere gentlemanliness or externally imposed precepts of benevolence:

Let due civilities be strictly paid.
The wall surrender to the hooded maid;
Nor let thy sturdy elbow's hasty rage
Jostle the feeble steps of trembling age:
And when the porter bends beneath his load,
And pants for breath; clear thou the crouded road.
But, above all, the groping blind direct,
And from the pressing throng the lame protect.
(II, 45–52)

The passage about Christmas (II, 437–450) provides the best illustration of Gay's humanitarianism. It offers additional proofs of the generosity, kindliness, and selflessness which his contemporaries were so quick to attribute to him. Christmas meant charity for Gay,[9] a special time to think upon and aid the poor, sick, and unfortunate. The combination of bad weather and good spirits that make up Christmas affects Gay with its strange paradox. Country symbols, such as "rosemary, and bays, the Poet's crown, . . . bright holly, . . . laurel green, and sacred mistletoe," indicate that Christmas is a "joyous period of the year," and yet Gay knows that storms and coldness make this time of the year one of misery for the poor. Gay recognizes that it is difficult to really feel joy with the knowledge that others are suffering. With Spenserian personification he invokes what should be the true spirit of these sacred moments:

> Now, heav'n-born Charity, thy blessings shed;
> Bid meagre Want uprear her sickly head;
> Bid shiv'ring limbs be warm; let plenty's bowle
> In humble roofs make glad the needy soul.
> See, see, the heav'n-born maid her blessings shed;
> Lo! meagre Want uprears her sickly head;
> Cloath'd are the naked, and the needy glad,
> While selfish Avarice alone is sad. (II, 443–450)

The naked and the needy beneath the humble roofs of the town would make the country cheer of Christmas a mockery, if meager Want and selfish Avarice were not for once subjected. But Gay realizes too that the selfish avarice of the rich is continually imposing meager want upon the poor throughout the year. The duty of the walker (or the good man) is to maintain the Christmas spirit throughout the year; Gay expresses his Dickensian sentiments thus:

> Proud coaches pass, regardless of the moan
> Of infant orphans, and the widow's groan;
> While Charity still moves the walker's mind,
> His lib'ral purse relieves the lame and blind.
> Judiciously thy half-pence are bestow'd,
> Where the laborious beggar sweeps the road.
> Whate'er you give, give ever at demand,
> Nor let old-age long stretch his palsy'd hand.
> Those who give late, are importun'd each day,
> And still are teaz'd because they still delay.
> If e'er the miser durst his farthings spare,

> He thinly spreads them through the publick square,
> Where, all beside the rail, rang'd beggars lie,
> And from each other catch the doleful cry;
> With heav'n, for two-pence, cheaply wipes his score,
> Lifts up his eyes, and hasts to beggar more. (II, 451–466)

Again Gay protests against human hypocrisy; the miser or extortioner, who preys upon the poor and creates the beggar, seeks to put down the pricking of his conscience and bribe the impartial judges of heaven by distributing his two-pence "thinly . . . through the publick square." And this is double bribery in the sense that the extortioner bribes the beggar, with money that would be rightfully his in a well-adjusted economy, to keep quiet about the social injustice that has been done to him. Such gestures only emphasize the greed and selfishness of false charity. True charity is to "give ever at demand," as much as possible and with as much good will as possible. Only those who do not overvalue money really know to what purposes it should be put.

The tone of this passage partakes directly of the famous verses of Paul's praise of charity:

> Though I speak with the tongues of men and of angels, and have not charity, I am become as sounding brass, or a tinkling cymbal.

The double reference to *heaven* in the above lines (443 and 465) of *Trivia* contributes another of the rare chords of Christian orthodoxy to Gay's poetry, primarily because of the essentially Christian origin of the concept of charity. The section is concluded on a strong religious note (i.e., strong for Gay and the early eighteenth century) with Gay's plea for prayer, the final gift of charity, when actual social charity and brotherly compassion are no longer of any avail:

> Where the brass knocker, wrapt in flannel band,
> Forbids the thunder of the footman's hand;
> Th' upholder, rueful harbinger of death,

Waits with impatience for the dying breath;
As vultures, o'er a camp, with hov'ring flight,
Snuff up the future carnage of the fight.
Here canst thou pass, unmindful of a pray'r,
That heav'n in mercy may thy brother spare? (II, 467–474)

Trivia may be considered then as the voicing of the beggar's social criticism by his fellow in isolation, the artist. But the artist as neoclassic poet is much less overtly critical than the beggar might be, if he were allowed to protest directly. This restraint is due to the neoclassicist's use of imitation, and his respect for the classical model he is following, even when he is pleasantly burlesquing it. The newsreel shifts its focus, as is proper with the progress poem, but it attempts to maintain a structural unity by selecting or focusing on themes proper to a burlesque georgic on the art of walking the streets. The town with all its dangers, disease, and crime is flashed on the screen, but for the riders—the rich and selfish ones—the film has been so speeded up that they cannot see the evils which they have caused by initiating this era of materialism. However, for the walkers—the poor and compassionate ones like Gay—the film has been geared for slow motion; they can pause and deliberate upon the life of the town, and compare its perversions of humanity with the self-sufficient functionalism of a well-lived country existence. The clown, after seeing the big city, is well satisfied to return home again.

CHAPTER IV

Wealth and Universal Darkness

> When we with superficial view
> Gaze on the rich, we're dazled too:
> We know that wealth, well understood,
> Hath frequent power of doing good;
> Then fancy that the thing is done,
> As if the power and will were one.
> Thus oft' the cheated croud adore
> The thriving knaves that keep 'em poor.

IN ADDITION to the directly presented social lessons of *Trivia*, Gay, in his role of didactic poet, often implied such lessons through satire. Satire, as a genre, obviously embodied the same principles for Gay as it did for Dr. Johnson who defined it as "a poem in which wickedness or folly is censured." With the exception of his last *Fables*, Gay's undeservedly neglected verse epistles probably show his keenest censure of the wickednesses and follies of the town. And though the sunshine of Gay's humor often plays about these poems, Gay, as satirist, is still judging his society with a voice of righteousness. Again it is the artist of merit as impecunious beggar who speaks in these epistles, and his attitude truly reflects that aura of gloominess which has been ascribed to the indignant satires of Gay and his fellow Scriblerians. The darknesses of Gay's gloom are split by rays of laughter, but the inevitable sense of spiritual isolation which accompanies the satirist's calling is thoroughly evident in these poems. The indignation of the beggar is voiced by the unpatronized artist, because the crime of neglect which is perpetrated against each of them springs from the same root, the misuse of wealth.

It is needless to retrace the development of satire from the Fescennine verses of the old Roman Saturnian Feasts through the consolidation of the form by Ennius and Lucilius and the innovations of Varro to its final perfection in Horace and Juvenal.[1] The English satires of the early seventeenth century by Hall and Donne have been recognized as more Juvenalian, more savage, more filled with the indignation of outraged virtue than the satire of the Restoration period expressed with such cynical disillusionment toward human dignity in the poems of Rochester. The materialism and mechanism which Swift, Pope, and Gay protest against in the name of Christian and classical values was a tidal wave against which neither tirade nor cynicism could erect dikes strong enough to keep the "virtue" of the ancients truly alive and pertinent. Thus, with the full flowering of English neo-classicism in the eighteenth century, Horace, because of his repute as the greatest moral philosopher of the Roman satirists, began to be more fully imitated as the best antidote against the utter decay of right reason. Dacier in his *Essay upon Satyr* maintains that the aim of Horatian satire is to instruct to action by reaching our hearts, and he summarizes for us the aims of Gay and the other Augustan satirists, as well as those of Horace, when he says,

In these two Books of his Satyrs, Horace would teach us, to conquer our Vices, to rule our Passions, to follow Nature, to limit our Desires, to distinguish true from False, and Ideas from things, to forsake Prejudice, to know thoroughly the Principles, and Motives of all our Actions, and to shun that Folly which is in all Men, who are bigotted to the Opinions they have imbibed under their teachers, which they keep obstinately without examining whether they are well grounded. In a Word, he endeavors to make us happy for our selves, agreeable, and faithful to our Friends, easie, discreet, and honest to all, with whom we are oblig'd to live.[2]

These precepts of subjugating vice, ruling our passions, and knowing ourselves thoroughly in order to conform to the Horatian concept of the *vir bonus* underlie the effort of the Tory satirists to combine a Cartesian rationalism with humanistic cultural values. They accept the dictum of Descartes that man is a rational creature whose reason, assisted by his will, his imagination, and his ability to reform when his frailties are subjected to the clarity of a searching ridicule, can control his passions according to the innate ideas of good with which he is endowed and can preserve himself in a state of equilibrium with ordered society. The Tory satirists share a liking for irony, a distrust of mechanistic science and fanatic religiosity, a tendency to satirize by debasing human dignity through the use of animal analogies, and a surface Hobbesian bitterness [3] (the pose of cynic in Gay) which only clothes a true self based on beliefs similar to those of the benevolists (the real Gay as sentimentalist). The core of religious faith which Swift, Pope, and Gay maintained (in opposition to Bolingbroke, for instance) lent a constant sincerity and idealism to their bent for satire.

Certain passages of Gay's epistles, as well as his second series of *Fables,* embody a sharpness and vehemence which is more characteristic of the formal verse satire of the Juvenalian type, but the primary tone of many of these poems is one of instructive raillery. We are very much reminded of Gay by Dacier's rather exuberant eulogy of Horace:

In the manner that *Horace* presents himself to us in his Satyrs, we discover nothing of him at first, that deserves our attachment. He seems to be fitter to amuse Children than to employ the thoughts of Men; but when we remove that, which hides him from our Eyes, and view him even to the Bottom, we find in him all the Gods together; that is to say, all those Vertues, which

ought to be the continual Practice of such as seriously endeavor
to forsake their Vices.[4]

Gay likewise insinuates himself upon the reader; at first, he
too seems to be merely pleasant and amusing, sounding the
same familiar chords which other and better poets have struck
before. He often employs the stock conventions of the verse
epistle. Frequently his initial paragraph is one of subtle flattery with an accompanying protestation that he does not
intend to flatter because flattery is a vice and would be an
insult to the recipient. He mockingly invokes some Muse or
other (usually a satiric one), depending upon the chief topic
of the epistle. He includes serious interpolations on the virtues and vices of his own nation. His poems are full of vignettes, dramatic dialogues, and character portraits of a
satirical sort with many ironical illustrations. And all of these
conventions are usually cloaked in a didactic moral tone.
But, as we have noted, there is a core of thought and belief
which serves as a foundation for a genuinely apprehensible
set of principles in Gay's work. The more we study his poetry
and drama, the more convinced we become of his ability to
instruct us in the difficult arts of following nature, of distinguishing the true from the false, and the idea from the
thing, and of knowing thoroughly the motivating forces or
beliefs behind our actions.

The modes through which this instruction is conveyed
naturally vary; and the verse epistle itself is an extremely
flexible form. Before we consider Gay's genuinely satiric
epistles, we must glance momentarily at a lesser type, common to the Restoration and eighteenth century, the versified
letter. In origin, it was probably modeled upon the lighter
verse of Horace, wherein a graceful, easy diction combines
with a pleasurable, easy hedonism. The letter could be on almost any topic, and verse was often used for no other reason
than humorous effect.[5] Gay's epistle *To a Lady on her pas-*

sion for old China rivals the poems of Prior, the acknowl-
edged master of this form. It is in the octosyllabic couplets
which both of these poets often employed in their lighter
songs, ballads, and fables for mildly satiric purposes. The
motif of "enthusiastic" overvaluation of some foible of
society (the theme of being in vogue applied to an article of
clothing, a knickknack, or a coiffure) has affinities with such
mock-heroic poems as Pope's *Rape of the Lock* and Gay's
own *Fan*. Gay's main object in this poem is to persuade
Laura to love him instead of devoting her passion to a China
Jar. The jar serves as a clever metaphor complimenting Laura
and womanly beauty;

> When I some antique Jar behold,
> Or white, or blue, or speck'd with gold,
> Vessels so pure, and so refin'd
> Appear the types of woman-kind. (ll. 28–31)

Of course, a mild irony operates in the comparison of Laura,
the town lady, with the nonfunctional China Jar whose
beauty is merely decorative. Man, on the other hand, is "a
strong earthen vessel, made for drudging, labour, toil and
trade;" yet, on second thought, Gay asks, and the cynical
note is all important, is the ruling passion for china any more
ridiculous than the scientist's pursuit of knowledge by examining fossils,[6] or the poet's pursuit of place by flattering
courtiers?

> If all that's frail we must despise,
> No human view or scheme is wise.
> Are not Ambition's hopes as weak?
> They swell like bubbles, shine and break. (ll. 55–58)

Again Gay asks what is real and what illusory, what is strong
and what brittle? The poem concludes that there are very
few pleasures upon which we can rely absolutely. Even the
man who "loves a country life" may be made miserable if

his wife constantly nags him to return to town; "and if he quit his farms and plough," he is very apt to be made a cuckold. A veil of cynicism overlays the charming banter of this poem, and gives to its conclusion an irrefutable logic to add to its "Cavalier" grace:

> Love, *Laura,* love, while youth is warm,
> For each new winter breaks a charm;
> And woman's not like *China* sold,
> But cheaper grows in growing old;
> Then quickly chuse the prudent part,
> Or else you a break a faithful heart.[7] (ll. 67-72)

The excellence of the light epistles with their mastery of humorous incongruity and mild irony, their ribaldry and sly pokes at the fashions of the town, has been overlooked because of the more powerful impact of Gay's major epistles. These key poems, also derived and imitated from Horace, are grounded firmly in the better-known traditions of classical satire and verse epistle. But because of the variance of subject matter, the classical verse epistle of the eighteenth century is primarily an imitation of Horace in tone rather than in structure. We may inquire briefly just how thorough is Gay's use of the classics. Are his Latinate phrases and epithets, and his references to the Muses, Apollo, Bacchus, and the Tritons the allusions of a scholar or the meaningless tags absorbed from the pamphlets and fashionable letters of the day? Or are they perhaps the reminiscences of once-loved books still fermenting in the memory although the taste is no longer sharp and the thoughts and images no longer clear? His expressions are frequently classical, but they are usually not too definite or easily traceable to their source. His classical allusions are employed most often in making epic analogies or ludicrous similes, and as bases for the creation of burlesque myths of his own. Dobson refers to a large paper copy of Maittaire's *Horace* (Tonson and Watts, 1715) which Gay owned and annotated extensively in his own handwriting.⁸ In addition to Homer, Virgil, and Ovid, in his *Epistle to Bernard Lintott* Gay mentions Horace as one of the great ancients whom all should know and study, "Horace [who] in useful numbers should be sung (l. 30)." It is obvious that, although he is most often indebted to Horace in his earlier writings, the satires and epistles of the Roman master contributed much to the critical vein of all of Gay's works, even the *Fables* which are singularly free from classical allusions of any sort.⁹ In addition to the obvious imitation of Horace's *Journey to Brundisium* in the *Epistle to Burlington*, Gay's epistles employ both the personal condemnation more characteristic of Horace's *Satires* and the expository presentation of a point of view characteristic of Horace's *Epistles* (paralleled, for instance, in Gay's discourse on art in the *Epistle to Methuen*). That Gay approximates an Horatian tone may be seen by a brief comparison of a passage from Horace's *Second Satire of the Second Book* with a passage from the *Epistle to Snow:*

> O magnus posthac inimicis risus! uter-ne
> Ad casus dubios fidet sibi certus? hic, qui
> Pluribus assuerit mentem corpusque superbum?
> An qui contentus parvo, metuens que futuri,
> In pace, ut sapiens, aptarit idonea bello?¹⁰ (ll. 89–93)

> Why did '*Change-Alley* waste thy precious Hours,
> Among the Fools who gap'd for golden Show'rs?
>   .   .   .   .
> Madmen alone their empty Dreams pursue,
> And still believe the fleeting Vision true;
> They sell the Treasures which their Slumbers get,
> Then wake, and fancy all the World in Debt. (ll. 14–37)

The fallacy of basing all one's hopes on "fickle Fortune," and overemphasizing the security which money supposedly brings, are Horatian themes quite pertinent to Gay, and it is interesting that the lines of Pope's paraphrase [10] of this *Second Satire* refer directly to the South Sea Bubble which constitutes the chief theme of Gay's *Epistle*. The barbed tones of these passages are similar in their probing for the reality behind the "Jest"; the satirist, as exposer (or psychologist), in the commentaries of both Pope and Gay, depicts the ordinary grasping citizen as "madman." Gay shares with Horace the desire for country peace and contentment, free from the cares of urban wealth and ambition; common sense leads Gay to Devonshire (in dreams at least) just as it led Horace to Brundisium.

The main object of satire, however, is to point out the social and moral evils of character and action which need remedying. Such is the aim of Gay's major verse epistles. *An Epistle to William Pulteney, Esq.* castigates the fop as one of the most reprehensible products of an overrefined civilization. The contemptuous tone which Gay uses to picture the character and activities of man as Sporus is reminiscent of the Juvenalian indignation and violence of Donne's *Satyre I*. As we have noted in *Trivia*, the fop is the ultimate in nonfunctional man, the antithesis of the hardworking rural swain. The fact that this epistle is to review for Pulteney the amusements which he and Gay shared on their visit to Paris in 1717–1718 gives Gay an opportunity to be more vehemently condemnatory than if he were speaking more directly of the social diseases of London. It cannot be denied however that the foibles and evils which are so typical of Paris are only the same as those of London carried (perhaps) to excess; it is not Paris or London which is really on trial, it is the broader concept of the town as representative of urban civilization. The veiled threat at the conclusion of this poem, "Should I let Satyr loose on English ground,/[Where] fools of various character abound," has really been fulfilled in many parts of the preceding two hundred and fifty lines. Implied comparisons, such as:

> For such a flutt'ring sight (the fops) we need not roam;
> Our Own Assemblys shine with these at home;

> Women of ev'ry nation are the same;

and

> We too, I own, without such aids may chance
> In ignorance and pride to rival France,

are plentiful throughout this epistle. Paris, as the recognized source of the many vagaries of the theme of being in vogue, is satirized freely; her *petit-maîtres,* her coquettes, and her operas must endure the abuse of *Trivia's* poet. We feel that Gay, even as "Trav'ler," still judges in terms of his ideal, the countryside, a constant standard against which to judge all cities. Gay now, when the times are past, can sagely "laugh at those follys which [he] strove to taste," knowing full well that Paris only suffers from a more advanced stage of the same disease which has afflicted London.

Gay immediately uses his favorite device of the debasing animal analogy to describe the *petit-maître* (or fop):

> In *Paris,* there's a race of animals,
> (I've seen them at their Operas and Balls)
> They stand erect, they dance when-e'er they walk,
> Monkeys in action, perroquets in talk;
> They're crown'd with feathers, like the cockatoo,
> And, like camelions, daily change their hue. (ll. 31–36)

The irony of undeserved praise, so common to Swift, is then employed to emphasize the foible of ostentatious finery:

> How happy lives the man, how sure to charm,
> Whose knot embroider'd flutters down his arm!
> On him the Ladies cast the yielding glance,
> Sigh in his songs, and languish in his dance; (ll. 43–46)

Gay, the silk-mercer's apprentice, who left his detested job and with it probable chances of financial success for the world of wit and poetry, is particularly contemptuous of the town taste which prefers external trappings to artistic merit:

> While wretched is the Wit, contemn'd, forlorn,
> Whose gummy hat no scarlet plumes adorn;
> No broider'd flowers his worsted ankle grace,
> Nor cane emboss'd with gold directs his pace;
> No Lady's favour on his sword is hung.
> What, though *Apollo* dictate from his tongue,
> His wit is spiritless and void of grace,
> Who wants th' assurance of brocade and lace.
> While the gay fop genteely talks of weather,
> The fair in raptures doat upon his feather;
> Like a Court Lady though he write and spell,
> His minuet step was fashion'd by *Marcell;*
> He dresses, fences. What avails to know?
> For women chuse their men, like silks, for show. (ll. 47–60)

The irony of a philosophy of clothes, so effectively exploited by Shakespeare, Swift, and Carlyle, emerges heavily in this poem. The quest of these three great masters to search out what is essential in man and for man also fascinates Gay. Is a man to be judged by his virtues or by his ability to perform the minuet, to fence, and to dress? By satirizing the criteria by which those of the town who are in vogue judge one another, Gay implies that a common sense estimate of evaluating human worth is lacking. We know from our analyses of his other works that Gay expects a man to be truly functional within the limits of his capacity, and in any circumstance to observe those basic moral virtues which any study of the catechism and the ancients would inculcate. But such methods of estimation have been subordinated to the false propriety of being in vogue; the search for the universal with its attendant attempts at standardization occasionally went amiss, and social aberrations, which were condoned or forwarded by those whom power, prestige, and wealth had glorified, were often accepted as the standard of social decorum. The fop, whom any man of common sense would recognize as something different, something provincial and peculiar to the city rather than universal, was often accepted by frivolous elements of high society as exemplifying the most correct, the most decorous, and the most universal characteristics of social behavior. The absurdity of such regard has been a stock theme for all satirists, and nowhere is the ridiculous vice of being in vogue better exemplified than in Gay's character portrait of this Parisian *petit-maître* (ll. 137–160), another Sporus, "a thing of silk, . . . [a] mere white curd of Ass's milk":

> Sudden a fop steps forth before the rest;
> I knew the bold embroidery of his vest.
> He thus accosts me with familiar air,
> "Parbleu! on a fait cet habit en Angleterre!
> Quelle manche! ce galon est grossièrement rangé;
> Voilà quelque chose de fort beau et dégagé!"
> This said: On his red heel he turns, and then
> Hums a soft minuet, and proceeds agen:
> "Well; now you've *Paris* seen, you'll frankly own
> Your boasted *London* seems a country town;
> Has Christianity yet reach'd your nation?
> Are churches built? Are Masquerades in fashion?
> Do daily Soups your dinners introduce?
> Are musick, snuff, and coaches yet in use?"
> Pardon me, Sir; we know the *Paris* mode,
> And gather *Politesse* from Courts abroad.
> Like you, our Courtiers keep a num'rous train.
> To load their coach; and tradesmen dun in vain.
> Nor has Religion left us in the lurch,
> And, as in France, our vulgar croud the Church;
> Our Ladys too support the Masquerade,
> The sex by nature love th' intriguing trade.
> Strait the vain fop in ign'rant rapture crys,
> *Paris* the barbarous world will civilize! (ll. 137–160)

In this passage, the affectation and rudeness of the fop is immediately apparent in the patronizing manner with which he treats Gay as the ignorant rustic. This is a new version of the theme of the country clown in the big city; and the fallacy of any particular society setting itself up as the absolute standard of decorum becomes obvious when we consider that the vogues of the London of *Trivia* are now but the ill-bred notions of a "country town" to the Parisian. Such relativism indicates the folly of any pretensions of absolutism in a decorum based on the drape of the sleeve, or the fashionability of masquerades, music, and snuff. Gay's ironic answer in this little dramatic dialogue makes it clear that he recognizes how really provincial it is for the Parisian to think that "the Parisian mode" is the only correct one. Such behavior is not only known in London, but all that is evil and vicious in that mode is practiced with the same peculiar intensity. Gay actually says, "In London many noble and wealthy fools have adopted Parisian customs: our tradesmen who work to supply the necessities and luxuries of the wealthy are not paid; the ruling classes, who should set good examples, do not go to Church, which is only considered appropriate for the vulgar and downtrodden who need consolation; and our fine ladies are also morally loose and devote themselves to nothing but selfish amusement." But "the vain fop," who is too stupid to apprehend the irony, thinks that such a state of affairs is wonderful, and that the imitation of Paris has rescued London from barbarity. Again the satire of Gay taunts us by its questioning of such manliness and such refinement.

Gay's most personal satire is contained in *A Panegyrical Epistle to Mr. Thomas Snow.* This poem is the best example of formal verse satire in Gay, and also the best example of his hatred for the financial dishonesty, increasingly prevalent with the rise of commerce and industry during the eighteenth century. Mr. Thomas Snow was a goldsmith banker, one of a profession which had evolved in the late seventeenth century, when, because of the insecurity of the Civil War period, wealthy nobles and merchants began to deposit their money, plate, and jewels in the vaults of the goldsmiths. The goldsmiths came to realize that only a small fraction of these valuables were ever withdrawn from day to day by their clients for their expenses, and that the greater fraction lay static in their strong rooms. There were no laws to prevent them from lending out these deposits, as long as they maintained a reserve sufficient to take care of any daily withdrawals which might be made upon them. Thus, the goldsmiths performed two of the chief functions of our modern banks, the lending of money and the receiving of deposits. And with the increase of speculation in the early eighteenth century, they began to use part of these deposits, not only for money-lending transactions, but also for the buying and selling of stocks.[11] By Gay's time, these goldsmith bankers had established a fairly extensive banking system, and although many were men of good repute, there were also many who sought to take advantage of the impecunious spendthrift or the avaricious gull.

When the South Sea (South America) joint-stock company was formed to make use of the commercial privileges gained from the treaty of Utrecht, financial inexperience on the part of both the government and the directors proved disastrous. The company had already assisted in the funding of a floating debt of £10,000,000 in 1711, and now in 1719

when from 6 to 8 per cent. was being paid on the [government] debt of £52,000,000, while the legal rate for private loans was 5 per cent., it offered to take over by instalments annuities to the amount of £31,000,000, and to pay £7,500,000 by the end of 1720, the annuities it acquired being converted into permanent stock at a low rate of interest. The very audacity of this offer convinced a credulous community that the Company had some wonderful money-making secret plan, and investors jumped at the chance of subscribing and of converting their holdings in the national debt into its stock. On 12 April it was able to make a fresh issue of £2,000,000 at £300 for each £100 of stock, on the 23rd it issued £1,500,000 at £400, in July, after the price had touched £1,060, it issued £4,000,000 at £1,000. All the more cautious speculators [unlike Gay] then began to sell out, and the infection quickly spread; by 21 September the price had dropped to £150. The Company never did any profitable trade, and when Walpole wound up its financial transactions, the shareholders only got £33 6s. 8d. for each £100 of Government stock they had sacrificed.[12]

The fever of speculation which attached itself to the dealings of the South Sea Company became contagious and quickly spread to other far more fantastic schemes (or bubbles) for which subscriptions were invited.[13] When it became apparent that the limited opportunities of trade which were available to the South Sea Company could not provide sufficient income for its vast undertakings and the much too high annual dividend (not less than 50 percent) which the directors had promised, the "bubble" burst, and with it all the smaller "bubbles" of the various wildcat joint-stock companies. In 1720 a "Bubble Act" was passed which declared illegal any company without a charter (increasingly difficult to obtain), and thus the formation of further joint-stock companies was effectively discouraged.

Gay and Pope invested in the South Sea Company, but Pope fortunately sold out part of his stock in time. Gay refused to sell on the chance that he might gain the full financial independence which he deemed so necessary to an artist's integrity and personal liberty. The chance failed, and Gay lost most of his money, although enough of the stock was left to transfer some to Pope in May, 1721, and in June of the same year to pay a debt to Henry Watson out of the

South Sea dividends. Gay, the artist, was beggar again, subject to the whims of patronage. It is natural that some bitterness would seep into his *Epistle to Snow,* and yet, this is a poem on a vicious social evil rather than a poem of personal spite, as Dr. Johnson mistakenly believed. Gay was upset, but he refused to shroud himself in the sheets of his valueless stock certificates. Common sense and a nobler scale of values prohibited such an overvaluation of wealth.[14]

At the height of this period of speculation, unscrupulous goldsmith bankers such as Snow perceived that stock-jobbing could be extremely profitable. They began to sell stock in wildcat companies; they bought from speculators items of stable value, such as plate and jewels, at a price beneath their real worth, or they exchanged stock for these items; they exchanged holdings in the national debt for South Sea stock; and, as the gist of Gay's epistle points out, they bought and sold the ridiculously high-priced third South Sea subscription (of £4,000,000 at £1,000) at a huge profit to themselves. Their tactics were eminently practicable, and when honest goldsmith bankers like Martin and Atwill became bankrupt, the dishonest ones like Snow were found to have amassed a wealth comparable to that of the ancient Peruvians. Gay paints an ironic picture of Snow, the Ulysses of Temple-Bar:

O thou, whose penetrative Wisdom found
The *South-Sea* Rocks and Shelves where Thousands drown'd.
When Credit sunk, and Commerce gasping lay,
Thou stood'st: No Bill was sent unpaid away.
When not a Guinea chink'd on *Martin's* Boards,
And *Atwill's* self was drain'd of all his Hoards,
Thou stood'st; (an *Indian* King in Size and Hue)
Thy unexhausted Shop was our *Peru.* (ll. 9–16)

The South Sea treasure hoard was no myth; it actually was discovered, only it was found not in South America, but in Change Alley.

Such a brazen example of the misuse of money, and of the
immoral lengths to which man will stoop to acquire this
most vicious of illusions, wealth, afforded Gay an excellent
opportunity to indulge his talent for satire, and the sharpness
of his wit was certainly not dulled by his sense of personal
involvement. A satiric portrait in the manner of Dryden and
Pope establishes the Scrooge-like character of Mr. Snow at
the beginning of the epistle. Gay addresses his victim directly
with the usual mock humility:

> DISDAIN not, Snow, my humble Verse to hear:
> Stick thy black Pen awhile behind thy Ear.
> Whether thy Compter shine with Sums untold,
> And thy wide-grasping Hand grow black with Gold:
> Whether thy Mien erect, and sable Locks,
> In Crowds of Brokers over-awe the *Stocks*:
> Suspend the worldly Business of the Day;
> And to enrich thy Mind, attend my Lay. (ll. 1–8)

The threefold emphasis on black, connoting evil, with its
effective contrast to the name of Snow points up the irony
of the epic tone. The magnification of the bent (in spirit,
at least) miser into the Achilles of the stock exchange is constantly elaborated in these eight lines. Gay's chief point is to
get Snow to pause in his mighty struggle (for money), lay
down his sword (the accountant's black pen), and rest his
mighty hand (the grasping, crooked fingers of an avaricious
man), so that he may enrich his mind by hearing Gay's
Homeric lay in praise of his heroic deeds. The lay is hardly
complimentary. The ironic phrase, "penetrative Wisdom" as
applied to Snow indicates the goldsmith's perversion of human reason. That which should be used to better the human
lot is perverted to clever scheming and the bankrupting of
"thousands" of helpless people. Snow's continued solvency
during the bursting of the South Sea Bubble is a tribute to his
materialistic passion for money rather than to his capacity to

exercise reason. His ruling passion of avarice provides a powerful springboard for his reason to jump off into precise but
crooked calculation. Against the reality of cold cash the
illusions of poetic imagination are pitted in conflict. Snow,
"whose Judgment scorns Poetick Flights," sold the illusory
contracts which were worth so much less than their declared
value.[15] The poets, here accused of embodying enthusiasm
rather than witty common sense, ("[they] live on Fancy,
and can Feed on Air") bought these third subscriptions at a
price ten times that which Snow had paid for them (probably
satiric exaggeration on Gay's part), dreaming fondly of the
day when they would resell them for "Millions," and cease
to be beggars. But the millions are only in "imaginary gold";
the market crashes and their stocks and contracts are fit only
"to furnish Boys [with] Paper Kites."

Many ambiguities of the relationship between materialism
and idealism are expressed in this poem. The chief antithetical
poles to be considered are business acumen and poetic imagination. The former, as represented by Snow, can produce
real gold and worthless paper (a contract instead of a poem);
the latter, as represented by "Poets," chiefly Gay himself,
produce only the imaginary gold of daydreams, yet on paper
they can produce something of genuine worth, a poem, an
insight into human motives and morals. What Gay satirizes in
this epistle is the foolishness of applying poetic imagination
to the field of business. In business, honesty and integrity are
gone, the universals are discarded for the momentary local-
ized advantages; but the poet (a clown in the realm of
finance) does not realize this:

> No wonder, that *their* Fancies wild can frame
> Strange Reasons, that a Thing is still the same
> Though chang'd throughout in Substance and in Name.
> (ll. 25–27)

A contract is not a poem.

In fact, a contract is not even a contract, it is a kite. The beggar (which Gay has become through his South Sea losses) is different from both the poet and the clown in that he is wise to the ways of business and municipal society. Ironically, he says that Snow is not like Pope's satiric victim, Vulture Hopkins, when, of course, Gay means he is just like him, and "with Ideal Debts [would] plague mankind." And to prove his point that poets can only be deluded by dreams of wealth, Gay tells a "Moral Tale." Gay always uses this device when he wishes to prove that he is in full control of his feelings, and yet make the salient point of the poem lucid. And although this tale tries to be objective, we can detect a not entirely detached bitterness in its tone because we know very well that this poet is Gay and the banker is Snow. Again human dignity is debased, not by the use of the beast analogy, but by its equivalent, man deranged, man void of reason. The scene is set in the asylum for the insane at Moor-Fields. One lunatic, a banker, offers to sell for £10,000 the imaginary estate which he, in his hallucination, has created within his cell. Another lunatic, a poet, is so impressed by the words in which the banker-lunatic has described his delusion that he offers to buy it. So they sign a contract. Then the banker, in a moment of sanity, realizes that all this transaction is worthless, the buying and selling of a vision; but in his avariciousness he wishes to make something on the deal, so he asks the poet for a penny to void the contract. But the poet will not be fooled so easily by the financial connivance of the banker. He takes his "Skew-r" stick and marks off ten notches, each equal to £1000, and completes the bargain. The moral is clear, and universally valid, wealth is illusory and worth nothing compared to artistic creation. And yet the anger which throbs beneath the satire is ample evidence that Gay too realized that a basic amount of money is necessary to maintain one's integrity, one's sense of personal independence.

Gay's venture on the South Seas had culminated in ship-wreck, and he feels doubly hurt because the ship was unsea-worthy.

The problem of the worth and place of poetry is further pursued with typical light Horatian raillery in Gay's *Epistle to [his] ingenious and worthy Friend, W[illiam] L[owndes], Esq., Author of that celebrated treatise in folio, called the LAND-TAX BILL.* The tone of this poem employs the quick-witted, good-hearted satire found in the *Spectator Papers* of "Mr. Steele and his friend" (l. 43), who were praised so highly in Gay's *The Present State of Wit* (3 May 1711) for their excellent style, their nice judgment, and their noble profusion of wit and humor. It is worth quoting a few paragraphs of Gay's praise of Steele, because they sum up so nicely the qualities which Gay feels that literature should propagate, the claims to consideration which art can demand, or should command, in a well-balanced society;

. . . There is this noble difference between him [Steele] and all the rest of our polite and gallant authors: the latter have endeavoured to please the age by falling in with them, and en-couraging them in their fashionable vices and false notions of things. It would have been a jest some time since, for a man to have asserted that anything witty could be said in praise of a married state; or that devotion and virtue were any way neces-sary to the character of a fine gentleman. Bickerstaff ventured to tell the town that they were a parcel of fops, fools, and vain coquettes; but in such a manner as even pleased them, and made them more than half inclined to believe that he spoke truth. Instead of complying with the false sentiments or vicious tastes of the age, either in morality, criticism, or good breeding, he has boldly assured them that they were altogether in the wrong, and commanded them, with an authority which perfectly well became him, to surrender themselves to his arguments for virtue and good sense.

It is incredible to conceive the effect his writings have had on the town; how many thousand follies they have either quite banished, or given a very great check to; how much countenance they have added to virtue and religion; how many people they have rendered happy, by showing them it was their own fault if they were not so; and, lastly, how entirely they have convinced our fops and young fellows of the value and advantages of learning. He has indeed rescued it out of the hands of pedants and fools, and discovered the true method of making it amiable and lovely to all mankind. In the dress he gives it, it is a most welcome guest at tea-tables and assemblies, and is relished and caressed by the merchants on the 'Change; accordingly, there is not a lady at Court, nor a banker in Lombard Street, who is not verily persuaded that Captain Steele is the greatest scholar and best casuist of any man in England.

Lastly, his writings have set all our wits and men of letters upon a new way of thinking, of which they had little or no notion before; and though we cannot yet say that any of them have come up to the beauties of the original, I think we may venture to affirm that every one of them writes and thinks much more justly than they did some time since.

Steele's contribution to Gay's appreciation of the sentimental, the nostalgic, and the pathetic in human affairs, is quite evident in this essay, written before any of Gay's major poetry appeared. The qualities for which Gay praises Steele are all to be found in his own later work. Themes, such as the attack on the fashionable vogues and vices of fop, fool, and coquette; the search for reality; the argument for devotion, marital sanctity, good sense, and learning in the gentleman (and everyone); and the rescuing of virtue from pedantry [16] so as to make it "amiable and lovely to all mankind," have occurred with great frequency in our examination of Gay's principles.

Such are some of the more universal values which poets propagate—and yet what is their reward? How powerful is their influence on men and manners (especially in the Lon-

don society of the Augustan period)? Gay tells us by an
ironic invidious comparison in this epistle to Lowndes. Mr.
Lowndes (1652–1724) was an M.P. for many years and later
a member of the Treasury staff; it was his duty to write up
the annual Land-Tax Bill which was automatically passed
as the first order of business at the opening of each Parliament. Gay's preference for the "Country" party may have
had a slight bearing on his choice of this particular Bill as an
example for his satire because, of course, it did burden the
landed gentry and benefit the merchant class. Lowndes' annual bills were naturally written in the dullest, most businesslike, legal prose, always the same except for the minor changes
due to circumstance. It was a hack task, and yet, the passage
of this bill created the main source of the government's reve-
nue. Gay sets up his ironic contrast immediately at the start
of the poem:

> When Poets print their works, the scribbling crew
> Stick the Bard o'er with Bays, like Christmas pew:
> Can meagre Poetry such fame deserve?
> Can Poetry; that only writes to starve?
> And shall no laurel deck that famous head,
> In which the Senate's annual law is bred?
> That hoary head, which greater glory fires,
> By nobler *ways* and *means* true fame acquires.
> O had I *Virgil's* force to sing the man,
> Whose learned lines can millions raise *per ann.*
> Great L—— his praise should swell the trump of fame,
> And *Rapes* and *Wapentakes* resound his name. (ll. 1–12)

Acclaim by fellow poets and critics, even when deserved,
is not edible; neither for that matter are the values propa-
gated, and the creative imagination shown on the poet's
paper. Gay feels that the poet should have some guarantee of
economic security in a society that values knowledge. And
the fact that he does not have such security is indirect proof

that his society does not value knowledge. The distortion of
the use of *words*, instruments of inspiration and knowledge,
to make money ("millions . . . per ann"), while the real use
of words for the rational communication of values is neglected, constitutes the basic perversion of society satirized
in this epistle. It is obvious that Lowndes' tax bills are nothing
but Snow's contracts expanded; i.e., they are words devoted
to the sole purpose of acquiring money. Yet, this is precisely
all that this type of society desires; therefore Gay by the use
of irony will translate their greedy values into what might
be a truthful expression of such values in the realm of art.
Urban civilization exalts money over art; why not exalt the
written expression of acquiring money over poetry? This
Gay proceeds to do in a burlesque eulogy of Lowndes' creative powers. Homer gained renown "by singing ev'ry
Grecian chief and town," but Lowndes is greater far because
his prose lists every landed person in all of England, and all
of their property that is to be taxed. Why even his style is so
smooth (?) that "we read with pleasure, though with pain
we pay!" [17] How shall we classify him then asks Gay with
mock seriousness; he is not Poet or Historian—suddenly it
comes to him:

> . . . Satyr is thy talent; and each lash
> Makes the rich Miser tremble o'er his cash;
> What on the Drunkard can be more severe,
> Than direful taxes on his ale and beer? (ll. 30–33)

Lowndes is more read than the wits at *Button's;* his text,
unlike the *Classicks* is "fix'd as Fate"; his words last a whole
year invariably while the *Spectator Papers* hardly maintain
interest for a week. And as a final encomium, though Cadmus
could raise an army by sowing dragon's teeth,

> Thy labours, L[owndes], can greater wonders do,
> Thou raisest armys, and canst pay them too.

> Truce with thy dreaded pen; thy Annals cease;
> Why need we armys when the land's in peace?
> Soldiers are perfect devils in their way,
> When once they're rais'd, they're cursed hard to lay.

(ll. 52–57)

The conclusion of the poem hardly seems to be in keeping with its chief theme, and one would think that Gay should have ended it with some climactic mock-heroic plaudit to Lowndes. The reference in lines 53 to 57 is probably to the large standing army of the past decade which drained the nation's resources for the purpose of perpetuating a class devoted to violence at the possible expense of some kind of government patronage for artists, or at least at the expense of some humanitarian reliefs. This epistle is then a fine example of Gay's satiric raillery and his use of irony to expose false social values. Lowndes, who was really a very dull man according to contemporary reports, is universally read because his word is *law* (in the most literal sense). His tax bills maintain a momentary aura of eternality because the government revenues depend on them. He is the politician's poet, the businessman's artist, the symbol of a new society which is beginning to count its wealth in coins instead of knowledge.

In such a society how can we prevent the poet from becoming beggar? Or what is more important, how can we prevent him from becoming a spiritual and intellectual pauper, forced to flatter the unworthy because of his need of actual bread? In a famous joint letter with Pope to Swift (December 1, 1731), after he had at last acquired his small fortune, Gay says:

I have nothing to take me off from my friendship to you. I seek no new acquaintance, and court no favour; I spend no shillings in coaches or chairs to levees or great visits, and, as I do not want the assistance of some that I formerly conversed with, I will not so much as seem to seek to be a dependent. . . . All the money I get is by saving, so that by habit there may be some hopes, if I grow richer, of my becoming a miser. All misers have their excuses. The motive to my parsimony is independence.[18]

And earlier on March 31, 1730, he had told Swift:

I hate to be in debt; for I cannot bear to pawn five pounds' worth of my liberty to a tailor or a butcher. I grant you this is not having the true spirit of modern nobility, but it is hard to cure the prejudice of education.[19]

Personal independence with its concomitant sense of being able to afford real and constant integrity seems to have been a primary goal of Gay in many of his endeavors. He resented deeply being forced to act the sycophant in even the slightest way, and probably that is why his *Epistle to a Lady, Occasion'd by the Arrival of Her Royal Highness* was not considered serious enough to warrant Gay a profitable place at Court, even when Caroline became queen. He could not flatter with that false sincerity so common to courtiers; his best effort for the new princess was a burlesque on how to write a eulogistic poem, followed by clever and undoubtedly pleasant compliments which lack genuine conviction, just as his *Epistle to the Dutchess of Marlborough* on the Duke's death lacks any feeling of genuine sorrow.

And "honest" Gay hated not being genuine. But since he was a poet above all else, a member of a craft traditionally dependent for its income on patronage, what could he do? He felt that enlightened patronage was justifiable and necessary; and yet, the majority of patrons in his own age not only lacked good taste, but also demanded abject flattery. Being possessed of such an aversion to flattering, the choice for Gay was a difficult one. It is to his credit that he finally attained his independence by the composition of a huge dramatic success, *The Beggar's Opera*, and the compilation of a large subscription list for *Polly*. It is even more to his credit that he maintained his integrity, and could write on the problem of patronage thus in his last letter to Pope:

As to your advice about writing Panegyric, 'tis what I have not frequently done. I have indeed done it sometimes against my judgment and inclinations, and I heartily repent of it. And at present, as I have no desire of reward, and see no just reason of praise, I think I had better let it alone. There are flatterers good enough to be found, and I would not interfere in any Gentleman's profession. I have seen no verses on these sublime occasions: so that I have no emulation: let the patrons enjoy the authors, and the authors their patrons, for I know myself unworthy.[20]

Gay perhaps was merely very tired in this letter, written just two months before his death, and yet the dignity and nobility of tone which is inherent in his answer is a refutation of the waning force of patronage more than equal to that more famous refutation made in Dr. Johnson's letter to Chesterfield a few years later.

The chief poetic expression of Gay's views on patronage is contained in the verse satire of his *Epistle to Methuen.* Sir Paul Methuen (1672–1757) was a diplomatist, M.P., and art collector. He had been lord of the Admiralty and of the Treasury; a very wealthy man, he was renowned for his hospitality and liberality. He was accomplished in many of the old social graces, horsemanship, fencing, and dancing, and he knew many foreign languages and was well read in the best authors. His fine collection of paintings was envied throughout England. He was in many senses an ideal person to whom to address an epistle on the degeneration of detached perceptive patronage. Gay compliments him thus as he voices his initial complaint:

> That, 'tis encouragement makes Science spread,
> Is rarely practis'd, though 'tis often said;
> When learning droops and sickens in the land,
> What Patron's found to lend a saving hand?

> True gen'rous Spirits prosp'rous vice detest,
> And love to cherish virtue when distrest:
> But e'er our mighty Lords this scheme pursue,
> Our mighty Lords must think and act like you.
> (ll. 1–8)

But Gay knows that "prosp'rous vice," not sick learning, determines the motives of the men of Augustan society, and thus, the position of the poet in such a society has become economically precarious:

> Why flourish'd verse in great *Augustus*' reign?
> He and *Mecaenas* lov'd the Muse's strain.
> But now that wight in poverty must mourn
> Who was (O cruel stars!) a Poet born. (ll. 15–18)

But a poet need not starve. With a passage of really excellent verse satire, Gay enumerates the present "ways for authors to be great":

> Write ranc'rous libels to reform the State:
> Or if you chuse more sure and ready ways,
> Spatter a Minister with fulsome praise:
> Launch out with freedom, flatter him enough;
> Fear not, all men are dedication-proof.
> Be bolder yet, you must go farther still,
> Dip deep in gall thy mercenary quill.
> He who his pen in party quarrels draws,
> Lists an hir'd bravo to support the cause;
> He must indulge his Patron's hate and spleen,
> And stab the fame of those he ne'er has seen.
> Why then should authors mourn their desp'rate case?
> Be brave, do this, and then demand a place.
> Why art thou poor? exert the gifts to rise,
> And banish tim'rous vertue from thy eyes. (ll. 20–34)

Be hack writer for a Sporus, and you need not be poor; banish virtue and you can secure a profitable place at court (and incidentally also in the *Dunciad*). Sacrifice integrity and

success is yours. Gay knows the answers, but he cannot play
the game. The bitterness of the following lines cannot be
denied:

> All this seems modern preface, where we're told
> That wit is prais'd, but hungry lives and cold:
> Against th' ungrateful age these authors roar,
> And fancy learning starves because they're poor.
> Yet why should learning hope success at Court?
> Why should our Patriots vertue's cause support?
> Why to true merit should they have regard?
> They know that vertue is its own reward.[21] (ll. 35–42)

Money buys creative endeavor in order to distort it and
place it at the service of vice; but learning and true merit
will not provide sufficient money for an artist to subsist, let
alone live with integrity and independence.

Gay feels that enlightened patronage, such as that which
flourished in Italy, may still be a possible answer. The patrons
of the Roman Empire and of the Risorgimento were both
men of wealth and true connoisseurs. And though few such
men are left in England, Gay feels that he prefers the appreciation of such sensitive and tutored patrons and critics to the
profit that he might get by prostituting even his "humble
lays." The contrast of Italy and England is drawn quite
clearly, and for once to England's detriment:

> Ask Painting, why she loves *Hesperian* air.
> Go view, she crys, my glorious labours there;
> There in rich palaces I reign in state,
> And on the temple's lofty domes create.
> The Nobles view my works with knowing eyes,
> They love the science, and the painter prize. (ll. 47–52)

Even now Rome honors artists such as the English painter
William Kent, who studied in Rome and was brought back
to England by the eighteenth-century English prototype of

the true patron, Richard Boyle, the Earl of Burlington.[22] Gay compliments Kent and his patron, Burlington, who not only obtained many projects for his protégé through his influence, establishing him as a "fashionable oracle," but also furnished him with apartments in his town house for some years. According to Gay's view the relationship between these two men is the ideal; the patron provides adequate material needs and the best opportunities for work, and then shares in the glory and good which the artist accomplishes through his genuine ability.

This was, for the period, an honest and fairly independent arrangement, one which we can accept because of the social peculiarities of an age discarding the last social remnants of feudalism for industrial individualism. But we must hesitate momentarily at the examples which Gay was perhaps compelled to choose. What does Gay really know about painting, architecture, and music in comparison with his knowledge of literature? The fact that he compares Kent to Raphael, Titian, and Guido makes us suspicious that Gay was merely tossing names about. His mourning for a lost taste is legitimate and probably true to some extent,[23] but to assert the name of Kent as evidence of a present approximation to the art of the Italian Renaissance is certainly an exaggeration on Gay's part. The opinion of Hogarth that Kent was a very mediocre painter has been confirmed by later critics; the praise of Kent shows that Gay himself could fall into the trap of flattering a friend. Gay was on firmer ground in praising Burlington and Kent for their furtherance of the Palladian style of architecture in England. Both of them had studied Vitruvius, Palladio, and Inigo Jones, and "Burlington's fair palace" and the buildings which he and Kent helped to design [24] were monuments to Burlington's sense of proportion and his desire to harmonize the whole of any structure.[25]

Burlington was also a patron of Handel (*Trivia*, pp. 497–

498), whose music Gay truly loved, and who composed the
score for Gay's Pastoral Opera, *Acis and Galatea*. Gay's taste
in music is commendable also; he frequently mentions
"learned" Corelli; and he is able to distinguish the beauties of
the genuine Italian opera from its French imitation, as we
discover in his amusing vignette (*Epistle to Pulteney*, 185–
204) about the Frenchmen whose abdominable singing
drowned out the voices on the stage. Gay can even become
quite rhapsodic about music:

> O sooth me with some soft *Italian* air,
> Let harmony compose my tortured ear!
> When *Anastasia's* voice commands the strain,
> The melting warble thrills through ev'ry vein; [26]
> Thought stands suspense, and silence pleas'd attends,
> While in her notes the heav'nly Choir descends.
> (*Epistle to Pulteney*, 205–210)

And, of course, the best proof of all is Gay's adaptation of his
lyrics to the music of *The Beggar's Opera* which satirized
the mongrel form of the Italian Opera, a fashionable foible
of the period. Gay believes that art should transcend national
limitations and parochial peculiarities of taste. That which
is universal in theme and beautiful in form should be admired
regardless of its executor.

Provincialism in taste is very often apt to produce envy
of one sort or another. The learned architect Burlington,
and the liberal, though ostentatious, Chandos must both suffer
from it; Gay asks them,

> Canst thou unhurt the tongue of envy hear?
> Censure will blame, her breath was ever spent
> To blast the laurels of the Eminent. (ll. 64–66)

The skill and good taste of Burlington makes him the victim
of the malice of the ignorant;

> While *Burlington's* proportion'd columns rise,
> Does not he stand the gaze of envious eyes?

> Doors, windows are condemn'd by passing fools,
> Who know not that they damn Palladio's rules.[27]
> (ll. 67–70)

The lavishness of Chandos in building a showplace like Timon's Villa is misunderstood by those jealous of his wealth and liberality:

> If *Chandois* with a lib'ral hand bestow,
> Censure imputes it all to pomp and show;
> When, if the motive right were understood,
> His daily pleasure is in doing good.[28] (ll. 71–74)

The superior artist, whether he be architect or poet, must always be the scapegoat for ignorance and local prejudice. Only the dunce, whose work is beneath notice and who flatters the perversions of a bigoted taste, can escape envy:

> Had *Pope* with groveling numbers fill'd his page,
> *Dennis* had never kindled into rage.
> 'Tis the sublime that hurts the Critic's ease;
> Write nonsense and he reads and sleeps in peace.
> Were *Prior, Congreve, Swift* and *Pope* unknown,
> Poor slander-selling *Curll* would be undone.
> He who would free from malice pass his days,
> Must live obscure, and never merit praise.[29] (ll. 75–82)

Naturally, these evidences of corruption in town morality and town taste reflect a feeling on Gay's part that civilization itself is corrupt and decadent. The commonplace idea of the Tory satirists that social values, as well as cultural and artistic skills, had degenerated since the time of the ancients, was bound to be prevalent in Gay's work. The theories of Burnet and his followers [30] about the parallelism of physical decay (the flood) and moral decay (the fall of Adam) were perverted by certain deists and religious pseudo scientists so as to infer that both of these events were mere ancient superstitions of primitive races.[31] The spread of such doubts and the twisted use of Descartes to refute Aristotle's ethics, as well as his science, led to the denial in some cases of original sin and overpraise of the accomplishments of the "moderns." Gay contributed to the attempts to preserve the elements of humanistic (both Christian and classical) learning and ethics which are mirrored in Temple's essay *Upon Ancient and Modern Learning*, Swift's *Battle of the Books*, and *The Memoirs of Martinus Scriblerus*.[32] What Swift, Pope, and Gay dreaded was the coming of an era of outright materialism, the signs of which were overwhelmingly evident to them. Such an era, lacking the old tried and true social and moral values, seemed right on top of them with its proofs of declining taste and art. With his old nostalgia for the past, primitivism, and periods of unusual artistic excellence, Gay had mused to his friend Fortescue, in *Trivia:*

> Behold that narrow street which steep descends,
> Whose building to the slimy shore extends;
> Here *Arundel's* fam'd structure rear'd its frame,
> The street alone retains an empty name:
> Where *Titian's* glowing paint the canvas warm'd,
> And *Raphael's* fair design, with judgment, charm'd,
> Now hangs the bell'man's song, and pasted here
> The colour'd prints of *Overton* appear.
> Where statues breath'd, the work of *Phidias'* hands,
> A wooden pump, or lonely watch-house stands.
> There *Essex'* stately pile adorn'd the shore,
> There *Cecil's, Bedford's, Villers'*, now no more.
>
> (II, 481–492)

Gay was in full accord with Pope in complimenting the Earl of Burlington for maintaining classical proportion and beauty in his estate, and for reviving "declining art," but the young Earl was a last dim light on a darkening social scene. Grotesque, mechanistic tastes and increasing poverty bore down upon the artist of erudition, skill, and integrity. Gay, too, must have felt with Pope that the Goddess of Dulness had succeeded and that the reign "Of *Night* primaeval and of *Chaos* old" was come again to London. The superb ending of *The Dunciad* expresses more than Gay's feeling, but Gay feels it with Pope:

> *Art* after *Art* goes out, and all is Night.
> See skulking *Truth* to her old cavern fled,
> Mountains of Casuistry heaped o'er her head!
> *Philosophy*, that leaned on Heaven before,
> Shrinks to her second cause, and is no more.
> *Physic* of *Metaphysic* begs defence,
> And *Metaphysic* calls for aid on *Sense!*
> See *Mystery* to *Mathematics* fly!
> In vain! they gaze, turn giddy, rave, and die.
> *Religion* blushing veils her sacred fires,
> And unawares *Morality* expires.
> For *public* Flame, nor *private*, dares to shine;
> Nor *human* Spark is left, nor Glimpse *divine!*
> Lo! thy dread Empire, CHAOS! is restored;
> Light dies before thy uncreating word;
> Thy hand, great Anarch! lets the curtain fall,
> And universal Darkness buries All. (ll. 640–656)

Without effective patronage, such as that of Burlington and Methuen, the false values of an avaricious society which bases its taste on the foibles of a fop, the stupid ostentation of the wealthy, or the bigotry of the provincial dunce will prevail more and more. The satire of Gay's best epistles is devoted to warning the public of its cultural decay. Augustan England is becoming a large brokerage office where the poor in wealth must give in to the poor in mind; and where the rich in merit must give in to the rich in bonds. When the artist is forced to become beggar, his society becomes even poorer than he.

CHAPTER V

The Beggar's View of Augustan Courtly Love

LOVE, usually considered the most basic of the passions, offers a good measure for examination and judgment of a society. Attitudes toward sex and the ideals of relationship between men and women are necessarily basic fodder for the satirist and the social commentator. Of them Gay makes good use. Much of his thought was devoted to such examination, and his judgments on sex conduct and love are expressed in all his works.

It is fair to assume that Gay was an expert in the psychology of the feminine mind, for it is certainly true that he had gained the allegiance of many women, including the noblest duchesses of the court. When the performance of *Polly* (later published in 1729) was suppressed, the ladies showed their response to his appeal by rallying to his support. An anonymous friend made the matter the subject of a mocking poem entitled *The Female Faction; or, The Gay Subscribers*. As quoted by Mr. Underhill, it runs:

> Thrice happy poet! whose unrivall'd lays
> Can hosts of Ladies in thy Quarrel raise,
> For thee, their Features do they cease to prize,
> And lose in Rage the Lustre of their eyes!
> On thy blest Lot, accept, without disdain,
> A Brother Bard's Congratulating Strain.[1]

Gay was well able to view in all aspects the usages of Augustan courtly love. In a sense his relationship to the noble duchesses recalls the medieval courts of love, and we can picture him as a sort of Chrétien de Troyes reading a lay to Marie de France or as an Andreas Capellanus prescribing precise rules of devotion for lovers at the mercy of female judges.

There was, however, an intrinsic difference between courtly love in an earlier day and in the Augustan period. Basically life and manners were in eighteenth-century London different from the chivalric mode of living in medieval Provence. The beloved lady was no longer the mistress of a feudal manor but a figure in town society. She was not actually regarded as a singular goddess or inspiration but was only referred to as such in words that she and the lover regarded as no more than conscious artifice. The eternal devotion of Jaufre Rudel had given way to the rule of unfaithfulness in the love game of the Restoration and Augustan periods. All concepts of loyalty were limited to marriage, though observance of marital fidelity was considered "Puritanical" and sneered at by the sophisticated husbands and wives embroiled in fashionable love pursuits.

The town fine lady who was the object of the new courtly love was honored by the foolish and despised by the wise in the Augustan period. She is depicted by Addison—with accents reminiscent of the satire of the Augustan period of Rome—in *Spectator*, No. 73, the best description of the type: [2]

An *Idol* is wholly taken up in the Adorning of her Person. You see in every posture of her Body, Air of her Face, and Motion of her Head, that it is her Business and Employment to gain Adorers. For this Reason your *Idols* appear in all publick Places and Assemblies, in order to seduce Men to their Worship. The Playhouse is very frequently filled with *Idols*; several of them are carried in Procession every Evening about the Ring, and several of them set up their worship even in Churches. They are to be accosted in the Language proper to the Deity, Life and Death are

in their Power; Joys of Heaven and Pains of Hell are at their disposal, Paradise is in their Arms, and Eternity in every Moment
that you are present with them. Raptures, Transports, and Ex-
tasies are the Rewards which they confer: Sighs and Tears,
Prayers and broken Hearts are the Offerings which are paid to
them. Their smiles make Men happy; their Frowns drive them
to despair. (p. 277)

As to the fashionable lover, the following description of his
code of behavior may be compared with the *De arte honeste
amandi* of Andreas Capellanus to show the difference between medieval lover and eighteenth-century gallant, who

must be well born; he must dress well but not ostentatiously; he
must be poised and witty, so that he is never out of countenance;
he must be skilled in making love, whether to women of the town,
to married women, or to young ladies of his own rank, and he
may conduct several love-affairs simultaneously, provided his
head is always master of his heart. He must not boast of his
amours, however, and he must be discreet: it is unpardonable to
betray the confidence of any woman of his own class. If he is so
weak as to entertain a serious passion he must conceal the fact
by an affectation of indifference or by overacted and conventional protestations of devotion. If he is married he must not show
any jealousy of his wife, nor may he let it be seen that he is in love
with her. The fashionable lady is his counterpart, except that she
has somewhat less freedom in love. Ideally she should be perfectly familiar with the world of intrigue without allowing herself to become involved in it; if she is a widow, or is married to
an uncongenial husband, she may indulge in illicit love, provided
she is not found out. In any case she will not expect complete
constancy from her husband.[3]

These are the fine ladies and gentlemen who set the standards and manners of the worldly society of the town—the
social leaders who devote themselves to being "in vogue."
Their foibles, petty deceits, and vanities are amusing to the

urbane gaze of Gay. But does he think them entirely harmless? He does not.

Instead he pillories them by showing their reflections distorted in characters of low life. He accepted the premises that the wealthy set the fashions and that, because the wealthy are not "virtuous," they often establish false standards of taste in dress, amusement, and morality. These are imitated by those lower in the social scale, and because the basis of being "in vogue" is self-interest, not to imitate the selfishness of the rich and powerful is to be vulgar. In *The Beggar's Opera*, Lockit (a warden in Newgate prison) berates his daughter, Lucy, because she let Macheath escape from prison for love rather than for a bribe:

Thou wilt always be a vulgar slut, Lucy— If you would not be look'd upon as a fool, you should never do any thing but upon the foot of interest. Those that act otherwise are their own bubbles. (p. 517)

Self-interest is fashionable, and the same ideas color all society from the noble lord to the highwayman. Macheath, in vowing constancy to Polly Peachum, employs burlesque analogies to bribery, vanity, and gambling, all typical symbols of social success:

Is there any power, any force that could tear me from thee? You might sooner tear a pension out of the hands of a Courtier, a fee from a Lawyer, a pretty woman from a looking-glass, or any woman from *Quadrille*. (p. 500)

The contrast between social vulgarity and true moral vulgarity is heightened throughout the play by incidents and references showing what is supposedly fashionable or polite. In these Gay's irony operates at its best. Lucy Lockit is effusively polite as she plies her rival, Polly Peachum, with poisoned gin. She excuses her previous jealous passion by

saying, "I was so over-run with spleen [high-society melancholia or neurotic depression], that I was perfectly out of
my self. And really when one hath the spleen, everything is
to be excus'd by a friend" (p. 524). The glass of "Strong-
waters" offered as a gesture of renewed friendship is another
symbol of gentility and is accompanied with the boast, "Not
the greatest lady in the land could have better in her closet,
for her own private drinking." Polly also from time to time
shows a liking for the foibles of the fine ladies. And the
prostitute, Jenny Diver, assumes one of the favorite poses
of the fine lady—that of the prude. Macheath greets her:

What! and my pretty Jenny Diver too! As prim and demure as
ever! There is not any Prude, though ever so high bred hath a
more sanctify'd look, with a more mischievous heart. Ah! thou
art a dear artful hypocrite. (p. 504)

It is unnecessary to belabor the point that the duchess and
the whore may be alike in more ways than one. Nothing
could show better the cynical aspect of Gay's view of Augustan love.

Imitation of the vogue can lead to more hypocrisy and
distortion than this. In *The Beggar's Opera*, Peachum has
black-listed [4] Bob Booty (a parody of Robert Walpole), an
old customer, because Bob was devoting himself too much
to females and not providing Peachum with enough profits.
Mrs. Peachum objects, and Peachum replies:

What a dickens is the woman always a whimp'ring about murder
for? No gentleman is ever looked upon the worse for killing a
man in his own defence; and if business cannot be carried on without it, what would you have a gentleman do? (p. 490)

Mrs. Peachum then obsequiously murmurs, "If I am in the
wrong, my dear, you must excuse me, for no-body can help
the frailty of an overscrupulous Conscience." Peachum com-
forts her by appealing, not to her gentleness, but to her

gentility; we can almost picture him putting a loving arm about her shoulders as he assures her that "murder is as fashionable a crime as man can be guilty of."

There is another side of the coin. Whether Gay is praising the true love of Polly, Cylene, and the rural wife or mocking the debased loves of Jenny, the Ducats, and the city fine lady, he is always voicing his firm belief in certain elements as absolutely necessary to love and marriage. These key attributes are devotion, faithfulness, cheerfulness, self-sacrifice, and the ability to create a home environment in which children may be reared virtuously. Such characteristics are simply, easily comprehensible to common sense, and supposedly basic to the benevolent spirit with which Gay thought mankind to be imbued.

Much of the laughter in *The Beggar's Opera* and *Polly* springs from farcical situations created by lust and lack of honor in love. Yet through the two, Polly, continually tempted and continually noble, represents continuing faithfulness to the beloved. She rebels against the vicious social code her parents advocate, which includes exploiting a lover for his money and then betraying him; she marries Macheath even when she knows he may soon be executed; she suffers transportation to the West Indies for him; she risks the loss of her honor; absurdly enough, she even becomes a soldier. Her initial aim was the honest completion of her love through marriage, but the normal fulfillments of marriage in a home and children were frustrated by Macheath's transportation. Later, he, as the pirate chief Morano, is not only unfaithful but evil; he contracts a bigamous marriage with Jenny, the genteel prostitute. His ambition and lust for money destroy his earlier good-natured charm and thwart Polly's loyalty. But love as usual is quite blind. The reins of judgment slip easily from Polly's hands. Despite all the ill-treatment he heaps on her, she still thinks that "my love . . . might reclaim him." This hopeful illusion illustrates an archetypal mode of futility. Gay laughs at his ridiculous Polly, but his account of her undeviating faithfulness shows, behind the mockery, his sentimental admiration for honest devotion in affairs of love.

Much more seriously presented is the heroine of *The Captives*, which is cast in the somewhat outmoded form of the heroic drama.[5] Cylene, the female captive, is a typical, angelic heroine, filled with loyalty and self-sacrifice in a manner to meet the tasteless demands of Gay's audience. Her husband, Sophernes, is a captured Persian prince, like Dryden's Almanzor, but Sophernes is shadowed into total eclipse by his wife's exalted virtue. Her devotion, indeed, seems as endless as some of the monologues. Although the moral force of the play is vitiated by its sentimentality, *The Captives* does fulfill the purposes of the exemplary drama.[6] The key scene (IV, vii) is laid in a dank dungeon. Cylene, by a ruse, has entered Sophernes' cell to give up her life so that he may reassert the rights of the Persian people. After a tender moment of recognition and renewal of affection, Cylene tricks her husband into an oath that he will grant her whatever she will ask. After he swears, she says,

> I thank thee. Thou hast given me all my wishes,
> For now thy life is safe; and sav'd by me.
> Here, take this veil; this shall secure thy flight,
> With this thou shalt deceive the watchful guard.
> O blest occasion! fly, my Lord, with speed;
> I never wish'd to part till now. (ll. 77–82)

He, of course, objects, refusing to save his life at the expense of hers. But she is adamant and threatens suicide until he consents to go and leave her. The last two speeches of the scene, though by no means great poetry, touchingly evoke genuine tragic love in a way reminiscent of Shakespeare's *Othello* and *Romeo and Juliet*: [7]

Cyl. From thy dear hands I take the galling chains.
Lest danger intercept thee, haste, be gone;
And as thou valuest mine, secure thy life.
Thou hadst no hope. Who knows but my offence
May find forgiveness! 'tis a crime of love;
And love's a powerful advocate to mercy.
Soph. O how I struggle to unloose my heart-strings,
That are so closely knit and twin'd with thine!
Is't possible that we may meet again?
That thought has filled my soul with resolution.
Farewell: may Heaven support thee, and redress us!
(ll. 116–126)

Thus true and lasting love can be demonstrated in Gay's works, but far more often does he offer pictures of the distortions of love in town. In *The Beggar's Opera* we are offered no sample of successful marriage like that of the Persian captives. Instead, marriage is constantly being viewed as an encumbrance. Peachum avers that "there is nothing to be got by the death of women—except our wives." Macheath, confronted by both Polly and Lucy, sings,

> One wife is too much for most husbands to bear
> But two at a time there's no mortal can bear.

Thieves and gentlemen share this distaste for the married state, and alike they seek fulfillment of the psychical and physical needs of love outside the moral bounds of matrimony. Possibly the gay lovers of Restoration comedy and of the Augustan courtly love game were truly in love, but the fact that their love never reached its natural fulfillment in marriage gave to it a certain air of spiritual prostitution. How far this immorality could go is shown in Peachum's attitude toward the marriage of his daughter Polly:

You know, *Polly*, I am not against your toying and trifling with a customer in the way of business, or to get out a secret, or so. But if I find out that you have play'd the fool and are married, you jade you, I'll cut your throat, hussy. Now you know my mind. (p. 493)

Mrs. Peachum, whose usual honeyed and motherly tones only emphasize her basic viciousness, is of the same mind as her husband. When Polly confesses that she has indeed been honorable enough to marry Macheath instead of fleecing him, Mrs. Peachum denounces her with rage:

I knew she was always a proud slut; and now the wench hath play'd the fool and married, because forsooth she would do like the Gentry. Can you support the expense of a husband, hussy, in gaming, drinking and whoring? have you money enough to carry on the daily quarrels of man and wife about who shall squander most? There are not many husbands and wives, who can bear the charges of plaguing one another in a handsome way. If you must be married, could you introduce no-body into our family, but a highwayman! Why, thou foolish jade, thou wilt be as ill us'd, and as much neglected, as if thou hadst married a Lord! (p. 494)

She is angry primarily because she feels that she has been cheated in a business deal; her daughter's virginity was a valuable business asset, now stolen by Macheath. Polly's offer of an excuse shows her primitive and basically natural impulses, the innocence of a country girl:

I did not marry him (as 'tis the fashion) cooly and deliberately for honour or money. But, I love him. (p. 495)

The absurdity of this explanation makes Mrs. Peachum faint. Polly and Mr. Peachum revive her with a cordial, and she is able to deliver herself of a businesslike rule for chastity that summarizes Gay's idea of deceit in love:

Yes, indeed, the sex is frail. But the first time a woman is frail, she should be somewhat nice methinks, for then or never is the time to make her fortune. After that, she hath nothing to do but to guard herself from being found out, and she may do what she pleases. (p. 495)

Nevertheless, Polly has already been married, and Mr. and Mrs. Peachum must make the best of a bad bargain. Peachum immediately conceives a plan for gaining profit. "Where," he asks Polly, "is the woman who would scruple to be a wife, if she had it in her power to be a widow whenever she pleas'd?" He suggests that she get all that Macheath has and then contrive to have him "peach'd the next Sessions" so that she can arrive at complete possession. Polly exclaims in horror, "What, murder the man I love!"—and her father answers, "Fye, *Polly!* What hath murder to do in the affair? Since the thing sooner or later must happen, I dare say, the Captain himself would like that we should get the reward for his death sooner than a stranger." In this suggestion he carries self-love to a true extreme for he attributes to another an altruism that would be to his own benefit. Such ludicrous cynicism primarily is intended to burlesque the egocentricity of town love.

Macheath himself is offered as almost the perfect example of self-love. When Peachum and his wife resolve to "peach" Macheath anyway, Polly, true to the standards of sentimental heroines of play books and romances, is ever faithful to her love, and warns the intended victim of the plot. He goes into hiding, but his own moral code depends entirely on self-gratification. The Augustan lover *par excellence*, he has no intention of being true to Polly. In the tavern scene (II, iii), he declares that he "loves the sex" and says that if it were not for him and the recruiting officers, Drury Lane (a favorite hangout for prostitutes) would be uninhabited. He boasts that he has made promiscuity a fine art. In Act II, Scene iv, he as the "maker" greets many of his "creations"—various types of prostitutes:

Dear Mrs. *Coaxer,* you are welcome. You look charmingly to-day. I hope you don't want the repairs of quality, and lay on paint.—*Dolly Troll!* kiss me, you slut; are you as amorous as ever, hussy? You are always so taken up with stealing hearts, that you don't allow your self time to steal any thing else.—Ah *Dolly*, thou wilt ever be a Coquette!—Mrs. *Vixen*, I'm yours, I always lov'd a woman of wit and spirit; they make charming mistresses, but plaguy wives.—*Betty Doxy!* come hither, hussy. Do you drink as hard as ever? You had better stick to good wholesome beer; for in troth, *Betty*, strong-waters will in time ruin your constitution. You should leave those to your betters. . . . Mrs. *Slammekin!* as careless and genteel as ever! all you fine ladies, who know your own beauty, affect an undress.—But see, here's *Suky Tawdry* come to contradict what I was saying. Every thing she gets one way she lays out upon her back. Why, *Suky*, you must keep at least a dozen Tally-men. *Molly Brazen!* (*She kisses him.*) That's well done. I love a free-hearted wench. Thou hast a most agreeable assurance, girl, and art as willing as a turtle. (p. 504)

In such company as this Macheath is at home and jovial, with poor "bitten" Polly forgotten. Fundamentally corrupt worldliness is shown bare in the philosophical discussion among "the ladies" on the question of being kept (p. 506); it is agreed that the "best sort of keepers" are the most generous. The attitude is the same as that of Mr. and Mrs. Peachum— money is the standard for measuring love. And since Peachum is a munificent briber when the occasion demands, it is not surprising that Jenny and Tawdry, when kissing Macheath, betray him to the constables by beckoning in their "boss" (Peachum).

Town love is nothing but a round of betrayals, and Macheath is himself adept at the game. When brought into Newgate, he is immediately confronted with Lucy Lockit, whom he previously seduced with the promise of marriage. But to him, as to the finest town gallant, promises mean nothing. Before Lucy comes in, he soliloquizes:

What signifies a promise to a woman? does not man in marriage itself promise a hundred things that he never means to perform? Do all we can, women will believe us; for they look upon a promise as an excuse for following their own inclinations. (p. 508)

To Lucy he recalls the promise, appealing to her tenderness as her husband-to-be and assuring her of the value of his word as a "man of honour." Lucy flares at him. "'Tis the pleasure of all you fine men to insult the women you have ruin'd," she says, and adds, "I could tear thy eyes out." But Macheath soon convinces her, at least momentarily, that he has not married Polly (although he has) and that he will make an "honest woman" of Lucy—and Lucy longs more for that label than for actual marriage itself.[8] Macheath denies Polly not because he loves her less, but only because he loves no one but himself.[9] He would be quite willing to marry Lucy too, since he is not averse to bigamy, but unfortunately for him Polly comes to Newgate to visit him, and there is a showdown among the three. Macheath denies his marriage and his love for Polly, because Lucy is in a better position to help him escape from Newgate and from hanging.

Polly sings once more of true and lasting love:

> No power on earth can e'er divide
> The knot that sacred Love hath ty'd.
> When parents draw against our mind,
> The true-love's knot they faster bind. (p. 515)

Macheath, the courtly gamester, instead sings:

> How happy could I be with either,
> Were t'other dear charmer away!

Actually, of course, he loves neither—only himself—and soon demonstrates the fact. After Lucy helps him to escape, he is promptly captured again, this time in the bed of Mrs. Coaxer, who, with her bawd, Mrs. Trapes, has laid a new trap for him. There is further betrayal in Lucy's attempt to poison Polly, an attempt which fails because Polly, startled at seeing Macheath again in custody, drops the glass of poisoned gin. Thus both girls are frustrated—the more so when, in Scene xv four more wives are brought in by the jailer to claim

Macheath, each "with a child a-piece." He pictures himself in song:

> Thus I stand like a Turk, with his doxies around;
> From all sides their glances his passion confound;
> For black, brown, and fair, his inconstancy burns,
> And the different beauties subdue him by turns. (p. 532)

He thus swaggers on the stage, a symbol of virile and in one sense "natural" man, as promiscuous as the beasts and as selfish. He must satisfy his all-consuming sexual drive at whatever cost to others. Such is the fine example of Augustan courtly lover, who does not devote himself to one woman, whether Idol or no, but makes of love a mere pastime. Gay puts Macheath before us and expects us to laugh at Macheath's immense potency; perhaps he even expects us to envy him; but most assuredly he does not want us to admire him.

Macheath's thorough selfishness in sexual matters is, however, outmatched by that of the despicable Filch, the thieves' apprentice who has turned into a childgetter. Lockit greets him in Act III, Scene iii, with a fitting reference to a creature lower in the chain of being than a human:

Why, boy, thou lookest as if thou wert half starv'd; like a shotten Herring. (p. 519)

Filch replies:

One had need have the constitution of a horse to go through the business.—Since the favourite Childgetter was disabled by a mishap, I have pick'd up a little money by helping the ladies to a pregnancy against their being call'd down to sentence.—But if a man cannot get an honest livelihood any easier way, I am sure, 'tis what I can't undertake for another Session. (p. 519)

Here is a ludicrous, bawdily funny figure. Yet behind him loom shadows. A society with conditions so bad as to make Filch plausible enough to be funny is open to sharp criticism.

Here sexual intercourse, which can be the warm expression of true love, has been most thoroughly debased. Even lust itself has been undermined. Love is moral and practical; lust is immoral and impractical; but begetting illegitimate children in order to cheat justice combines immorality with a sort of practicality. This is sex as simply business for all concerned; a breed farm for criminals represents the complete perversion of the chivalric code of courtly love. Gay's irony touches a high point when he has Lockit say of the professional childgetter:

Truly, if that great man should tip off, 'twould be an irreparable loss. The vigor and prowess of a Knight-errant never sav'd half the ladies in distress that he hath done. (p. 519)

The satire on society and sex in *The Beggar's Opera* thus ranges from catlike gentleness to outright savagery. It ends on a note of compounded mockery. What happens to Macheath, that symbol of distorted love in urban civilization, provides a key to the standards of that civilization's view. The beggar (Gay as the satirist) claims that the moral—that punishment is meted out only to the poor—demands Macheath's death. The Player insists that this ending would not "comply with the taste of the town" (p. 531). Gay (as pretended cynic) succumbs to the Player. The moral of the play is dismissed as the town in its ethical degradation dismisses morality.

In discussing the attack in *The Beggar's Opera* on evil social attitudes with the solemnity the subject deserves, it is sometimes easy to forget that the manner of presenting social criticism is that of burlesque and good-natured farce. Indeed if a veil of comic humor were not drawn between the audience and the attitudes and actions in the drama, the play would be simply a distressing and unpleasant indictment of a society more fit for a grim sociological report than for theatrical entertainment. But the laughter is there to soothe and alleviate the ferocity of the social attack. *The Beggar's Opera* well illustrates the perceptive remark by T. S. Eliot in his essay on Philip Massinger that great farce has "the ability to perform that slight distortion of all the elements in the world of a play or a story, so that this world is complete in itself." Gay's farce-created world gives latitude for all sorts of absurdities in sex relationships.

His last play, *Achilles*,[10] has in a way even more ribaldry than *The Beggar's Opera*. It deals with the period when Achilles is in forced hiding. His mother, Thetis, knowing that he is doomed to die at Troy, wishes to put him in some refuge where none can find him and persuade him to join the Greek forces going to attack the Trojans. She decides to disguise him as a girl and put him in the palace of Lycomedes. This shameful doffing of his sex is contrary to Achilles' code of honor, but he has no choice, for he has sworn to obey his mother. We find him living, sullen and wrathful, disguised as the Lady Pyrrha among the many daughters of Lycomedes and Theaspe. Thus a young and virile man is spending all the hours of day and night in company with young and lovely girls. The possibilities of the situation are obvious. When you add the fact that Lycomedes is a confirmed lecher, who immediately attempts to seduce his ward, the Lady Pyrrha, the comic possibilities are much increased. Gay exploits them to the full.

The lustful hopes of Lycomedes give rise to some of the broader strokes of humor in the play. The king employs one of his great ministers, Diphilus, as a go-between, but the Lady Pyrrha firmly repulses all the suggestions of Diphilus. The minister then reports to the king that the Lady is merely playing the coquette (one of the regular roles of the Idol) and is really ambitious for the power that being the king's mistress will give her:

Lycom. But, dear *Diphilus,* I grow more and more impatient.
Diph. That too by this time is her Case.—To save the Appear-
ances of Virtue, the most easy Woman expects a little gentle
Compulsion, and to be allow'd the Decency of a little feeble Re-
sistance. For the Quiet of her own Conscience a Woman may
insist upon acting the Part of Modesty, and you must comply with
her Scruples.—You will have no more trouble but what will
heighten the Pleasure. (p. 613)

The king is deceived by this persuasion and goes in person
to approach Pyrrha. When "she" refuses his proposals, he
tries to use force. The result is that he is violently thrown
down, with the breath thoroughly knocked out of him. Justice thus farcically triumphs, virtue is exonerated in an unreal
situation.

Theaspe, the queen, is meanwhile concerned about her
husband's wandering fancy and determines to frustrate his
intentions by marrying Pyrrha to her nephew, Periphas. She
broaches the subject to Pyrrha, who is with "her" favorite
"sister," Deidamia. Pyrrha stalls for time. "She" says that
Periphas will be welcome when he returns from the siege of
Troy, renowned for martial deeds. The inverted relationships throw a comic but dismal light on self-seeking human
motives.

At the outset of the disguise, Achilles has already expressed
his opinion that he cannot live among the girls without causing trouble. When Thetis expresses the hope that he will
remember his disguise and fears that he, "among the ladies,
might be so little Master of [his] passions as to find [him-
self] a Man," Achilles replies with a song of little consolation:

> The Woman always in Temptation,
> Must do what Nature bids her do;
> Our Hearts feel equal Palpitation,
> For we've unguarded Minutes too.

By Nature greedy,
When lank and needy,
Within your Fold the Wolf confine;
Then bid the Glutton
Not think of Mutton;
Can you persuade him not to dine? (Air III; p. 599)

His intention of being a wolf among sheep he thoroughly justifies by making Deidamia pregnant. Achilles and Deidamia are then faced with their different conceptions of honor:

Ach. Was there ever a Man in so whimsical a Circumstance!
Deid. Was there ever a Woman in so happy and so unhappy a one as mine!
Ach. Why did I submit? why did I plight my Faith thus infamously to conceal my self?—What is become of my Honour?
Deid. Ah *Pyrrha, Pyrrha,* what is become of mine!
Ach. When shall I behave my self as a Man!
Deid. Wou'd you had never behav'd yourself as one! (p. 619)

Achilles, a pompous, military boor at heart, is unable to see the desperation of Deidamia, who has lost her own honor without being able to explain how, and prates of his own dissatisfaction:

For Heaven's sake, *Deidamia,* if you regard my Love, give me Quiet.—Intreaties, Fondness, Tears, Rage and the whole matrimonial Rhetorick of Woman to gain her Ends are all thrown away upon me; for, by the Gods, my dear *Deidamia,* I am inexorable. (p. 620)

The masquerade of Achilles is exposed by Ulysses, who comes disguised as a merchant to the palace. He unpacks two bundles of goods, one of lovely silks, one of armor; all the others look at the silks, but Pyrrha begins to examine the armor. "She" is therefore unmasked, and Achilles is able to marry Deidamia and go off to war, a man of honor once more.

In *Achilles* Gay takes the opportunity to make sharp and even misogynistic comments on female motives and wiles. The play is studded with prose epigrams against women, reminiscent of Pope's best satire. The clean conciseness of Gay's thrusts give an acid tone to his criticism of the female mind and temperament. Their fundamental enmity for each other is reflected in the speech addressed to Achilles:

You are so very touchy, *Pyrrha*, that there is no enduring you.— How can you be so insociable a Creature as to deny a Friend the Liberty of laughing at your little Follies and Indiscretions? For what do you think Women keep Company with one another?

(p. 600)

Diphilus, the procurer and cynic, expresses a very low opinion of the chastity and honesty of women in general:

Things of this Nature shou'd be always transacted in Person, for there are Women so ridiculously half-modest, that they are asham'd in Words to consent to what (when a Man comes to the Point) they will make no Difficulties to comply with. (p. 612)

And indeed the women in the play display all sorts of unpleasant traits—obstinacy, prudery, ambition, jealousy, and snobbery. Far from being charitable toward a sister's fall from chastity, they delight in it:

Lesb. Now, dear *Artemona*, can any Woman alive imagine that Shape of hers within the compass of common Modesty?
Art. But how can one possibly have those Suspicions?
Phil. She is a Woman, Madam; she hath Inclinations and may have had her Opportunities that we know nothing of. (p. 628)

One can even feel sympathy for Periphas, when he offers the conventional objection of the courtly lover to matrimony. Addressing Theaspe, he says:

How cou'd you, Madam, imagine I had any Views of this kind!— What, be a Woman's Follower with Intention to marry her! Why, the very women themselves wou'd laugh at a Man who had so vulgar a Notion of Galantry, and knew so little of their Inclinations.—The Man never means it, and the Woman never expects it; and for the most part they have every other view but Marriage.

(pp. 622–623)

Later in a soliloquy he carries the theme farther, bringing forth a military metaphor in speaking of the battles of marriage:

Had I so little Taste of Liberty as to be inclin'd to marry; that Girl is of so termagant a Spirit!—The bravest Man must have the dread of an eternal Domestic War.—In a Tongue-combat Woman is invincible, and the Husband must come off with Shame and Infamy; for though he lives in perpetual Noise and Tumult, the poor Man is only ridiculous to his Neighbours.—How can we ever get rid of her?—*Hercules* conquered the seven-headed *Hydra*, but his Wife was a venom'd Shirt that stuck to him to the last. (p. 624)

All of this is offered in *Achilles* in sportive vein, with the convincing unreality of farce. The mockery of fashionable attitudes toward sex is light. Even the attempt of Lycomedes to force his attentions on Pyrrha is little more than straight burlesque.

In *Polly*, however, a similar situation is treated comically but with an underlying serious vein of criticism of the truly vicious. Clearly, the immorality cultivated by "the vogue" is not entirely a laughing matter. The Ducats, representative of the wealthy but ignorant bourgeoisie, epitomize all that is cheap and vulgar in the *nouveaux-riches*. Mr. Ducat is a rich planter; born in the Indies, he has no knowledge of town ways but a great desire to learn them. Who then is chosen as instructress? Mrs. Trapes, a transported bawd, who has learned her principles by imitating the "great" of London. Witness her advice to Ducat:

Though you were born and bred and live in the *Indies*, as you are a subject of *Britain* you shou'd live up to our customs. Prodigality

there, is a fashion that is among all ranks of people. Why, our very
younger brothers push themselves into the polite world by
squandering more than they are worth. You are wealthy, very
wealthy, Mr. *Ducat;* and I grant you the more you have, the taste
of getting more should grow stronger upon you. 'Tis just so with
us. But then the richest of our Lords and Gentlemen, who live
elegantly, always run out. 'Tis genteel to be in debt. Your luxury
should distinguish you from the vulgar. You cannot be too expensive in your pleasures. (p. 539)

She reinforces this recommendation of extravagance, debt,
and showy luxury by singing an air praising the manners of
the polite world and the custom of ignoring the rights of
any but yourself. Mrs. Trapes is, in short, telling Ducat to
make himself into a ruthless wastrel. Fundamentally, fashionable gentility compels the rich to spend their money in such
ways as to transform harmless foibles into dangerous vices.
They should use their wealth to gain power so that they in
turn will be imitated and by this imitation spread corruption.[11] Mrs. Trapes sings finally,

> Morals and honesty leave to the poor,
> As they do at London.

Ducat is persuaded that he must squander money on the
"superfluities" of life—first of all on a beautiful mistress.
Poor Ducat, shamefaced, has confessed that he is still having
sexual relations with his wife and that she is "unreasonable
enough to expect to have [him] always to herself." Mrs.
Trapes sets out to improve this unfashionable state of affairs.
"Keep mistresses," she says. To help him find one, she suggests that he take advantage of her "fresh cargo of ladies just
arrived," because

We are not here, I must tell you, as we are at *London*, where we
can have fresh goods every week by the waggon. My maid is
again gone aboard the vessel; she is perfectly charm'd with one
of the ladies; 'twill be a credit to you to keep her. I have obliga-

tions to you, Mr. *Ducat,* and I would part with her to no man alive but your self. If I had her at London, such a lady would be sufficient to make my fortune; but, in truth, she is not impudent enough to make herself agreeable to the sailors in a publick-house in this country. By all accounts, she hath a behaviour only fit for a private family. (p. 541)

Ducat is convinced, and says that "if we can agree upon the price I'll take her into the family." He is congratulated by Mrs. Trapes on his wish to spend money on a real "delicacy."

The "delicacy" turns out to be Polly, who thinks that Mrs. Trapes (her father's old friend) is going to get her an honest job as servant to Mrs. Ducat.

Ducat at first balks at the price of a hundred pistoles, but Mrs. Trapes attacks him with sophistic reasoning:

Trapes. Mr. *Ducat.* Sir. . . . I had many a stratagem . . . to inveigle her away from her relations! she too herself was exceeding difficult. And I can assure you, to ruine a girl of severe education is no small addition to the pleasure of our fine gentlemen. I can be answerable for it too, that you will have the first of her. I am sure I could have dispos'd of her upon the same account for at least a hundred guineas to an alderman of *London;* and then too I might have had the disposal of her again as soon as she was out of keeping; but you are my friend, and I shall not deal hard with you. . . .
Ducat. But, dear Mrs. *Dye,* a hundred pistoles say you? why, I could have half a dozen negro princesses for the price.
Trapes. But sure you cannot expect to buy a fine handsome christian at that rate. You are not us'd to see such goods on this side of the water. For the women, like the cloaths, are all tarnish'd and half worn out before they are sent hither. Do but cast your eye upon her, Sir; the door stands half open. (p. 546)

It is not the reasoning of the bawd but a view of Polly that convinces Ducat:

Ducat. I'll have her. I'll pay you down upon the nail. You shall leave her with me. Come, count your money, Mrs. *Dye.*

Trapes. What a shape is there! she's of the finest growth.

Ducat. You make me mis-reckon. She even takes off my eyes from gold.

Trapes. What a curious pair of sparkling eyes!

Ducat. As vivifying as the sun. I have paid you ten.

Trapes. What a racy flavour must breath from those lips!

Ducat. I want no provoking commendations. I'm in youth; I'm on fire! twenty more makes it thirty; and this here makes it just fifty.

Trapes. What a most inviting complexion! how charming a colour! In short, a fine woman has all the perfections of fine wine, and is a cordial that is ten times as restorative.

Ducat. This fifty then makes it just the sum. So now, Madam, you may deliver her up. (p. 547)

Fortunately for Polly, Mrs. Ducat is jealous, and "will have none of [Ducat's] hussies about [her]." When Polly rejects Ducat's advances, she finds she has an ally and is firm, though Ducat makes her status appallingly clear to her:

Polly. 'Tis barbarous in you, Sir, to take the occasion of my necessities to insult me.

Ducat. Nay, hussy, I'll give you money.

Polly. I despise it. No, Sir, tho' I was born and bred in England, I can dare to be poor, which is the only thing now-a-days men are asham'd of.

Ducat. I shall humble these saucy airs of yours, Mrs. *Minx.* Is this language from a servant! from a slave!

Polly. Am I then betray'd and sold!

Ducat. Yes, hussy, that you are; and as legally my property, as any woman is her husband's, who sells her self in marriage. . . . Your fortune, your happiness depends upon your compliance. What, proof against a bribe! Sure, hussy, you belye your country, or you must have had a very vulgar education. 'Tis unnatural. . . . Besides, hussy, your consent may make me your slave; there's power to tempt you into the bargain. You must be more than woman if you can stand that too.

Polly. Sure you only mean to try me! but 'tis barbarous to trifle with my distresses.

Ducat. I'll have none of these airs. 'Tis impertinent in a servant, to have scruples of any kind. I hire honour, conscience and all, for I will not be serv'd by halves. And so, to be plain with you, you obstinate slut, you shall either contribute to my pleasure or my profit; and if you refuse play in the bed-chamber, you shall go work in the fields among the planters. I hope now I have explain'd my self. (pp. 551–552)

Polly is nearly helpless, the victim of poverty and of her own loyalty to Macheath. Yet, as "rural" heroine, she sturdily defends her honor:

My freedom may be lost, but you cannot rob me of my virtue and integrity: and whatever is my lot, having that, I shall have the comfort of hope, and find pleasure in reflection. (p. 552)

She is saved by circumstance. At just the right moment news comes that the pirates have invaded the island. Polly gets the aid of Mrs. Ducat, who is glad to get rid of her, and escapes to the jungle. Dressed as a soldier, she sets out to find her wandering husband. Ducat, the forsaken and despised slave-owner, is left to the consolation of his servant, Damaris:

But you [Ducat] are too rich to have courage. You should fight by deputy. 'Tis only for poor people to be brave and desperate, who cannot afford to live. (p. 553)

Beneath the glitter of this ridicule of Ducat is bitter comment on the ugliness to which sexual relations can be reduced. The references to the slave trade are by no means incidental. Polly is sold, with Ducat as buyer, Mrs. Trapes as seller, and Mrs. Trapes's parlor the auction block. The fashionable Idol could play with love and dispense her favors whimsically, with only a little danger of losing her reputation; she is protected by wealth and position. But the girl of lower class, caught by the "rules" of courtly love, finds herself in the slave mart. When love becomes a commodity, so does the girl unfortunate enough to be caught in the immoral business of flesh selling. The resultant effects on the psychology of all concerned and on society itself are lamentable.

Gay's works can be seen as fairly full commentary on the distortions of love that characterize "town" life. Just how much this was based on earlier literary models, just how much on Gay's burning social views, just how much on Gay's own personal life and attitudes—here is a question that cannot easily be settled.

Gay was a bachelor. He seems never to have found a woman with whom he thought he could establish a relationship satisfactory enough for marriage. It may be that he vainly sought the image of the mother he lost at the age of nine—a woman who could make real the idealistic picture of contentment around a Devonshire hearth such as he described in *Rural Sports*. Possibly, however, he considered such scenes of happiness with a rural mother and frolicking children as unreal and unattainable—only a dream into which he could retreat.

He may, on the other hand, simply have felt that his economic status was too insecure for marriage. He did not have the income necessary to support a "lady." He might have married a rich widow, such as Mrs. Drelincourt, but probably had scruples against it, since such a match would have had a touch of the mercenary in it. The "affair" with Mrs. Drelincourt, which lasted from 1727 to 1731, was no more than a remote attachment, a blossom that never opened despite Swift's encouragement.[12] Nothing came of it whether because Gay was repelled by the problems of wealth and independence involved or because he felt that she did not meet the demands of his dreams. After all, a bachelor in his forties does not accept the idea of marriage easily.

Finally there is the question of the author's relationship to

the beautiful and captivating Duchess of Queensberry.[13] He
knew her well and possibly was so in love with her that, although she was unattainable, he could not bear the thought
of marrying anyone else. Certainly he was in her company
most of the time. They enjoyed one another's wit and clever-
ness and used to write joint letters to mutual friends, Swift,
Pope, Mrs. Howard, and others. Manuscripts of these letters [14] show that the Duchess and Gay wrote alternately, the
one taking up a paragraph where the other had left off. Such
intimacy between a member of the nobility and a man of
letters was unusual and not in accord with the ordinary standards of decorum of the day. The very writing of the letters
implies physical as well as mental closeness.[15]

The age was certainly licentious, as it appears in records,
such as the letters of the observant and gossipy Lady Mary
Wortley Montagu. Gay, though fat, was a handsome man
with an individual charm, highly attractive to women. He
shared with the Duchess many interests in which the stolid
Duke could not participate. But do these facts imply that poet
and lady were lovers? Not in the light of other circumstances.
Though Gay was financially competent at the period when
he came to stay for long visits at the Queensberry home and
thus not actually dependent upon his host, he was not
such a man as to betray his obligations as a guest. It is true
that it was the Duchess who was banished from court for
protesting too vehemently against the suppression of *Polly*,
but the Duke also took Gay's part and threw his influence to
the support of the poet then and on other occasions. Gay
seems to have been a truly devoted friend of the Duke, who
valued the writer's business ability and entrusted him with
the management of many financial affairs. "Honest" John
Gay was not the man to indulge in an affair with a friend's
wife behind his back; as this chapter has shown, such an act
would have been directly contrary to his deep-felt views of

love and friendship. There seems to have been no blemish
on his relations with the Duke and Duchess. They erected
for him a monument with words engraved upon it that
seem, even with allowance for the exuberant idealization in
epitaphs, to betoken heartfelt love for a man who was to
them both

> The warmest friend;
> The most benevolent man:
> Who maintained
> Independency
> In low circumstances of fortune;
> Integrity
> In the midst of a corrupt age
> And that equal serenity of mind,
> Which conscious goodness alone can give,
> Through the whole course of his life.

Their respect for his character and his abilities seems to
have been unbounded. It seems to be reflected in further
words on the monument:

> Favourite of the Muses,
> He was led by them to every elegant art;
> Refin'd in taste,
> And fraught with graces all his own;
> In various kinds of poetry
> Superior to many,
> Inferior to none,
> His words continue to inspire,
> What his example taught,
> Contempt of folly, however adorn'd;
> Detestation of vice, however dignified;
> Reverence of virtue, however disgrac'd.[16]

This is a gentle epitaph indeed for a man who dealt somewhat ungently with the faults and foibles of his day. He
knew the evils of courtly love game conventions in high

society and the savage difficulties of love among the poor and the criminal. These evils he mocked with the seeming cynicism of a man who has become doubtful as to human morality. Yet the flow of wit and the mordant criticism were instinct with a kindliness and an integrity that made his strictures on love in his day palatable to contemporaries and to generations afterward until the present.

CHAPTER VI

Lobbin Rapin

Love in citys never dwells,
He delights in rural cells
    Which sweet wood-bine covers.
What are your Assemblys then?
There, 'tis true, we see more men;
    But much fewer lovers.

SINCE the basic outlines of the pastoral tradition are undoubtedly familiar to most readers, only the briefest review
would seem necessary for an analysis of Gay's place in this
tradition. Gay shared with Rapin, Fontenelle, and Pope the
pretty notion that the pastoral was the first of all literary
forms because man's first occupation was that of shepherd.
Of course, we now know that bucolic literature was more
the product of displaced rural poets seeking relief from the
conflicts and frustrations of an urban life. While at the court
of King Ptolemy in Alexandria, Theocritus, the originator of
eclogue conventions, recalled the primitive simplicity of his
boyhood in Sicily and wrote down his memories with a compassionate nostalgia and a tone quite similar to that of Gay's.[1]
Virgil, whose ornate allegorical eclogues set the pattern for
most future pastoral poets,[2] wrote his poems to please the
patrons at the court of Augustus. The allegorical disguises
of Virgil were later expanded by Renaissance poets such as
Mantuan so that the contrast of town and country was emphasized by satire on the former. In addition, the shepherds
of the eclogues came to discuss the more complex problems

of current religious and political significance instead of their simple loves and labors. However, their protests were relatively ineffective, as shown, for example, in the neglect of Spenser and his pastoral admonitions at the court of Queen Elizabeth. The pastoral form finally became, in the later seventeenth century, "a court plaything, in which princes and great ladies, poets and wits, loved to see themselves figured and complimented, and the practise of assuming pastoral names became almost universal in polite circles . . . court life became one continual pageant of pastoral conceit." [3]

Because of the traditional connections between court patron and artist, the pastoral vogue became reflected in the art and learning of the early neoclassical period. The absurdities of such an attempt at escape by the nobility from the boredom of their licentious lives was bound to give at least an air or tone of preciosity to the art which sprang from such an impetus. The pictures of Fragonard and those of his English contemporaries combined classical and modern dress in portraits such as that of Nell Gwyn as shepherdess with an exquisitely coiffured wig; the filmy landscapes of Boucher and Watteau were peopled by courtly nymphs on rose-bedecked swings; the formal gardens of Versailles, whose symmetrical regularity offended Pope, were full of artificial fountains, artificially cut trees and hedges, and picturesque pseudoclassical sculpturings which made tangible the artificial concept of pastoralism existing in the courtly mind. Despite the clarity and intelligence of many of the critics, even the literary criticism of the age becomes tainted with the prevailing attitude. The simple shepherds of Rapin's *Discourse of Pastorals* are often fathered by figures from the romances of D'Urfé, although their mothers are to be found in the eclogues of Theocritus and Virgil. The works of Fontenelle, Walsh, and Pope, show a similar preference for this conventional court-infected pastoral as opposed to the

more native type of eclogue represented in the impulse behind the work of Theocritus, Spenser, or Ambrose Philips.
Gay himself probably subscribed to Rapin's theory which
accounts for his friendly attempt to aid Pope in his controversy with Philips by burlesquing in *The Shepherd's Week*
Philips's attempts at the native eclogue. A brief examination
of Rapin's *Discourse* will clarify the pastoral theory which
caused Gay to fail in the creation of a revitalized pastoral
poem, when he tried to exemplify this theory in *Dione,* and
yet to succeed when he breached its rules in *The Shepherd's
Week.*

   After analyzing the classical conception of pastoral, hinted
at in Aristotle and Lucretius and employed by Theocritus
and Virgil, Rapin formulates the proper subjects for pastoral
poetry, "sports, Jests, Gifts, and [inexpensive] Presents:

The[r]efore let Pastoral never venture upon a lofty subject, let
it not recede one jot from its proper matter, but be employ'd
about rustick affairs: such are mean and humble in themselves;
and such are the affairs of Shepherds, especially their Loves, but
those must be pure and innocent; not disturb'd by vain suspitious
jealousy, nor polluted by Rapes; The Rivals must not fight, and
their emulations must be without quarrellings.[4]

The environment of the country as ideal Golden Age must
be expressed with no intrusions of urban immorality and
crime:

all things must appear delightful and easy, nothing vitious and
rough: A perfidious Pimp, a designing Jilt, a gripeing Usurer, a
crafty factious Servant must have no room there, but every part
must be full of the simplicity of the Golden-Age, and of that
Candor which was then eminent.[5]

The investigation of fable, manners, thought, and expression
is then pursued with relation to pastoral poetry. Rapin determines that the fable or plot must be plain and simple and

"agreeable to the Person it treats of." The thought must be plain and pure, "nor must [it] contain any, deep, exquisite, or elaborate fancies," for these would not be consistent with the state of persons and things to be found in the country. The expression "must be soft, and gentle, and all its Passion must seem to flow only, and not break out." [6] These three elements are summed up as the pastoral necessities of simplicity, brevity, and delicacy.

The question of manners involves the decorum of shepherds. Rapin disapproves of much of the allegorical references to contemporary events in the eclogues of Virgil and Theocritus; he rules out the Theocritan pastorals on fishermen, hunters, farmers, and others who are not strictly shepherds; he dislikes Mantuan's representation of the shepherd as a rustic full of "clownish stupidity," yet he maintains that the shepherd must not be too "polite and elegant." Rapin's summary of correct manners reflects the humanistic ideals of Gay's *Rural Sports* rather than those of the burlesque *Shepherd's Week*, although many of the same principles permeate both poems beneath the differing modes of expression:

[Shepherds] must be such as theirs who liv'd in the Islands of the Happy or Golden Age: They must be candid, simple, and ingenuous; lovers of Goodness, and Justice, affable, and kind; strangers to all fraud, contrivance, and deceit; in their Love modest, and chast, not one suspitious word, no loose expression to be allowed.[7]

Because the pastoral, in accord with all classical forms of literature, aims to instruct as well as delight, and

since tis a product of the Golden Age, it will shew the most innocent manners of the most ancient Simplicity, how plain and honest, and how free from all varnish, and deceit, to more degenerate and worse times: And certainly for this tis commendable in its kind, since its design in drawing the image of a Country and

Shepherd's life, is to teach Honesty, Candor, and Simplicity, which are the vertues of private men.[8]

Rapin's view of the pastoral gradually permeated the English critical mind along with the other "rules" of Gallic neoclassical criticism. By the time (1704) Pope wrote his *Discourse on Pastoral Poetry*, the French version of the correct pastoral had become an accepted critical convention.[9] Pope employs this convention judiciously, combining with it hints from Addison's *Essay on the Georgics*[10] and dicta from his old mentor, Walsh; the most important being that the pastoral should reflect the life of the shepherd as it was lived in the nebulous Golden Age of peace and innocence which existed as an ideal in the minds of most neoclassicists. Pope's own pastorals were practically made-to-order illustrations of these conventional rules; the names, the stylized settings, and the observance of the happy medium between rusticity and elegance combine to form a generalized picture of Golden Age simplicity and neoclassical nature. The error of certain now well-refuted critics in condemning Pope for not being Wordsworth lay in their failure to recognize what Pope was trying to do:

Pope's plan necessitated the emphasizing of the setting as opposed to the soliloquy or dialogue put in the mouth of the shepherds. Not only was the season definitely determined by the description but even the time of day was suggested, and the poems so arranged that as the seasons came in proper order, the time of day moved from morning to noon, evening, and night . . . like scenes in a drama. . . . Thus Pope's *Pastorals* fixed this kind of dramatic form upon the eclogue so definitely that the eighteenth century never lost sight of it.[11]

The precision of such a plan, and the need to remove any elements extraneous to the neoclassical pastoral naturally resulted in a different type of poetry; and because such a version of the pastoral had become a type, supposedly with the authority of the ancients behind it, Pope and his friends were outraged at the praise bestowed on Ambrose Philips when he so brazenly ignored the conventions of this particular genre.

If we disregard the animus about this controversy expressed by Pope, Philips, and Addison in certain of the *Guardian* papers and also overlook the fact that the real cause of Philips's failure to create a native pastoral sprang from his lack of poetic ability, we can see plainly that the whole argument revolved about a conflict as to the correct form of the pastoral eclogue. Gay was persuaded by Pope to ridicule the departures of Philips from the normal conventions of this genre. The original intention of the two friends was to ridicule the realism (the names and supposedly vulgar themes) of Philips and reduce it to absurdity by writing a parody so overly realistic that the contrast of Philips's ridiculous rural subject matter with the literary form employed would utterly demolish his pretentions to a place as pastoral poet superior to that of Pope's. The argument was concerned primarily with the degree of realism to be injected into the pastoral. Pope, of course, recognized that knowledge of rural affairs was absolutely necessary:

But with a respect to the present age, nothing more conduces to make these composures natural, than when some Knowledge in rural affairs is discovered. This may be made to appear rather done by chance than on design, and sometimes is best shewn by inference; lest by too much study to seem natural, we destroy that easy simplicity from whence arises the delight.[12]

But Philips believed that a complete portrayal of rustic manners was to be the chief object of the pastoral rather than a presentation of an ideal Golden Age. Thus, he sought to oppose his native eclogue to the conventional eclogue of Pope and his school. Unfortunately, Philips's choice of ex-

emplary subject matter was rather inadequate, and he laid
himself open to ridicule.[13]

Gay's burlesque poem, *The Shepherd's Week*, was meant
then to point up the incompatibility of describing modern
British rural matter (actual country scenes and life) in the
strict form of the Virgilian eclogue. The proof that Gay was
ridiculing Philips's departure from the conventional eclogue
rather than the eclogue form of tradition itself (although
the debasement of the tradition was inescapable in a burlesque poem) is most apparent in his proem. This discourse
itself is written in a pseudo archaic style with much euphuis-
tic alliteration, and with an amusing mixture of medieval and
Elizabethan terms. It is a mongrel style which contrasts
strongly with the precise modern neoclassical prose that Gay
handled so well. The initial paragraph of this ironic essay
immediately proclaims that it is a "great marvell" that "no
Poet . . . hath hit on the right simple Eclogue after the
true ancient guise of Theocritus, before this mine attempt";
Philips is denied his due and ignored even as he was most
vehemently defending his position as writer of the true pastoral. Gay usurps all of Philips's arguments and claims them
as his own reasons for writing:

> such it behoveth a Pastoral to be, as nature in the country af-
> fordeth; and the manners also meetly copied from the rustical
> folk therein; . . . albeit, not ignorant I am, what a rout and rab-
> blement of critical gallimawfry hath been made of late days by
> certain young men of insipid delicacy, concerning, I wist not
> what, Golden Age, and other outragious conceits, to which they
> would confine Pastoral.

Gay's own critical side is disavowed; contemporary rural
manners are to be described, and the Golden Age and the life
of its ancient shepherds are to be forgotten. "This idle trump-
ery" of the convention was not known to Theocritus; "he
rightly, throughout his fifth Idyll, maketh his louts give foul

language, and behold their goats at rut in all simplicity." Foul
language and coarse subject matter was naturally entirely
against the rules of Rapin and Pope. After ironically com-
paring the "new-fangled [pastoral] fooleries" of courtiers
with the "plain downright hearty cleanly manners of true
homebred country folk," Gay promises "to set before (the
gentle reader), as it were a picture, or rather lively landschape
of thy own country, just as thou mightest see it, didest thou
take a walk into the fields at the proper season," just as Milton
did in *L'Allegro*. Actual rural tasks will occupy his shepherds
and shepherdesses instead of courtly and conventional "pip-
ing on oaten reeds" or "gathering nosegays." Gay, in the guise
of Philips, makes it a point to eulogize Spenser, who, like
Theocritus, was thought by the strict neoclassicists to be not
entirely decorous. Pope praises Spenser with quite a few reservations:

Spenser's *Calendar*, in Mr. Dryden's opinion, is the most complete
work of this kind which any Nation has produced ever since the
time of Virgil. Not but that he may be thought imperfect in some
few points. His Eclogues are somewhat too long, if we compare
them with the ancients. He is sometimes too allegorical, and treats
of matters of religion in a pastoral style, as the Mantuan had done
before him. He has employed the Lyric measure, which is contrary to the practice of the old Poets. His Stanza is not still the
same, nor always well chosen. This last may be the reason his
expression is sometimes not concise enough: . . . the old English
and country phrases of Spenser were either entirely obsolete, or
spoken only by people of the lowest condition. As there is a difference betwixt simplicity and rusticity, so the expression of simple thoughts should be plain, but not clownish.[14]

Gay praises Spenser for his ludicrous names, but then drops his
burlesque to make almost exactly the same reservations against
Spenser as Pope did; he is too rustic instead of being precisely
simple; he discusses extraneous religious subjects; he has not

characterized certain of his months by appropriate description. The strict similarity with Pope's *Discourse on Pastoral* is ample evidence of Gay's upholding the neoclassical banner beneath his ironic burlesque. Gay then apologizes for his use of a "no language ever spoken," but in conclusion he hopes that "some lover of Simplicity [the distinguishing mark of the neoclassical pastoralists] shall arise, who shall have the hardiness to render these mine eclogues into such more modern dialect as shall be then understood, to which end, glosses and explications of uncouth pastoral terms are annexed."

But whatever Gay meant to do in the way of burlesquing Philips's type of pastoral soon became subject to the upheaval of old emotional reactions to the countryside and its life. John Aiken in 1806 summed up the actual result of what had happened when Gay had completed his writing of *The Shepherd's Week:*

but such is the charm of reality, and so grateful to the general feelings are the images drawn from rural scenes [that they pleased both the sophisticated who caught on to the parody of Philips and also those who enjoyed Gay's acute perception expressed in his] faithful copies of nature . . . While he pursues his primary design of burlesque parody, he paints rural scenes with a truth of pencil scarcely elsewhere to be met with; and even pathetic circumstances are intermixed with strokes of sportive humor.[15]

What gives poetic life to these poems is Gay's fundamentally respectful attitude toward the functionalism, healthfulness, and naturalness of the country which we found exemplified in *Rural Sports.* However, the chief point with which we are concerned in this chapter is that, with the exception of "Saturday" (modeled upon Virgil's sixth eclogue), all of the eclogues center upon the theme of love. The conventional eclogue had become closely associated with the old courtly concept of the civilizing power of love, and despite the fact that this was meant to be a burlesque poem, we find *The Shepherd's Week*, like most other eclogues, varying between the pastoral of the tranquillity of hope (youthful shepherds and successful love) and the pastoral of the tranquillity of despair (old shepherds mourning a better age, or lovers lamenting the loss of the beloved). Love, as the topic of the eclogue, could not be escaped; but it could be transformed to fit the purposes of parody or distortion. *The Shepherd's Week* was meant to show absurd violations of such neoclassical rules as that of Rapin's who asserts,

And therefore those who make wanton Love-stories the subject of Pastorals, are in my opinion very unadvis'd; for all sort of lewdness or debauchery are directly contrary to the Innocence of the *golden* Age.[16]

Gay's favorite device of the sex tease is often purposefully employed in these seven eclogues to run counter to Rapin's dictum. In "Monday," the two song contestants try to outdo each other by reciting their moments of titillation while playing country games (ll. 103–110), and Cuddy presumably wins a point by describing how Buxoma fell from the seesaw and what an interesting sight he spied.[17] Gay's device of the satirical ending with a clever twist is shown in "Friday" where the Dirge of Bumkinet and Grubbinol concludes with the triumph of physical love over devotion to the dead beloved:

> Thus wail'd the louts in melancholy strain,
> 'Till bonny *Susan* sped a-cross the plain;
> They seiz'd the lass in apron clean array'd,
> And to the ale-house forc'd the willing maid;
> In ale and kisses they forget their cares,
> And *Susan Blouzelinda's* loss repairs.
>
> (ll. 159–164)

And "Saturday" introduces a ribald, teasing passage of lewdness which is all Chaucer and no Rapin:

To the near hedge young *Susan* steps aside,
She feign'd her coat or garter was unty'd,
What-e'er she did, she stoop'd adown unseen,
And merry reapers, what they list, will ween.[18]

(ll. 13–16)

The significance of the titillating passages in *The Shepherd's Week* resides in the naturalness with which physical attraction is portrayed. Gay's attitude toward rural sex is that of Jean de Meun, or that of Spenser's portrayal of the Garden of Adonis rather than that of Guillaume de Loris and Spenser's picture of the Bower of Bliss.[19] The physical relationship of man and woman in a healthy environment is spontaneous, and, when allowed to be expressed without feelings of guilt, it satisfies fundamental psychological needs of creativeness, communion, and security. In the country environment of *The Shepherd's Week*, the teasing assumes much less importance because the natural impulses aroused may be realized instead of frustrated or pursued with guilt or callousness as in the city. The impression conveyed in each of the eclogues is not one of bestial lust, but one of genuine love for the partner, a love very apt to be fulfilled in marriage. The country wife of *Rural Sports* may very well be a picture of the country maid of *The Shepherd's Week* ten years later. The environment almost demands such a conclusion to a rural love affair because the lovers have had to share rustic labors and rustic domestic tasks with and for each other all their lives.[20] The shepherd may have a wandering eye and polygamous instincts as the lamenting Marian has discovered, but the very needs of his daily existence will probably bring him back to the devotion of such a love as Gay portrays in "Tuesday":

Whilom with thee 'twas *Marian's* dear delight
To moil all day, and merry-make at night.
If in the soil you guide the crooked share,
Your early breakfast is my constant care.

And when with even hand you strow the grain,
I fright the thievish rooks from off the plain,
In misling days when I my thresher heard,
With nappy beer I to the barn repair'd;
Lost in the musick of the whirling flail,
To gaze on thee I left the smoaking pail;
In harvest when the Sun was mounted high,
My leathern bottle did thy drought supply;
When-e'er you mow'd I follow'd with the rake,
And have full oft been sun-burnt for thy sake;
When in the welkin gath'ring show'rs were seen,
I lagg'd the last with *Colin* on the green;
And when at eve returning with thy carr,
Awaiting heard the gingling bells from far;
Strait on the fire the sooty pot I plac't,
To warm thy broth I burnt my hands for haste.

(ll. 49–68)

It is this eclogue convention of the lover's complaint which
serves Gay best as a means of illustrating both the chief differences in town and country reactions to frustrated love
and the basic similarities apparent in the natures of all women.
Marian finds it most difficult to pursue her duties after Colin
Clout has deserted her for "Cic'ly, the western lass who tends
the kee." In her lament she voices country love in terms of
labor, duty, self-sacrifice, and devotion:

Ah Colin! canst thou leave thy Sweetheart true!
What I have done for thee will *Cic'ly* do?
Will she thy linnen wash or hosen darn,
And knit thee gloves made of her own-spun yarn?
Will she with huswife's hand provide thy meat,
And ev'ry Sunday morn thy neckcloth plait?

(ll. 31–36)

Her constant love has an element of purity in it; it is expressed in images of kindness, peace, and security:

> Have I not sate with thee full many a night,
> When dying embers were our only light,
> When ev'ry creature did in slumbers lye,
> Besides our cat, my *Colin Clout,* and I?
> No troublous thoughts the cat or *Colin* move,
> While I alone am kept awake by love.
>
> (ll. 87–92)

Though Marian is momentarily deprived of the opportunity to imitate the jolly hostess of the *Epistle to Burlington* ("who nineteen children bore"), her sorrow is not entirely debilitating. The necessity of fulfilling her daily tasks does afford some release for her grief-stricken existence. Goody Dobbins's cow must needs be served by Marian's bull; she earns a groat, and her tears are dried. Love is only a part of her life. When it vanishes, the country maid has something else of value left, a useful role as a contributing member of her society.

However, if we examine the town eclogue, *The Toilette,* we see that the urban shepherdess, Lydia, lives an entirely barren life, and without love her existence is a vast boredom. Her lament for Damon is not, like Marian's, a sorrowing for the loss of a beloved man, but a complaint about the lost youth and gay times which his love gave her. His desertion, perfectly in accord with the fickleness of love as a token of the courtly love game, is frightening because it tells her she is getting old:

> Now twenty springs had cloath'd the Park with green,
> Since *Lydia* knew the blossom of fifteen;
> No lovers now her morning hours molest,
> And catch her at her Toilette half undrest; (ll. 1–4)

She sits before her mirror primping; "she smooths her brow, and frizles forth her hairs,/And fancys youthful dress gives youthful airs." But it is no use:

> O Youth! O spring of life! for ever lost!
> No more my name shall reign the fav'rite Toast,
> On glass no more the di'mond grave my name,
> And rhymes mispell'd record a lover's flame:
> Nor shall side-boxes watch my restless eyes,
> And as they catch the glance in rows arise
> With humble bows; nor white-glov'd Beaus encroach
> In crouds behind, to guard me to my coach.
> Ah hapless nymph! such conquests are no more,
> For *Chloe's* now what *Lydia* was before! (ll. 23–32)

Without the attentions of an idolator, with no duties to perform and no husband or children to care for, boredom and fretful dissatisfaction with herself arises. We are reminded of the neurotic fine lady of Eliot's *Wasteland*, who also sat before her glass and asked like Lydia, "What shall I do? how spend the hateful day?" She considers various possibilities; religious devotions are rejected because going to chapel with "ancient matrons . . . and gray religious maids" would be an admission of her decay; shopping would be fun, but the china shop only reminds her of the day when Damon, buying her a present, first met her rival, Chloe. Anger gets the best of her, and with a good dose of sour grapes, she makes a passionate resolution to let Chloe have Damon and thus suffer the consequences of a town marriage:

> Fly from perfidious man, the sex disdain;
> Let servile *Chloe* wear the nuptial chain.
> *Damon* is practis'd in the modish life,
> Can hate, and yet be civil to a wife.
> He games; he swears; he drinks; he fights; he roves;
> Yet *Chloe* can believe he fondly loves.
> Mistress and wife can well supply his need,
> A miss for pleasure, and a wife for breed. (ll. 79–86)

"Thus love-sick *Lydia* rav'd," until her maid appears with a new hat and cleverly servile compliments on how youthful and pretty her mistress looks. Lydia is easily convinced and hurries off to the playhouse where she is soothed and flattered by the fortune hunter, Harry. Town love of this sort has no moral or purposeful basis; it cannot rise above the mere trifles of vanity, flattery, and pleasure, and so it is a bauble for sale to the highest bidder. If no genuine communion or mutual respect is established between the participants, any wayward circumstance or better prospect for either "lover" will destroy it.

In the *Epistle to Burlington* Gay had rebuked the Idols with the admonition to be "virgins still in town, but mothers here" in the country. His ironic appeal that they even up the score with regard to the national birth rate naturally fell on the deaf ears of the prudes, coquettes, *femme fatales*, and prostitutes of the court and city. Satire on these types and their attitudes and modes of living interjects many a mocking note into Gay's poetry. The eclogue form again offered him the most suitable medium for this sort of satire; the distorting of the Virgilian form with its precise rules lent itself admirably to the depiction of perversions of social conventions and universally respected moral values. The mock pastoral of Swift, Gay, and Lady Mary Wortley Montagu was meant to condemn the vices [21] of the town, not by posing the contrast of a simple Golden Age, but by depicting directly the vicious manners of urban society in a form fraught with the associations of peace, virtue, and innocence. *The Tea-Table* serves as a fine example of Gay's satire on two of the most common types of town female, the prude and the coquette. Gay, the psychologist of feminine character, exposes the deceitfulness of the two town shepherdesses (fine ladies), Doris and Melanthe, who are discussing two other shepherdesses, Sylvia, the coquette, and Laura, the prude:

DORIS

Sylvia the vain fantastic Fop admires,
The Rake's loose gallantry her bosom fires;

> *Sylvia* like that is vain, like this she roves,
> In liking them she but her self approves.
>
> MELANTHE
> *Laura* rails on at men, the sex reviles,
> Their vice condemns, or at their folly smiles.
> Why should her tongue in just resentment fail,
> Since men at her with equal freedom rail?
>
> (ll. 13–20)

These representative urban women are then described in alternating speeches. Doris portrays Sylvia, the coquette, as an easy and willing victim of the courtly love game; she represents the pseudo shepherdess of the town pastoral-masque to perfection:

> Last *Masquerade* was *Sylvia* nymphlike seen,
> Her hand a crook sustain'd, her dress was green;
> An am'rous shepherd led her through the croud,
> The nymph was innocent, the shepherd vow'd;
> But nymphs their innocence with shepherds trust;
> So both withdrew, as nymph and shepherd must.
>
> (ll. 21–26)

But Sylvia is growing old (life's chief horror for the fine lady) and "art her roses and her charms repairs." She is morally loose in her conduct, and when the Fop (like Sir Clement Willoughby in *Evelina*) attempts her honor in a hackney coach, Doris suspects that Sylvia has yielded. Doris has often seen her wandering off to meet "her spark" at dusk in the park, and she has seen her permit *Cynthio* to tie her garter. She is no better than a refined prostitute in Doris's opinion:

> Her favours *Sylvia* shares among mankind,
> Such gen'rous love should never be confin'd.
>
> (ll. 91–92)

To Sylvia, marriage is unbearable constraint; to her, love is universal in the sense that all men should have a piece of it.

Melanthe, on the other hand, portrays Laura, the prude, as the very symbol of urban hypocrisy. Laura pretends to despise men and love, yet, at the same time she is practically a nymphomaniac.[22] She disparages tragedies of love but snickers gleefully at the filthiest jests of Restoration comedy. Because she is homely,

> *Laura* despises ev'ry outward grace,
> The wanton sparkling eye, the blooming face,
> The beauties of the soul are all her pride,
> For other beauties Nature has deny'd;
> If affectation show a beauteous mind,
> Lives there a man to Laura's merits blind? (ll. 39–44)

According to Melanthe all men are blind to Laura's protestations of the value of *"Platonic* Love" except her footman, who is satisfied secretly by "more gen'rous acts." Gay's cynicism toward this type of city female is summed up by Melanthe's irony:

> If pure Devotion center in the face,
> If cens'ring others show intrinsick grace,
> If guilt to publick freedoms be confin'd,
> *Prudes* (all must own) are of the holy kind!
> (ll. 79–82)

The holy prude will really satisfy anyone in the secrecy of her closet where no one can know she has violated the conventions of her fashionable pose. Hypocrisy, such as that of Peachum and Lockit in business affairs, is no less prevalent in the realm of urban social relationships. We are not at all surprised at the warm greetings and pretensions of affection shown to Sylvia and Laura at the conclusion of this eclogue when they come to visit Doris and Melanthe for a game of Ombre.

A difference in economic status and social class seems to be a factor in determining Gay's depictions of love attitudes

and the actions resulting from them. Urban love, as pur-
chasable item in a discreet sale, is probably just the best
available substitute for the gentlemen and fine ladies who are
imitators of the court rather than properly of it. In reality,
only the truly wealthy members of the court circle can afford to take part in the perversions of a real pastoral game.
The following passage shows one of the most precious
versions of the courtly love game; the debasement of country love, simplicity, and innocence by the hypercivilized
shepherdesses of the reign of Louis XIV, and more pertinently, the reign of Charles II, is portrayed in all its lust and
vice:

> When the sweet-breathing spring unfolds the buds,
> Love flys the dusty town for shady woods.
> Then *Totenham* fields with roving beauty swarm,
> And *Hampstead* Balls the city virgin warm;
> Then *Chelsea's* meads o'erhear perfidious vows,
> And the prest grass defrauds the grazing cows.
> 'Tis here the same; but in a higher sphere,
> For ev'n Court Ladies sin in open air.
> What Cit with a gallant would trust his spouse
> Beneath the tempting shade of *Greenwich* boughs?
> What Peer of *France* would let his Dutchess rove,
> Where *Boulogne's* closest woods invite to love?
> But here no wife can blast her husband's fame,
> Cuckold is grown an honourable name.
> Stretch'd on the grass the shepherd sighs his pain,
> And on the grass what shepherd sighs in vain?
> On *Chloe's* lap here *Damon* lay'd along,
> Melts with the languish of her am'rous song;
> There *Iris* flies *Palaemon* through the glade,
> Nor trips by chance—'till in the thickest shade;
> Here *Celimene* defends her lips and breast,
> For kisses are by struggling closer prest;
> *Alexis* there with eager flame grows bold,
> Nor can the nymph his wanton fingers hold;

Be wise, *Alexis;* what, so near the road!
Hark, a coach rolls, and husbands are abroad!
Such were our pleasures in the days of yore,
When am'rous *Charles Britannia's* scepter bore;
The nightly scene of joy the *Park* was made,
And Love in couples peopled ev'ry shade. (ll. 101–130)

This is the pastoral tradition, not as the strict literary form
of Rapin, but as the social perversion underlying Watteau's
paintings of a superficially idyllic French Arcadia. Watteau's
court shepherdesses gambol about the countryside, but that
does not make them "rural" in any of the best senses which
Gay has associated with the word. They really reflect townspeople (in their courtly aspect) going to the country for a
summer vacation; but they do not absorb any country virtues; instead they bring the town and all its vices with them
and lead exactly the same sort of existence as they did before.
The distortion is expressed by such parallel actions as defrauding the cows of food by pressing down the grass with
their bodies, and of defrauding the husbands by yielding the
honor and love of a marriage to the lust-filled pleasures of a
wanton lover. The preservation of town attitudes is best expressed by the fact that court ladies sin just as well "in open
air" as they do in town. The boredom of this momentary
pastoral pastime soon overcomes the wealthy courtiers, and
they return to town where vice can be indulged more suitably
and more luxuriously. Gay sums up the departure in both
time and attitude with this cynical comment:

But since at Court the rural taste is lost,
What mighty summs have velvet couches cost!
(ll. 131–132)

In contrast to the perversions expressed by the noble class
in their pastoral game of courtly love, we have the urban
perversions of love forced by insecure economic circumstances on the lowest classes of the London milieu. The un-

faithfulness of Sabina, the fine lady, to her dead husband, Fidelio in *The Funeral* [23] is despicable when contrasted with the faithfulness of the rural maids, Marian, Sparabella, and Hobnelia, but it is nothing compared to the lack of devotion of certain of the lower classes mirrored in the act of Cloacina, the sewer goddess (*Trivia*, ll. 115–140). After being seduced by the dung collector while disguised as a cinder wench, she becomes pregnant; and after nine months "(cautious of disgrace), . . . Alone, beneath a bulk she dropt [her] boy." This, as we know, was the actual practice of unwed mothers of the lowest strata of society; maternal love, certainly the most universally appealing of all types of love because it is the natural outcome of true mutual affection, here succumbs to the contagion of such urban evils as unjust distribution of wealth, ignorance, and lust, and is forced to expire amid the most pathetic frustrations.[24]

Gay is not so blinded by his faith in the rural environment that he fails to recognize that here, too, perversions of love may exist. In the person of the country squire Gay finds another Ducat, fully as willing to take advantage of the menial position and economic insecurity of the lower classes. In "Wednesday" of *The Shepherd's Week*, Sparabella, in singing her "Dumps" or love complaint, relates how the Squire made attempts upon her person, and promised her that "Dick, in liv'ry striped with lace,/Should wed [her] soon to keep [her] from disgrace." But good little Sparabella refuses both the Squire's footman and his fee out of devotion to her wandering Bumkinet. This vignette, reminiscent of an oft-repeated incident in English literature,[25] is expanded in one of Gay's best eclogues, *The Birth of the Squire, In Imitation of the POLLIO of VIRGIL*. After Gay has mockingly invoked the Muses, he purposefully evokes the exalted, hopeful tone which caused Virgil's *Pollio* to be regarded as a Christian prophecy of the Messiah: [26]

See the pleas'd tenants duteous off'rings bear,
Turkeys and geese and grocer's sweetest ware;
With the new health the pond'rous tankard flows,
And old *October* reddens ev'ry nose.
Beagles and spaniels round his cradle stand,
Kiss his moist lip and gently lick his hand;
He joys to hear the shrill horn's ecchoing sounds,
And learns to lisp the names of all the hounds.
With frothy ale to make his cup o'er-flow,
Barley shall in paternal acres grow;
The bee shall sip the fragrant dew from flow'rs,
To give metheglin for his morning hours;
For him the clustring hop shall climb the poles,
And his own orchard sparkle in his bowles. (ll. 11–24)

Gay then foretells the future life of this babe in terms of a
conventional Squire's biography. The youth is stirred to
emulation by his father's tales of the chase; his fiery spirit is
never subjected to "the long tyranny of grammar schools,"
and so he revels in his ignorance. Amazingly enough, he
grows up to survive the perils of the hunt so that "in late years
[he may] be sent/To snore away Debates in Parliament,"
and eventually become a Justice of the Peace. His final end is
pictured by Gay in a Hogarthian scene which is a vivid symbol of country degradation caused by misused wealth. Gay's
ability to create static drama, as opposed to the active drama
of *The Beggar's Opera*, is shown here by the way he freezes
a symbolic moment in all its dramatic tension:

Methinks I see him in his hall appear,
Where the long table floats in clammy beer,
'Midst mugs and glasses shatter'd o'er the floor,
Dead-drunk his servile crew supinely snore;
Triumphant, o'er the prostrate brutes he stands,
The mighty bumper trembles in his hands;
Boldly he drinks, and like his glorious Sires,
In copious gulps of potent ale expires. (ll. 101–108)

Obviously, the Squire leads a full life, "censuring the State in his old age, and deflowering maidens" in his youth. Possibly the arduous labors of his mature occupation are more than compensated for by the joys of his salad days. In using his powerful position to take illicit advantage of the natural physical impulses of the country, the Squire has created a debt of social responsibility which must be paid later by unceasing perseverance in statesmanship. The consequences of his fiery adolescence are poignantly displayed by Gay:

> When rip'ning youth with down o'ershades his chin,
> And ev'ry female eye incites to sin;
> The milk-maid (thoughtless of her future shame)
> With smacking lip shall raise his guilty flame;
> The dairy, barn, the hay-loft and the grove
> Shall oft' be conscious of their stolen love.
> But think, *Priscilla*, on that dreadful time,
> When pangs and watry qualms shall own thy crime;
> How wilt thou tremble when thy nipple's prest,
> To see the white drops bathe thy swelling breast!
> Nine moons shall publickly divulge thy shame,
> And the young Squire forestall a father's name. (ll. 49–60)

Without doubt, the Squire's disregard for human dignity and welfare, as well as his ineptitude in Parliament, meet with Gay's just scorn. The Ducats of this world must be condemned even though they are part of the country environment.

But no rural perversions of love can ever hope to equal those found in the great city. The cynical *Epistle to Pulteney* substantiates the conclusions drawn in *The Beggar's Opera* and *Polly* with regard to the problem of love as a business commodity. In answer to Pulteney's inquiry, Gay depicts the sale of love as flesh payment for gambling debts:

> You ask me, if *Parisian* dames, like ours,
> With rattling dice prophane the *Sunday's* hours;

If they the gamester's pale-ey'd vigils keep,
And stake their honour while their husbands sleep.
Yes, Sir; like *English* Toasts, the dames of *France*
Will risque their income on a single chance . . .
Corinna's cheek with frequent losses burns,
And no bold *Trente le va* her fortune turns.
Ah, too rash virgin! where's thy virtue flown?
She pawns her person for the sharper's loan. (ll. 73–88)

The fact that lives of boredom must seek a release in gambling for money, a pseudo value, is distressing enough, but that the loss of money can be paid with pseudo love is infinitely worse in Gay's eyes. The sordidness of diseased city love in its timeless aspects is pointed up by lines 76 to 78; from Vittoria of Webster's *White Devil* to Mrs. Jackson of Farrell's *Judgment Day*, who pays off her racing debt by inviting three strangers to her apartment, the pattern is the same. The act of love becomes a commodity, lust is advertised by the saleswoman, and flesh is sold on the auction block in "milady's closet."

In addition, this epistle presents other cases of pseudo whores and introduces us to the methods by which they gain wealth and power instead of mere paltry fees. The French fop first tells us (ll. 167–172) of one young miss whose career may be gauged according to the value of the gifts she receives. At the height of her popularity this young lady was bedecked with the necklaces and jewels of fifty lovers but now she is forced to sin for cheap scarfs and stockings. Gay's mouthpiece next portrays for us the religious hypocrite who attempts to secure power by clandestine relations with members of the clergy:

This next, with sober gait and serious leer,
Wearies her knees with morn and ev'ning prayer;
She scorns th' ignoble love of feeble pages,
But with three Abbots in one night engages.
This with the Cardinal her nights employs,
Where holy sinews consecrate her joys. (ll. 173–178)

But the aims of the religious whore are obviously purely mercenary. This relationship seems to confuse elements of love, divine in origin, with human lust. But of course, Gay has the sanction of classical myth to excuse his depictions. After all, his tale of Vulcan and Patty (*Trivia*, I, 223–282) is merely an adaptation of Leda and the Swan; the god's aim is bestial in both instances, only Vulcan secures Patty by the gift of the patten instead of by forcible rape. Gay has perceived that the dichotomy in the feminine attitude with regard to matrimony springs from an essential confusion in the mind of every coquette between the kindly father image every woman seeks in a lover, and its substitute for the wealth-greedy females whom Gay portrays, the aging profligate who buys only flesh instead of love, and who gives only money instead of the security of genuine devotion. The emotional transference of attributes of fatherliness to those of divinity and vice versa is of course a common psychical phenomenon.

However, the sex-tease, both as a device used by Gay to titillate the reader, and as a method used by the flesh sellers, is best exemplified by the genuine town whores. In warning the unwary clown of their wiles, Gay describes one thus:

> 'Tis she who nightly strowls with saunt'ring pace,
> No stubborn stays her yielding shape embrace;
> Beneath the lamp her tawdry ribbons glare,
> The new-scower'd manteau, and the slattern air;
> High-draggled petticoats her travels show,
> And hollow cheeks with artful blushes glow;
> With flatt'ring sounds she sooths the cred'lous ear,
> My noble captain! charmer! love! my dear!
> In riding-hood near tavern-doors she plies,
> Or muffled pinners hide her livid eyes.
> With empty bandbox she delights to range,
> And feigns a distant errand from the *'Change;*
> Nay, she will oft' the Quaker's hood prophane,

And trudge demure the rounds of *Drury-lane*.
She darts from sarsnet ambush wily leers,
Twitches thy sleeve, or with familiar airs
Her fan will pat thy cheek; these snares disdain,
Nor gaze behind thee, when she turns again.
(*Trivia*, III, 267–284)

The whore is almost an archetypal symbol of human corruption; she represents the perversion of our most noble impulse, love, and the perversion of the human body by her
misuse of it. She represents the ultimate in nonfunctional
living and the selling of human dignity for money. The
whore, too, is primarily unique to urban civilization and
represents again the evils of the town in miniature. Because
of the scarcity of population and a more wholesome approach
to sex in the country, her profession is unnecessary there.
The town on the other hand seems to be full of abused young
girls who have fallen victims to some *homme fatale* like
Macheath. It is ironic justice that the destroyed should destroy. In the whore the diseased mental attitudes of the town
toward love are realized symbolically in the yielding shape
and hollow cheek. The tale of the yeoman then (*Trivia*, III,
285–306) actually summarizes for us Gay's contrast of urban
and country environments as each influences love relationships. The yeoman, representative of health, innocence, and
natural sexual impulses, comes to town. By selling his herds
for gold he becomes a "gull" for the sterile prostitute, who is
herself often a country girl fallen victim to the diseases of urban love. In obeying his natural impulses, not knowing he is
being tricked for his wealth, he becomes "unmindful of his
home, and distant bride," the representatives of rural virtue
and true love realized in marriage. He is taken to "her cob-
web room," where his natural impulse is satisfied by mere use
of another human being's body and where the whore's unnatural impulse to sell human flesh for money is satisfied by

her stealing of his purse. The usual result is voiced by Gay's
pitying apostrophe:

> Ah hapless swain, unus'd to pains and ills!
> Canst thou forego roast-beef for nauseous pills?
> How wilt thou lift to Heav'n thy eyes and hands,
> When the long scroll the surgeon's fees demands!
> Or else (ye Gods avert that worst disgrace)
> Thy ruin'd nose falls level with thy face,
> Then shall thy wife thy loathsome kiss disdain,
> And wholesome neighbours from thy mug refrain.
>
> (ll. 299–306)

Country health has been diseased by urban syphilis; country
money, earned by functional labor, must be expended on
nonfunctional surgeon's fees; true country love is destroyed
by a moment of urban unfaithfulness; and country honor
has been lost in the eyes of the still morally virtuous country
neighbors. The terrible irony is that the victim of poverty,
when young and healthy (and maybe fresh from the country), is destroyed by the rich; and when older, poorer, and
diseased (and very much of the town), the victim more often
helps to destroy her own class instead of those who have
perpetrated this crime against her.

That the pastoral of tradition has found a unique proponent
in John Gay cannot be questioned. His employment of the
form both for satire on inacceptable usage and for a clever
elucidation of the distortions of love in the Augustan period
resulted in poetry of lasting interest. His basic attitude toward the country life emerges clearly, however, as something
transcending either of the above results. *Rural Sports, The
Shepherd's Week*, and many of his pastoral lyrics and ballads
all embody those elements which we think of as constituting
the essence of true pastoralism, simplicity of taste, direct expression of the most basic human emotions, and close affinity
with nature. The complexities of a town existence which
Gay knew so well, the interweaving of conflicting emotions

and pseudo emotions, the anxiety of spirit, and the search into the paradoxicalness of life are expressed by Gay through modifications of the pastoral, through burlesque and satiric poems which operate on various and variable levels of meaning. William Empson has attempted to indicate some of the ambiguities involved in the expansion of pastoral themes to cover the relationships between urban life (as invariably condemned) and proletarian literature. He feels that

> The essential trick of the old pastoral, which was felt to imply a beautiful relationship between rich and poor, was to make simple people express strong feelings (felt as the most universal subject, something fundamentally true about everybody) in learned and fashionable language (so that you wrote about the best subject in the best way). From seeing the two sorts of people combined like this you thought better of both; the best parts of both were used.[27]

Mr. Empson further asserts that the attitude of the Puritans in distrusting beauty helped to destroy this conventionally polite pastoral, so that only the mock pastoral could be successful with the upper (the patrons) and the lower (the beggars) classes who were less consciously Puritan, or bourgeois, in their attitude. But the patron and the beggar have their vast differences also. Because of the "absurdly artificial" quality of the conventional pastoral, which often mingled its praise of simplicity with extreme flattery of a wealthy and sophisticated patron, parody became necessary so that the insincerity of the upper classes could be shown simultaneously with the invocation of the essential worth of the poor man, despite his ridiculousness;

> The simple man becomes a clumsy fool who yet has better "sense" than his betters and can say things more fundamentally true; he is "in contact with nature," which the complex man needs to be; . . . he is in contact with the mysterious forces of our own nature, so that the clown has the wit of the Unconscious; he can

speak the truth because he has nothing to lose. Also the idea that
he is in contact with nature, therefore "one with the universe"
like the Senecan man, brought in a suggestion of stoicism; this
made the thing less unreal since the humorous poor man is more
obviously stoical than profound.[28]

The pertinence of Empson's words to a study of Gay is revealed in *The Shepherd's Week* where the "clumsy fool" is
depicted as better morally for having close contact with
nature, more honest and direct because he is so poor, and
stronger because he has learned to endure hardships with
stoicism. What Gay brings out in his pastorals is a feeling of
human dignity inherent in country lives and loves. We both
laugh at and sympathize with these absurd but lovable shepherds and shepherdesses, whose lives are meant only to burlesque the distortion of a conventional literary form, and yet
who enchant us with their freshness, vigor, and health. The
most plausible explanation is that from the unconsciousness
of Gay, emotions, more deeply rooted than any rational defense of a literary genre could ever be, surged up into the
well of conscious art. To love properly, that is, kindly and
sincerely, is an all important principle of conduct with John
Gay, just as to pity the poor is an equally necessary part of
human awareness. The jaded conventional pastoral did not
really allow any sincere expression of these fundamental beliefs. For that matter neither do most town eclogues or ballads, but their satire on the distortions of urban relationships
and perversions of value have a didactic and wholly practicable worth in pointing out how the adoption of false standards subdues the natural impulses which lead to a genuine
devotion to these two principles. Gay in choosing to contrast the differing values of town and country by picturing
their attitudes toward love, has given us many trustworthy
hints about his own moral concepts and many precise illustrations of certain tendencies in Augustan society.

CHAPTER VII

Bob Booty and the Beast

Shall I not censure breach of trust,
Because knaves know themselves unjust?
All there, in duty, to the throne
Their common obligations own.

IT SEEMS very appropriate that Gay, the commentator on
Augustan moral attitudes, should excel in the composition
of fables, the most moralistic of all literary genres. That this
form offered him full scope for the exercise of his talent for
both direct narrative and social criticism as well as his talent
for burlesque and satire is evident from the frequency with
which he uses the essential fable structure of moral and
illustrative beast story in many of his other works. The
definition of *fable* which Dr. Johnson gives in the *Life of
Gay*,

A *Fable*, or Apologue, . . . seems to be, in its genuine state, a
narrative in which beings irrational, and sometimes inanimate,
arbores loquantur, non tantum ferae, are, for the purpose of moral
instruction, feigned to act and speak with human interests and
passions.

is really more in accord with Gay's general practice than
Dr. Johnson believed. Gay's deviation from the strict form in
his occasional use of the "Tale, or . . . abstracted Allegory"
lends a needed variety to a genre which is likely to become
tedious after continual reading. Monotony rather than
diversity is the danger. Where Dr. Johnson finds it "dif-

ficult to extract any moral principle" from some of the
Fables, it may be suspected that fables such as I: xvi and
I: xxxix are meant where Gay is probing satirically into the
psychological motives of human nature without making any
explicit value judgment. But such fables are rare; we have
noted the moral preoccupation of Gay in most of his dramas
and poems; his fables are therefore naturally much concerned with moral truth in so far as it can ever be ascertained.
Gay's participation in the classical search for universal
standards is expressed most clearly in these beast tales and
beast satires. At their best, they appeal immediately to man's
common sense, his highest faculty according to the concepts
of Gay and his friends of the Scriblerus Club. They are the
products of a man's reasoned examination of human nature;
they are his decisions on what is expedient and moral in
human action, expressed with symbolic artistry.

Although many of his beast tales are derived from Hindu,
Arabian, and Persian sources, Aesop has received the major
portion of credit for inventing the fables best known to
our Western culture. It is these well-known and well-
respected tales, as brought to artistic perfection by Phaedrus,
which form the basis of the genre, and which have been drawn
upon for themes and morals by so many later fabulists. The
beast tale, as distinguished from the beast satire, always has
a purely general moral tendency instead of a more personal
satiric quality. In its direct proposal, or illustration, of a
simple moral truth, it shares similarities with the Theocritean
pastoral, or the lyrical pastoral of Drayton; it is spontaneous
in its feeling, clear in its reasoning, and obvious in its allegory.
The beast fable of the Middle Ages, best exemplified by the
famous epic of *Reynard the Fox* and its influence on the
tales of Chaucer, Langland, Gower, Lydgate, and the
Scottish Chaucerians, introduced personal elements behind
the screen of the fable. These beast fables are more properly

called beast satires, because the medieval allegory employs beasts and their actions for the purpose of satirizing various contemporary persons, institutions, or attitudes. The beast satire may be more appropriately compared to the Virgilian-Mantuan tradition of the conventional pastoral where subtle condemnation of specific people and evils is veiled in the guise of the shepherd's discussions and actions.

Just as we turn to *The Shepherd's Calendar* for any introductory investigation of the classical eclogue in combination with native English elements of the pastoral tradition, so we may turn to Spenser's *Prosopopoia* for the first hints of classical influence on the English medieval beast satire. The stories of Reynard were allegorical narratives usually containing a unified series of actions, but when Spenser interrupted his satiric tale of the Ape and the Fox [1] to make direct condemnations of begging soldiers and illiterate priests, then he brought in hints of the episodic classical satire with its strong personal opinions and use of the direct rebuke. It is believed that Spenser fixed the form of the beast satire in England until the advent of the humanitarian attitude toward animals in Thomson's *Seasons*.[2] Except for increased admixtures of classical satire, the use of beast disguise for personal satire continued to be employed in Spenser's manner down to the time of Gay and his contemporaries.

La Fontaine, the greatest of modern fabulists, divides the fable into two parts:

L'apologue est composé de deux parties, dont on peut appeler l'une le corps, l'autre l'âme. Le corps est la fable; l'âme, la moralité.[3]

According to this division, we may look upon the bodies of Gay's fables as more original and more personal than those of La Fontaine, the souls of his fables as striving for the expression of the universal standards which both he and La Fontaine shared as neoclassicists. But because of the per-

sonal intent of Gay's satire (in the *Second Series* especially),
he was apt to slip occasionally into more particularized
attack.[4] A good example is in the different handlings by the
two modern fabulists of Aesop's "The Wolf and the
Shepherds," where La Fontaine's humorous and precise
evocation of a charming wolf who would have been content
to eat vegetables if he had not seen men eat sheep [5] is to be
compared with the debate version of Gay's where a didactic
shepherd's dog attempts to persuade an obstinately oratorical
wolf of the immorality of eating sheep, only to lose his
argument when the wolf reminds him that the dog's masters
eat thousands of sheep to his one (Fable I: xvii). The closest
analogies between these two renowned fabulists are to be
observed in the similarity of their neoclassical attitudes, as
shown in the soul, or moral, of their respective poems. La
Fontaine subscribes to the same ordered view of the universe
and its chain of being as we have traced in Gay. Providence
is to be trusted and the evil beast of many of La Fontaine's
fables is often one who leaves his place to strive for a better
one.[6] Contentment and peace of mind are the virtues to be
upheld, with ambition and envy as the vices to be deplored
and satirized. Wisdom and right reason are extolled by both
poets; avarice, ingratitude, pride, and vanity are rightfully
denigrated as passions contrary to the utilization of man's
highest faculties. They both reject the mechanistic view
of existence common to Hobbes and Descartes. La Fontaine
also respects utilitarianism and along with Gay he lauds
functional living and the exercise of one's abilities in the cause
of worthwhile duty.

It has been agreed by most critics that the fables (story
bodies) of Gay are mostly original or are so modified by
contemporary applications or subjective tones that they
are tantamount to original compositions.[7] Plessow thinks
that Gay, in attempting to preserve his contemporary rep-

utation for originality, actually strove too hard to make his
fable plots novel:

Im allgemeinen hat dieses Bemühen nach Selbständigkeit den
Fabeln unseres Dichters im hohem Masse geschadet. Denn gerade
die erfundenen Fabeln sind oft nur geistreiche Erdichtungen,
deren Handlungen kalt lassen; die Reden der Personen interes-
sieren nicht oder wir können ihnen nicht glauben, weil die
rhetorische Absicht zu sichtbar ist.[8]

There are germs of truth in this judgment, if it is applied
discriminately to certain weaker fables or weaker passages
of generally successful fables such as II: i or I: v, where
the boar and the ram are only indistinguishable mouthpieces
for Gay's favorite themes rather than realized fable
characters. As Plessow maintains, "the rhetorical appearance
is too noticeable"; Gay's animals do not speak and act
in ways very consistent with their natures in some of these
poorer poems.

    This tendency to make the animals mouthpieces for the
author's ideas is of course much more evident in Gay's
second series of *Fables,* which are almost all beast satires.
The new "scientific" philosophy of Descartes with its
emphasis on order, analysis, and factual truth drew a very
sharp line between man, the possessor of reason, and animals,
the nonrational creatures of passions. However, at the end
of the seventeenth century, Locke formulated his postulate
that animals do perceive, retain impressions, and are imbued
with a faculty called "brute reason." [9] Man is different
from beasts only in his superior reasoning power; yet,
his actions often gave satirists like Varro, Spenser, Dryden,
and Gay an opportunity to show that brute reason, because
it had constructed a virtuous yet practical code of conduct superior to that of mankind, was often more to be
admired than human reason. The ambiguities of action

resulting from the operations of these two faculties, as
Gay's age perceived them, renewed the contrast implicit in
the medieval hierarchy of beings which is brought out with
such terrifying significance in the animal imagery of *King
Lear*. The neoclassicists, especially those of Gay's group,
still subscribed strongly to the idea of the division on the
chain of being between man and beast; but they preferred
to present this contrast in the beast allegory of Swift and
Mandeville, or the beast satire of La Fontaine and Gay,
literary forms which more closely approximate classical
genres.

To overemphasize the bitterness and cynicism of the
Second Series of Gay's *Fables* would be a gross, though
forgivable, mistake. Gay is in no sense a disciple of
Hobbesian philosophy; he considers the "natural man" virtuous, while Hobbes, of course, considered him to be irrational and egocentric. We have noted previously that the
Scriblerus group, despite their "gloom," were primarily humanistic in their view of human nature and certainly shared
more affinities with benevolist doctrine. To Gay, it is civilized man rather than natural man who shares the rapacity
of wild and voracious beasts; primitive man, whether he
be of the *Indies* or of Devon (see the *Introduction to the
Fables*), is regarded as the most virtuous, because, common-
sensically speaking, he is the best reasoner, the most reasonable. Swift and Gay believed, as we know, in the exaltation
of plain common sense. In Fable II: xiv, the owl who "assumed the pride of human race," is identified with that dis-
torter of reason, the pedant; in Fable I: xli, this proud bird
proves the stupidity of false wisdom by attacking this very
quality (common sense) which, when used properly, enables
man (as rural farmer here) to see through the illusions of
civilized society. The Second Series, where Hobbesian man
in all his irrationality and egocentricity is pictured, deals

almost exclusively with the vices which we have seen Gay connect with the town. Sophisticate man, basking in the false pride (Fable I: xlix) [10] of a falsely reasoned society, is really the victim of his own passions as we saw in *Polly*. It was at this time that Gay, becoming more closely allied with the now organized Opposition Party (1727–1732), found a focal point for his satire on false reason, an epitome of the townsman in the person of Sir Robert Walpole, the ignobly noble Machiavellian monster-prince, half lion and half fox.

These satiric fables of 1738 which Gay had told Swift [11] were "mostly on Subjects of a graver and more political turn," are addressed to different kinds of men, thus renewing the satire on social types and professions begun earlier in the *Epistles*. They differ from the First Series of *Fables*, addressed to Prince William, in their increased satiric vehemence, and in the subordination of the fable proper to a lengthy introductory moral (usually a brief essay on some particular theme of Gay's which he has dealt with in a previous drama or poem). They may also be considered as an apologia for his satiric practice in that they verge toward the structure of the formal verse satire. As we know from our examination of his *Epistles*, Gay had an essentially classical concept of satire; in the *Epistles* and *Fables* he employs the usual conventions of condemning vice whatever its origin, protestations of nonpersonal attack, and outspoken exhortations to preserve the welfare of the nation. His chief significance to the English theory of formal verse satire lies in his contribution with Swift of *le mythe animal*, the utilization of the beast fable for criticism of contemporary events, and his continuance of the Renaissance preoccupation with the terrible problem of man as beast or angel.[12]

The difference between the satiric and the comic has been defined as a matter of the closeness of pursuit by an author to a single object or related group.[13] Since the preponderance

of satire will depend upon the intensity of the author's virulence, it is evident that the satiric quality of Gay's Second
Series of *Fables* depends upon the extent of his condemnation
of town (or court) vices, and his growing antipathy toward
Walpole. The humanistic leanings and humanitarian feelings
of Gay reacted strongly against the multitude of evils per-
meating the London social scene. He felt that only a severe
change in the moral attitude of individuals and a sincere
transference of value aims away from the accumulation of
wealth and power for self-aggrandizement, away from the
absurd necessity of keeping in vogue, and away from the
false distortions of natural impulses, would suffice to remedy
these Augustan social evils. To effect such a change was
certainly part of the poet's task according to any neoclassicist, but because of his connections with the Opposition
Party members, Gay found it somewhat too easy to believe
that the roots of most of these evils could be laid to the
misconduct of the Walpole government with its intimate
court alliances. As a member of this party, Gay thought he
saw all about him evidences of the arbitrary ministerial tyranny and corruption of a greed-stricken regime. In its place
Gay would have preferred to see exemplified the concepts
of benevolent monarchy outlined in Bolingbroke's *Idea of
a Patriot King*. This treatise, which contained the core of the
political philosophy of the Opposition in the 1720s, probably
determined what few commonplace views Gay had on
politics. His close association with Bolingbroke during the
period of the Scriblerus Club and his later intimacy with
Pulteney are reflected in his reiteration of many of the dicta
of *The Patriot King* as themes for his *Fables:*

> The good of the people is the ultimate and true end of gov-
> ernment. . . . Now, the greatest good of a people is their liberty:
> and, in the case here referred to, the people has judgd it so, and
> provided for it accordingly. Liberty is to the collective body,

what health is to every individual body. Without health no
pleasure can be tasted by man: without liberty no happiness can
be enjoyed by society. The obligation, therefore, to defend and
maintain the freedom of such constitutions, will appear most
sacred to a PATRIOT KING. (Cf., *An Epistle to Pulteney*, ll. 244–254)

. . . He will make one, and but one distinction between his
rights, and those of his people: he will look on his to be a trust,
and theirs a property. (Cf. Fable II: viii, ll. 49–64)

. . . royal blood can give no right, nor length of succession
any prescription, against the constitution of a government. The
first and the last hold by the same tenure. (Cf. Fable II: xi, ll.
7–12)

To espouse no party, but to govern like the common father
of his people, is so essential to the character of a PATRIOT KING, that
he who does otherwise forfeits the title. . . . The true image of
a free people, governed by a PATRIOT KING, is that of a patriarchal
family, where the head and all the members are united by one
common interest, and animated by one common spirit: and
where, if any are perverse enough to have another, they will be
soon borne down by the superiority of those who have the same;
and, far from making a division, they will but confirm the union
of the little state. (Cf. Fable I: i, ll. 66–74)

Parties, even before they degenerate into absolute factions, are
still numbers of men associated together for certain purposes,
and certain interests, which are not, or which are not allowed
to be, those of the community by others. A more private or personal interest comes but too soon, and too often, to be super-
added, and to grow predominant in them: and when it does so,
whatever occasions or principles began to form them [are neg-
lected]. (Cf. Fable II: ii, ll. 31–54; and Fable II: iv, ll. 143–154)

. . . [A bad prince] will not mend the administration, as long
as he can resist the justest and most popular opposition. (Cf.
Fable II: v, ll. 45–66)

This a PATRIOT KING will do. He may favour one party and dis-
courage another, upon occasions wherein the state of his kingdom makes such a temporary measure necessary. But he will
espouse none, much less will he proscribe any. He will list no

party, much less will he do the meanest and most imprudent thing a king can do, list himself in any. It will be his aim to pursue true principles of government independently of all: and, by a steady adherence to this measure, his reign will become an undeniable and glorious proof, that a wise and good prince may unite his subjects, and be himself the centre of their union, notwithstanding any of these divisions that have been hitherto mentioned.

. . . Nothing less than the hearts of his people will content such a prince; nor will he think his throne established, till it is established there. (Cf. Fable II: vi, ll. 47–54) [14]

The later satire on Walpole in *The Beggar's Opera, Polly,* and the *Fables* springs as much out of Gay's sometime position as occasional writer for the Opposition Party as it does out of any personal animus against Walpole, toward whom he had mixed feelings somewhat analogous to those of Pope, who both lunched with and satirized Sir Robert. Walpole had subscribed to the 1720 edition of Gay's *Poems on Several Occasions* and he had agreed to Gay's appointment in 1722 as one of the Commissioners of the Lottery, but any really friendly relationship between these two men had evaporated by the time Bolingbroke and Pulteney organized the Opposition Party in 1727, probably because of the failure of the Queen Caroline–Walpole alliance to recognize Gay's merits in any material sense and because of Gay's close friendship with Walpole's foremost Tory critics.[15] Gay usually employs the methods of the *Craftsman* in his beast satire against Walpole. He disavows any political motive in his allegories and protests that his only concern is with general vice, while anyone at all aware of the Augustan political conflicts would immediately recognize the specific ironical intent of any selected passage: [16]

> I meddle with no state-affairs,
> But spare my jest to save my ears.
> Our present schemes are too profound

> For *Machiavel* himself to sound:
> To censure 'em I've no pretension;
> I own they're past my comprehension.
> (Fable II: ii, 11–16)

The "present schemes" of Walpole are not really "too profound for Machiavel," because to Gay Walpole shares the dual role of Machiavelli, the master political pragmatist, and that of Borgia, the ruthless prince.[17]

Fable I: vii depicts the relativity of justice in present-day governments employing the Machiavellian characters of the Lion and the Fox. "A Lyon, tir'd with State affairs," the king who neglects his duties to his people like the despised Hanoverians, resolves to turn his kingdom over to the Fox, his Viceroy (Walpole). Another fox, a member of the Walpole party, eulogizes the Viceroy Fox for all his virtues, but a Goose comments,

> Foxes this government may prize
> As gentle, plentiful and wise;
> If they enjoy these sweets, 'tis plain,
> We geese must feel a tyrant reign.
> What havoc now shall thin our race!
> When ev'ry petty clerk in place,
> To prove his taste, and seem polite,
> Will feed on geese both noon and night. (ll. 35–42)

The fox, as Machiavellian manipulator, reflects Walpole's ambition, and his vanity in accepting gross flattery. Gay and the other (presumably snow-white) geese are forced into the precarious situation where they (equal claimants to public welfare) are to be used by Walpole and his bribe-controlled petty officials only as a means of satisfying private interests.

Fable II: ii has long been recognized as the key political fable among Gay's beast satires. Its real importance lies in the introductory moral essay "To [Gay's] Friend in the Country." The main theme is that courtiers (townspeople deluxe) are usually the tools of knaves and that there is no place for an honest man (the friend's brother seeking a place) in such a court. The successful Gay is no longer a beggar; he can assert the artist's social and moral criticism directly without the veil of irony:

> I've heard of times, (pray God defend us,
> We're not so good but he can mend us,)
> When wicked ministers have trod
> On kings and people, law and God;
> With arrogance they girt the throne,
> And knew no int'rest but their own.
> Then virtue, from preferment barr'd,
> Gets nothing but its own reward.
> A gang of petty knaves attend 'em,
> With proper parts to recommend 'em.
> Then, if his patron burn with lust,
> The first in favour's pimp the first.
> His doors are never clos'd to spies,
> Who chear his heart with double lyes;
> They flatter him, his foes defame,
> So lull the pangs of guilt and shame.
> If schemes of lucre haunt his brain,
> Projectors swell his greedy train;
> Vile brokers ply his private ear
> With jobs of plunder for the year.
> All consciences must bend and ply,
> You must vote on, and not know why;
> Through thick and thin you must go on;
> One scruple, and your place is gone. (ll. 31–54)

This passage reflects typical vices attributed to Walpole by the Opposition, such as purchasing votes by bribery, teaching corrupt methods to the English electorate, seeking arbitrary power, keeping spies, promoting faction, ruling by dividing the nation against itself, and giving important jobs to his own family. It also reflects the town evils which

were discussed in previous chapters—the impoverishing of
the virtuous, the debased sycophancy demanded by patrons,
political or artistic, the overvaluation of money, and the
stooping by projectors and brokers like Snow to criminal
schemes to obtain wealth—Gay again voices directly the
antithetical country attitudes toward which his ideals are
compelled:

> Wherever those a people drain,
> And strut with infamy and gain,
> I envy not their guilt and state,
> And scorn to share the publick hate.
> Let their own servile creatures rise,
> By screening fraud and venting lyes:
> Give me, kind heav'n, a private station,
> A mind serene for contemplation,
> Title and profit I resign,
> The post of honour shall be mine. (ll. 63–72)

The moral problem and its resolution is stated so explicitly
in the introduction that the illustrative fable is anticlimactic.
The bitterness and close pursuit of the topical evil have been
so well brought out previously that the tale of the "greedy
vulture," who usurps the power from the royal Eagle
(George II here) and surrounds himself with other equally
vicious bird companions, falls rather flat as does the cry of
the virtuous Sparrow (Gay) who says most sincerely, "I court
no favour, [and] ask no place" amid such corruption.

Examples could be multiplied many times in these beast
satires of Gay's overt or veiled references to Walpole's
suppression of educated intelligence, honesty, goodness,
justice, and liberty, as well as to his evil influence in causing
George I or George II to abrogate the tenets of the ideal
patriot king. However, a few typical ones must suffice. The
classical convention of answering an Adversarius while
defending one's principles of satire is best brought out in

Fable II: iv, and the "Friend" to whom it is addressed may
well be the same Fortescue of Pope's imitation of the *First
Satire to the Second Book of Horace.* Again Gay asserts his
independence of court and patrons and his right to "censure
breach of trust" in any aspect of his nation's government.
The fable of "The [ambitious] Ant in Office" who was
"made chief treas'rer of the grain" clearly satirizes the graft
policies of Walpole, ex-Secretary of the Treasury and financial genius. At the annual auditing of the ant-nations granary
accounts, the hoard is found to be very low, but the "Ant in
office thus reply'd" to criticism:

> Consider, Sirs, were secrets told,
> How could the best-schem'd projects hold?
> Should we state mysteries disclose,
> 'Twould lay us open to our foes.
> My duty and my well-known zeal
> Bid me our present schemes conceal:
> But, on my honour, all th' expence
> (Though vast) was for the swarm's defence.
>   (ll. 113–120)

"State mysteries" was one of Walpole's favorite excuses for
refusing to explain his policies to his Tory critics and "the
swarm's defence" was his reason for maintaining a standing
army in peacetime, a reason unacceptable to the Opposition
Party, who often accused him of having an elite SS guard
and of manufacturing artificial dangers to the throne or
foreign plots of invasion so that he himself could benefit
from the levying of higher taxes and the greater opportunities for graft which would be thus afforded. But this enrich-
ment of the ant in office ceases, when, after three years of
successful treachery, the ministerial tools realize that "we
little knaves are greater fools" because for each small grain
that they have stolen, the Walpole ant has pilfered a thousand
more for himself, his kin, and his favorite spies. They realize

that "all the magazine contains/Grows from our annual toil and pains," and that by accepting bribes to cheat the tribe, they are only cheating themselves (ll. 144-154). Wishful thinking on Gay's part characterizes the ending of this beast satire. Oddly enough, the pattern of Augustan London or modern Washington is not followed. Unrealistically, "the cunning plund'rer is detected," and "his [private] hoard is restored to public use." Gay reiterates that money must be fluid and functional and devoted only to public welfare instead of being stored up in the coffers of the corrupt rich or used to build magnificent private estates.

Bolingbroke's and Gay's objections to intermediary ministers between a king and his people are best exemplified in Fable II: vi, addressed significantly again "To a Country-Gentleman," who is described by the first seventeen lines of the introductory moral as "a man of pure and simple heart/[who] through life disclaims a double part":

> So shines his light before mankind,
> His actions prove his honest mind.
> If in his country's cause he rise,
> Debating senates to advise,
> Unbrib'd, unaw'd, he dares impart
> The honest dictates of his heart;
> No ministerial frown he fears,
> But in his virtue perseveres. (ll. 10–17)

In contrast to the good man of the country, we have the townsman in his role of the vicious politician:

> But would you play the politician,
> Whose heart's averse to intuition,
> Your lips at all times, nay, your reason
> Must be controul'd by place and season.
> What statesman could his power support,
> Were lying tongues forbid the court?
> Did princely ears to truth attend,

What minister could gain his end?
How could he raise his tools to place,
And how his honest foes disgrace?
  That politician tops his part,
Who readily can lye with art;
The man's proficient in his trade,
His power is strong, his fortune's made.
By that the int'rest of the throne
Is made subservient to his own:
By that have kings of old, deluded,
All their own friends for his excluded:
By that, his selfish schemes pursuing,
He thrives upon the publick ruin. (ll. 18–36)

This fable possesses a three-part structure instead of the usual two, with double illustrations of the moral, the first being a tale from Plutarch about Antiochus, the king, who outstrips his royal train in the chase and spends the night in discussion with a *"Parthian* clown," another of Gay's sage shepherd-philosophers; and the second being a beast fable about a Squire and his "snappish cur."

The problem of the proper method of governing is the topic of discussion between the clown of the Plutarch story and his royal guest. The clown maintains that "we country-folk" believe the king "is sound at heart, and means our good," but that since he has mistakenly transferred his power to selfish ministers, he has cut off his subjects' rights of redress. In refusing to burden himself with regal cares, he has lost touch with the true welfare of his people, and laid himself open to accusations of negligence, dishonesty, and tyranny. In an acute epigram the clown sums up the case for direct rule, "From kings to coblers 'tis the same:/Bad servants wound their masters fame" (ll. 47–64). The king, after thinking it over all night, accepts the advice of the clown, and when his ministers, courtiers, and flatterers find him the next morning, he tells them that he has finally discovered how

they have misled him by their counsels, lined their own
pockets, and separated him from his people, and then he
banishes them all (more wishful thinking). The moral is
made most explicit by Gay in Bolingbroke's terms:

> Thus wicked ministers oppress,
> When oft' the monarch means redress.
>   Would kings their private subjects hear,
> A minister must talk with fear.
> If honesty oppos'd his views,
> He dar'd not innocence accuse;
> 'Twould keep him in such narrow bound,
> He could not right and wrong confound.
> Happy were kings, could they disclose
> Their real friends and real foes!
> Were both themselves and subjects known,
> A monarch's will might be his own. (ll. 91–102)

The parallel in the relationship between Walpole and George
II (as ruled by Caroline) is obvious. Significantly, this fable
shows Gay's respect for royalty; as a Patriot, he follows
Bolingbroke's belief that kings are more apt to be misled
by bad advisors like Walpole than be inherently evil in themselves (a modified democratic version of the old Tory notion
of the divine right of kings).

The beast satire proper is well executed in this fable, and
the symbolic contrast of illusion and reality brought out to
reinforce further the more explicit statements of parts one
and two. The Squire is alienated from his tenants, old friends,
and servants by Yap, who seeks to have his own way by
defamation of everyone who does not fawn on him. The
illusion of his friendship for his master is voiced in typical
town fashion by his lies and slander about the master's true
friends. Yap is deadly afraid of the reality of truth:

> No honest tongue an audience found,
> He worried all the tenants round,

> For why, he lived in constant fear,
> Lest truth by chance should interfere. (ll. 129–132)

But in Gay's best humorous manner, employing an excellent ludicrous analogy, Yap is described as succumbing to the town evil of lust:

> It happen'd, in ill-omen'd hour,
> That *Yap*, unmindful of his power,
> Forsook his post, to love inclin'd;
> A fav'rite bitch was in the wind;
> By her seduc'd, in am'rous play
> They frisk'd the joyous hours away.
> Thus by untimely love pursuing,
> Like *Antony*, he sought his ruin. (ll. 147–154)

Meanwhile, an "honest neighbor" (again a farmer who represents native wisdom and the rural respect for truth) enters to remove the veil of illusion from the Squire's eyes by telling him that his tenants love him just as much as ever; it is just that they have been kept away from him by Yap's "snarling insolence." Truth is pictured as conquering once more and "the dog (would it were Walpole!) was cudgell'd out of place."

Fable II: ix is the most direct condemnation of Walpole's methods of bribery. It is addressed in unmistakable terms, "To a Modern Politician." Gay's theme that money will purchase anything is very evident in this tale where wealth buys justice and control of the government. The Jackal, who again is a deluder of the royal Lion (George II), is forced to bribe the hog, the wolf, and the fox to maintain his corrupt rule, in much the same fashion as Walpole and the Duke of Newcastle were accustomed to bribe members of Parliament to vote for their measures, and in this manner, as the Opposition continually asserted,[18] steal the people's liberty with their own tax money. However, the Leopard, a symbol for

Pulteney, exposes him through the confessions of those whom
he has bribed, because these false hirelings hope to escape
punishment for their parts in "the secret frauds" and to receive new bribes from the Leopard. But the Leopard spurns
them with an axiom from Gay's political philosophy for
statesmen:

> He, who the publick good intends,
> By bribes needs never purchase friends;
> Who acts this just, this open part,
> Is propt by ev'ry honest heart. (ll. 123–126)

The deplorable results of bribery, excessive pensioning,
and the sale of places are shown in Fable II: x, where "The
Degenerate Bees" turn to useless lives of luxury and idleness,
and where the "Patriot" Bee is dismissed from the hive for
upholding the old traditions of honest toil. An excellent
sketch of Walpole as the Opposition was prone to characterize or caricature him opens the beast satire proper:

> A Bee, of cunning, not of parts,
> Luxurious, negligent of arts,
> Rapacious, arrogant and vain,
> Greedy of power, but more of gain,
> Corruption sow'd throughout the hive.
> By petty rogues the great ones thrive.
>   As power and wealth his views supply'd,
> 'Twas seen in overbearing pride;
> With him loud impudence had merit,
> The Bee of conscience wanted spirit;
> And those who follow'd honour's rules
> Were laugh'd to scorn for squeamish fools:
> Wealth claim'd distinction, favour, grace,
> And poverty alone was base. (ll. 37–50)

The ideal Ruler as he was pictured by the Opposition is
best presented in Fables I: i and II: xi, which deal with the

ancient humanistic theme of the education of a prince, making the chief purpose of the First Series of *Fables* more explicit, but actually meant by Gay to be as fully applicable to the education of kings, noblemen, prime ministers, or government officials of any sort. *The Idea of a Patriot King* is in the tradition of Plato, Erasmus, and Castiglione rather than that of Machiavelli, and its methods of educating the ideal paternal monarch are reflected in both of these fables. (That the Duke of Cumberland neglected both *The Idea* and *The Fables*, and that his sister-in-law and Lord Bute perverted them in the education of George III, does not impair the valid aspects of many of these principles.) Fable I: i castigates the false flattery to which a Prince is subjected and advises him that true friends about the throne may be discerned by their honesty and willingness to administer "sweet reproof." The virtues of generosity, mildness, and kindness are inculcated as the best evidences of true justice; and ironically, the later "Butcher" is warned while an infant that "Cowards are cruel; but the brave/Love mercy, and delight to save" (ll. 33–34). The beast tale itself tells of the discussion between a man, saved from a tiger by the royal Lion, and his rescuer. The Lion boasts of his supreme power, based on the evidence of mutilated carcasses in his den (ll. 55–60). The man objects to this type of monarchy; he advocates,

> Be lov'd. Let justice bound your might.
> Mean are ambitious heroes boasts
> Of wasted lands and slaughter'd hosts;
> Pyrates their power by murders gain,
> Wise kings by love and mercy reign.[19] (ll. 66–70)

The Lion agrees to the reasonableness of this advice, but he cannot resist giving the dig of the punch lines:

> . . . Yet tell me, friend,
> Did ever you in courts attend?

> For all my fawning rogues agree
> That human heroes rule like me. (ll. 79–82)

The use of power politics for needless conquest is clearly forbidden the ideal monarch of Gay's political philosophy. The main impetus for this attitude on Gay's part is his love of peace and contentment, and his objection to the "using" of other men for the satisfaction of private interests (only a monarch or prime minister being powerful enough to "use" a whole nation in a war). Secondary considerations may perhaps be traced to reactions against the violence of the Duke of Marlborough's wars, and Walpole's maintenance of a standing army. The malcontent countryman of Fable II: vii discovers that the soldier's life is wholly unsatisfactory:

> Nor did the soldier's trade inflame
> His hopes with thirst of spoil and fame:
> The miseries of war he mourn'd,
> Whole nations into desarts turn'd.
>   By these have laws and rights been brav'd;
> By these was free-born man inslav'd:
> When battles and invasion cease,
> Why swarm they in the lands of peace? (ll. 129–136)

The concept of soldier, especially as foot soldier or pawn, is recognized by Gay, as it always had been by humanists and humanitarians, as a paradoxical mixture of mechanism (strict discipline) and bestiality (the utter immorality of killing and of despoiling when victorious). What Gay sees [20] is the reality of this concept as it is hidden under the illusion of heroism, the absurd ideal with which the "great man" cloaks his utilization of mankind for the debasement of human dignity; compulsion, fear, and wrath rather than liberty and courage are the actual motivating forces of the common foot soldier.

The Prince must always be aware that true nobility must prove itself anew in every generation by its action. Fable II: xi, "To a Young Nobleman," illustrates that the value of in-

herited rank is a mere illusion in the beast tale of the pack
horse "with blood," who is forced to work and live with
common horses. He is rebuked by the carrier horse and
remonstrated with for the Mohock tendencies of his youth:

> Vain-glorious fool, (the Carrier cry'd,)
> Respect was never paid to pride.
> Know 'twas thy giddy, wilful heart
> Reduc'd thee to this slavish part.
> Did not thy headstrong youth disdain
> To learn the conduct of the rein?
> Thus coxcombs, blind to real merit,
> In vicious frolicks fancy spirit.
> What is't to me by whom begot?
> Thou restif, pert, conceited sot.
> Your sires I rev'rence; 'tis their due:
> But, worthless fool, what's that to you?
> By outward show let's not be cheated:
> An ass should like an ass be treated. (ll. 80–100)

The ideal Prince (or noble) is well pictured in the introductory satiric essay on earning one's right to be called *Noble* by
one's merits: [21]

> Let virtue prove you greatly born. . . .
> (Your ancestors) serv'd the crown with loyal zeal,
> Yet jealous of the publick weal
> They stood the bulwark of our laws,
> And wore at heart their country's cause;
> By neither place or pension bought,
> They spoke and voted as they thought.
> Thus did your sires adorn their seat;
> And such alone are truly great. (ll. 12–26)

While Gay was obviously no political theorist, he did possess political principles, maintained with sincerity though bor-
rowed from (or better, shaped by) his association with the
men who later became the leaders of the Opposition Party.

Politics, as expanded and organized by Walpole's methods, became one of the worst social evils of our civilization; like war, it was of town manufacture to a great extent and it robbed people of their liberty and their right to control their own government. Money, the great town value, became an even greater vice because of its political value and its unique ability to purchase both honesty and justice. Political maneuvering deprived the people of their rightful recourse to their King, and the corruption seeped into court circles, where access to the monarch became an important political, and thus financial, asset. Political and courtly influence combined to destroy competency and honesty in government administration; self-interest (power and money for the clever and ambitious and just money for the stupid and dishonest) became the all-important criterion of judgment. In attacking the Walpole regime and contrasting it with the patriotic spirit of the Opposition, Gay, like the other Opposition authors, tried to show that the good of the people was the end of government, and that this good could be best attained through a maintenance of the constitution by a patriot king whose first concern would be for the liberty and welfare of his subjects.

Gay's *Epistle to Pulteney*, dedicated as it is to a statesman and friend, concludes with a serious passage on government and defines for us the virtues of the ideal king:

> Hear all ye Princes, who the world controul,
> What cares, what terrors haunt the tyrant's soul;
> His constant train are anger, fear, distrust.
> To be a King, is to be good and just;
> His people he protects, their rights he saves,
> And scorns to rule a wretched race of slaves. (ll. 241–246)

We note in this passage that Gay emphasizes the goodness of the benevolent monarch, his regard for justice, and his concern for the rights of his people. Gay feels that the king should not only disavow any tyrannical display of unjust power but that he should serve as a safeguard against any usurpation of power and exercise of despotism by any of his appointed ministers. The king should be the real ruler of his people, a people whose human dignity is respected rather than flaunted. Gay cannot advocate the supremacy of England, right or wrong; he must maintain his personal integrity with regard to liberty:

> . . . There are, I must confess,
> Things which might make me love my country less.
> I should not think my *Britain* had such charms,
> If lost to learning, if enslav'd by arms; (ll. 227–230)

Intelligence and education in Britain's culture and a liberty fully commensurate with the individual citizen's capacity to govern himself are the two chief tenets of Gay's political philosophy. This is not democratic egalitarianism, although Gay's humanitarian feelings might have led a more searching mind to question the ordering of men on the social chain. It is a belief in benevolent order imposed by a king who rises above politics to maintain a just law and a truly practicable liberty. The country imagery with its associations of virtue betoken the sincerity behind Gay's plea to Britain to cherish the liberty of her subjects without which there can be no prosperity and no happiness:

> Happy, thrice happy shall the monarch reign,
> Where guardian laws despotic power restrain!
> There shall the ploughshare break the stubborn land,
> And bending harvests tire the peasant's hand:
> There liberty her settled mansion boasts,
> There commerce plenty brings from foreign coasts.
> O *Britain*, guard thy laws, thy rights defend,
> So shall these blessings to thy sons descend! (ll. 247–254)

It is significant that the analogy most commonly employed by Gay in exemplifying the political theories of his party is that of the country father and his children. The king as father should serve as the center of all action and as giver of order and direction according to the laws of the constitution. The king should prevent discord and faction among various "parties" seeking to rule over one another, just as a father prevents one child from tyrannizing over another. Such an ideal monarch in preserving the good of all would automatically preserve the good of each individual. The theory of Gay and his friends was commendable, but, as the case of Pulteney [22] himself proved, it was much more realizable in the imaginary realm of a Pohetohee than in eighteenth-century England.

CHAPTER VIII

The Double View

If I lash vice in gen'ral fiction,
Is't I apply or self-conviction?
Brutes are my theme. Am I to blame,
If men in morals are the same?

IT IS MOST APPARENT from any extended analysis of the works of Gay that he possesses a double view of the nature of man, a view inherent in the very concept of the beast fable. Was man, with all that the term used humanistically implies, a creature of reason and dignity or was he after all a beast, a creature of passion and self-interest? The complexity of the problem for Gay is realized when we remember how, paradoxically, he considered an opposite view: that the creatures of civilization, of urban societies, were corrupt and that the most primitive man, the man living a life most like that of the beasts, was the most virtuous. Such conflicting views and the perception which Gay devotes to each facet of these views, lend tension to his poetry. They result in a vitalization of his rural depictions; they afford an effective means of satire for his primarily neoclassical and humanistic philosophy; and they explain, to a great extent, his recurrent use of animal imagery and analogies.[1]

As we have noted in the previous chapter, Gay, as a neo-classicist, preferred to present his various views of this relationship of man and beast in traditional classic patterns such as the beast tale and the beast satire, allowing the moral lessons to be inferred from the implicit contrast of actions supposedly typical of each. Neoclassical satiric devices, especially irony and raillery, are employed constantly to bring out the contradictions in these actions. And just as we were surprised by the similarity in the emotions (or instinctive reactions) which man and beast share, so we are surprised by the similarity of many of their direct actions, and the parallelism of the motives which prompted these actions. Gay must often have been aware of the paradox so succinctly expressed by Ezra Pound's *Meditatio:*

> When I carefully consider the curious habits of dogs
> I am compelled to conclude
> That man is the superior animal
>
> When I consider the curious habits of man
> I confess, my friend, I am puzzled.

It is very pertinent to any study of Gay to realize just what his various conclusions about this paradoxical relationship were and to note how they are expressed. Starting with the commonly held Aristotelian view that man, because of his reason, deserves a higher place on the scale of being, Gay employs the two types of classical satire to cast doubt upon this assumption. In the objective satire of Horace, Gay equates man with beast, i.e., he acts blindly without reason just as an animal would do. As the product of the shaping forces of his environment, he can be so molded that he will subdue his natural (or good) impulses and become the victim of habit, as when he follows fashionable foibles.[2] This sly and gentle satire on becoming accustomed to petty vice is most typical of the First Series of Gay's *Fables*, and is well illustrated by Fable I: xiii, about *"The tame* Stag," who was caught and made a pet in a Lord's household. At first, this timid creature "flys and hides from all mankind," but after awhile he makes himself at home, "and man, that was his terror, scorns" (ll. 17–26). The analogy between man and beast is then very

cleverly brought out by a little tale about a country maid,
reminding us of the career of Mrs. Waters in *Tom Jones:*

> Such is the country maiden's fright,
> When first a red-coat is in sight,
> Behind the door she hides her face,
> Next time at distance eyes the lace,
> She now can all his terrors stand,
> Nor from his squeeze withdraws her hand;
> She plays familiar in his arms,
> And ev'ry soldier hath his charms;
> From tent to tent she spreads her flame:
> For custom conquers fear and shame. (ll. 27–36)

The problem of the relationship of man and beast is eventually one of exaltation versus debasement in the realm of
human values, the primary concern of Gay, the neoclassicist.
And the great weapon of the satirist, which enables him to
indicate the full extent of the evils which he is attacking, is
reversal; the portrayal of human and animal actions in such
a way that the horror of the evil is readily apparent, because
being like the animal exalts and being like man debases. In
his more involved satire of the Juvenalian type, Gay brings
out the full extent of this debasement, especially in the town,
by placing man below the beast, who appears to act only
from instincts of mere sensation. This indictment maintains
that the corruption of human reason, or the avid passion of
the "enthusiast" which is so peculiar to mankind, is actually
worse than the mere yielding to natural passion; and of
course, such an indictment utilizes the concept that "brute
reason," being so close to the common sense of the primitive
and noble reason of Pohetohee and Cawwawkee, is basically
more moral than the specious human reason which civilized
man so cleverly uses to disguise his evil and passionate
enthusiasms. Often these Juvenalian satires of Gay seem to
indicate that in Augustan London the fear of Gulliver's

Houyhnhnm master that "the corruption of that faculty (reason) might be worse than bestiality itself" has been realized. Fundamentally, Gay holds that man, because of his divine gift of reason, is superior to the beast and thus is rightfully entitled to his superior place on the great chain of being. But, as satirist, Gay can point out how "brute reason" and its instinctive, primitive code of pragmatic virtues (similar to that possessed by the noble savages of *Polly*), occasionally make it appear that beasts are more moral than man:

> But is not man to man a prey?
> Beasts kill for hunger, men for pay.[3]
> (Fable I: x, ll. 55–56)

The beasts follow nature, which has "design'd [them] beasts of prey" (Fable I: xvii); each of them has been appointed by God to his own place, there to share nature's bounty and cooperate with each other if possible (Fable I: xlii). It is only man, the victim of the civilization which his distorted reason has created, who wants to rise above his destined place or to fool others into thinking that he is better than he is (Fables I: xxiv; I: xlv).[4]

As we have seen before, Gay considers that it is just this attempt to rise higher that makes man sink lower in the scale of being; he blinds himself to his own viciousness and cannot really see which way he is going, up or down. It is this false pride that makes the town pirates of *Polly* think they are superior to the noble savages; it is this distorted view of himself that causes Gulliver to think himself superior to the Houyhnhnms until he is shocked into the realization that he is really closer to a Yahoo, a subhuman race that is also subbestial.[5] Lockit's speech in the third act of *The Beggar's Opera* must be reiterated, because it is the key to this entire segment of Gay's view of man:

. . . Lions, Wolves, and Vulturs don't live together in herds,
droves or flocks.—Of all animals of prey, man is the only sociable
one. Every one of us preys upon his neighbour, and yet we herd
together. (p. 518)

It is the "custom of the world," i.e., of civilized, urbanized
man, to betray friends in a manner which no animal who
followed nature would ever think of doing. Man is thus the
worst of all the beasts, according to this particular seg-
mentary view, as the Philosopher of Fable I: xv discovers
when a Pheasant answers his question as to whether the animals of the forest flew from man's "figure or [his] nature."
He eavesdrops as she tells her nestlings in the safety of their
rural woodland home:

> No dangers here shall circumvent,
> Within the woods enjoy content.
> Sooner the hawk or vulture trust
> Than man; of animals the worst;
> In him ingratitude you find,
> A vice peculiar to the kind.

The sheep who gives his fleece is slain; the bees who give wax
and honey are robbed; and the goose who gives his quill to
the aid of science is eaten (ll. 28–42):

> Man then avoid, detest his ways,
> So safely shall prolong your days.
> When services are thus acquitted,
> Be sure we pheasants must be spitted.

The Philosopher might be tempted to cry out in his shame,
"O God, a beast, that wants discourse of reason," would be
more grateful and more generous than such a creature.

The man—beast relationship, as a purely literary device for
the expression of problems involving exclusively human moral
and social judgments, is bound to be the foundation of most
of the *Fables*.[6] In this strict sense of symbolic representation,

the beasts are apt to have no significance as beasts, i.e., beings on a scale of ordered existence; instead they serve merely as masks for human types in human situations. This use of animals is of course strictly in the classical tradition of Horace, Erasmus, and Spenser; the beast, although he may represent a conventional virtue or vice which has been generally connected with his character (the fox is a sneak), is nevertheless only a man with a Halloween mask and his speech and reason and the circumstances of his plight give away his humanity immediately. Most of the *Fables* which can be classified as classical beast satires directed against Walpole are of this type, and a reference to the *Fables* discussed in the previous chapter will make clear how the identification of the fox, vulture, baboon, ant, and others with Sir Robert brings out not the characteristics of the beast but the supposed characteristics of the Prime Minister. The disproportionate emphasis on the introductory moral essays of the Second Series of *Fables* provides sufficient evidence that Gay was often more interested in the propagation of a moral, social, or political point of view than he was in the vitality of the beast characters.

Some of the accompanying beast fables in the Second Series are excellent because of the quality of Gay's perception and the virulence of his satire, but a few of the poorest sink to the level of mere illustrative stories. This "true" fable type may be bitter and cynical in the vein of Jonson's *Volpone*, as are many fables of the Second Series, or they may be gentler and more pathetic like the oft-misinterpreted Fable I: 1, "The Hare and many Friends." To apply the cynical irony beneath this tale in a strict biographical fashion verges on the ridiculous. The theme, after all, is on the false friendships of the court, the acquaintances who promise to aid you in acquiring a "place" and who then forget you. The hare is an honest, decent creature who never makes trouble; she deserves help

as did Gay. But the fable, strictly in the Aesopian tradition, is
on ingratitude and false friendship, not on the valued love and
companionship which Gay actually shared with Swift, Pope,
Arbuthnot, and the Queensberrys. And because this tale is so
traditional and true to type, it should be regarded justly as an
illustrative story, not as a personal lament.

The underlying "philosophy" upon which the *Fables* are
constructed depends upon the theory of the ordering of men
and beasts on a scale of being precariously subject to disar-
rangement by the variability of man. However, a few other
ramifications must be mentioned to give a full picture of
Gay's attitude toward and expression of this question. The
fable in its origins was, of course, the animistic beast tale,
a form through which man expressed his identity with animals as they lived together in the closest possible physical relationships, a form which shows to some extent the survival
of man's fear that the intelligence shown by these inferior
animals was often prompted by some benevolent or malevo-
lent divinity, temporarily occupying this house of flesh and
hair and claws. This fear, which somehow underlies any
personification of the nonrational beings on the scale of
being, was also extended to trees and inanimate objects such
as stones and favored local pools. Thus, the intelligence which
Gay imposes upon the sun, the cloud, the pin, the needle,
and the dunghill are all perfectly justifiable, not only according to the fable tradition, but also in accord with the psychology of emotion which Gay expresses in the man-season,
man-beast, and man-flower affinities of *Rural Sports* and
The Shepherd's Week. Such identities of relationship occur
most often, as we have noted, in the rural imagery of Gay's
poetry, where the similarities of human and inhuman objects [7]
have impinged upon Gay's perception with the vitality which
comes from insights, half unique (and only half realized)

in the poet's own mind and half the product of memories of conventional images which constantly recur in the archetypal poetry of mankind whenever man feels "poetically." That Gay should be "feelingly" aware of this affinity, somewhat substantiated by the findings of anthropological investigation, is additional proof of his genuine sensitivity. We have only to refer back to the chapter on *The Shepherd's Week* to recall how Blouzelinda represents the very essence of wild flowers in her fresh beauty, how Bumkinet shared with the swine his grief at her loss, how he and Grubbinol feel the onslaught of winter in their very beings, and how the folklore and superstitions [8] of these country folk reflect the continued but subdued vitality of a more intimate relationship of man with beasts and with the natural phenomena of their environment. And it is significant to note that Gay frequently employs the primitive beliefs mirrored in the Ovidian myths of the *Metamorphoses* to bring out the threefold parallelisms in emotions, motives, and actions shared by the gods of the Greek hierarchy with men and beasts.

The final aspect of this relationship between man and beast, as viewed by Gay, has been discussed in the sections of *Rural Sports* and *Trivia* that deal with Gay's humanitarianism. This ultimately civilized attitude is, of course, the very opposite of the preromantic feeling of affinity for animals. Humanitarianism of this sort observes the decorum of that *noblesse oblige* which man, according to *An Essay on Man*, owes to his inferiors and helpmates on the scale of being. Necessity may require that certain beasts must be utilized by man for food and clothing, but beyond reasonable limits man should not go. It is his duty, under natural law, as the superior in the scale, to protect the beasts who contribute to his welfare rather than to tyrannize over them and waste their contributions through useless butchery (Fable I:

xv; and Fable I: xxxvi). But man often pursues the latter course most unjustly, and thus, as Pope asserts, he corrupts the innate morality of animals by his bad example:

> (Beasts, urged by us, their fellow-beast pursue,
> And learn of man each other to undo.)
> (*Windsor Forest*, ll. 123–124)

And Gay, in agreeing with Pope, makes it very clear that such corruption of animals is most apt to occur in town. In Fable I: xxx, the Partridge accuses the city Spaniel of degeneracy from his race:

> Thou fawning slave to man's deceit,
> Thou pimp of lux'ry, sneaking cheat,
> Of thy whole species thou disgrace,
> Dogs should disown thee of their race!
> For if I judge their native parts,
> They're born with honest open hearts,
> And, ere they serv'd man's wicked ends,
> Were gen'rous foes or real friends. (ll. 13–20)

The Dog answers this rural bird-moralist scornfully,

> Clowns are to polish'd manners blind;
> How ign'rant is the rustick mind! (ll. 23–24)

and boasts, "Thus train'd by man, I learnt his ways."

Gay's objections to bear baiting and whipping horses are constantly reinforced by the many references [9] in the *Fables* to butchering, the misuse of animals for cruel sports, and the waste of their bounty by needless killing. This genuine regard for animals reflects a real appreciation of the mutual benefits which man and beast can give to each other if they preserve the rural relationship epitomized by that of the shepherd and his dog. A sort of sympathetic identification with each other takes place as man comes to realize the qualities which they share in common as parts of nature; but this sympathetic identification is a rational perception by intelligent man, not the intangible emotional affinity which we have noted above. Such appreciation seems to be a direct anticipation of the new view of animals expressed by Thomson in *The Seasons,* an understanding of the beast in its own character as well as an understanding of its rightful place in natural society.

The antithesis expressed by Shakespeare in his two views of human nature, that of Hamlet that man is "noble in reason . . . [and] like a god, . . . the paragon of animals," and that of Lear that he is but a "poor, forked, animal" when stripped to the core of his being, is most applicable to the double view of Gay. It is important that we determine which of these views is truer to Gay's inmost beliefs. Certainly, the resolution of this problem is automatically contained in the fact of Gay's neoclassicism. He was a humanist upholding the Christian and classical values that he, Swift, and Pope sought to preserve in an age which they believed to be one of growing materialism, mechanism, and secularism, an age of weak morality and poor taste, an age of greed and injustice. These are the reasons for the "gloom of the Tory Satirists," and the reasons why they felt they must employ their satiric talents for the purpose of exposing these evils in the hopes that they might be cured. Gay, as orthodox Christian, faced with the fact of Death, the leveler, believes with Steele, Butler, Shaftesbury, and his age (in opposition to Hobbes and Mandeville) that man's soul at least is inclined toward goodness:

> The only true and real good
> Of man was never vermine's food.
> 'Tis seated in th' immortal mind;
> Virtue distinguishes mankind,
> And that (as yet ne'er harbour'd here)
> Mounts with the soul we know not where.[10]
> (Fable II: xvi, ll. 149–154)

And as a classicist, he agrees with Hamlet rather than Lear:

> What dignity's in human nature,
> Says Man, the most conceited creature,
> As from a cliff he cast his eye,
> And view'd the sea and arched sky!
> The sun was sunk beneath the main,
> The moon, and all the starry train
> Hung the vast vault of heav'n. The Man
> His contemplation thus began.
>   When I behold this glorious show,
> And the wide watry world below,
> The scaly people of the main,
> The beasts that range the wood or plain,
> The wing'd inhabitants of air,
> The day, the night, the various year,
> And know all these by heav'n design'd
> As gifts to pleasure human kind,
> I cannot raise my worth too high;
> Of what vast consequence am I!
>
> (Fable I: xlix, ll. 21–38)

But Gay makes it clear that it is the insufferable pride and egotism of man that debases his human dignity and makes him blind to the evil aspects of his nature. The relativity of such a vain viewpoint (a time-honored satiric device) is asserted by the remonstrance of the flea:

> Not of th' importance you suppose,
> Replies a Flea upon his nose:
> Be humble, learn thyself to scan;
> Know, pride was never made for man.
> 'Tis vanity that swells thy mind.
> What, heav'n and earth for thee design'd!
> For thee! made only for our need;
> That more important Fleas might feed.[11]
>
> (Fable I: xlix, ll. 39–46)

Gay, in accord with his friends, was seeking a truth beyond this relativity of viewpoint, a genuine universal truth. But these truths are often most difficult to find; Gay as usual can discover approximate certainties in nothing but the truths of human nature gained through self-analysis, "Be humble, learn thyself to scan." The morals [12] of all the *Fables* are predicated so that we may learn to know ourselves, which is much more important than knowing the external world. He devotes an entire Fable (II: vii) to this task; it is dedicated "*To Myself*," and in it Gay examines his motives and desires in the vein of Pope's *Epistle to Arbuthnot*. The introductory essay sums up in a direct manner his appraisal of himself and what he has discovered about "right conduct." He admits that his view may be somewhat biased; "Your faults . . ./My partial eyes could never find." But he contends that he has never "been opportunely mean and base"; nor has he "resign'd/ truth, honour, virtue, [and] peace of mind" to the requirements of the time. He realizes it is difficult for a man to be both rich and honest; therefore he is resigned to choose honesty, "write, practice morals, and be poor." After many years, he is now firmly convinced that happiness is not based on wealth; nor is it based on the acquisition of a power such as Walpole's, because the guilt of conscience and the anxiety which come with the amassing of great wealth or great power destroys "intrinsick and . . . true" happiness. Real happiness is found not in any particular spot, not even in the humble cottage necessarily, but only in the virtuous human heart. The fable proper, which incidentally is not a beast fable, concerns "*the* Countryman *and* Jupiter." It is somewhat like Goldsmith's *Tale of Asem*. The discontented Peasant, spent with toil, wishes he were someone else. Jupiter obligingly enables him to see the much greater cares of those (the wealthy man and the prime minister) with whom he might wish to exchange places. The clown is taught to distinguish between reality and illusion; "first learn to know/true happiness from outward show." With the "optick glass of intuition," he no longer "views the world with partial eyes" like the rest of mankind. He sees truly and rejects the lives of lawyer, statesman, and soldier. "Thus, weighing life in each condition," he chooses to return to the country and the labor of spade and plough. It is important to note that the Clown is chosen to represent the man, who, in his discontent, still has the most reason to be content. The wisdom of divinity is justified in this poem, and the conclusion that Gay (as Jupiter) arrives at is that human dignity is based on the possession of an "honest mind," the sole pursuit of justice, and the inculcation of virtue. The reward is contentment and true happiness. Man's lot is a difficult one, but he should play whatever role is assigned to him with this true dignity and courage. Only through such a course of right and rational action can he transcend the level of the beast, because as Pohetohee maintained, without "virtue, honour, and courage, man is but a brute in disguise."

For purposes of summation, the trial scene of Macheath (Morano) at the end of *Polly* serves to bring out as briefly as possible Gay's final conclusions about the town and country pastoral contrast:

Poh. Trifle not with justice, impious man. Your barbarities, your rapin, your murthers are now at an end.
Mor. Ambition must take its chance. If I die, I die in my vocation. . . . We must all take the common lot of our professions.
Poh. Would your European laws have suffer'd crimes like these to have gone unpunish'd!
Mor. Were all I am worth safely landed, I have wherewithal to make almost any crime sit easy upon me.
Poh. Have ye notions of property?
Mor. Of my own.

Poh. Would not your honest industry have been sufficient to have supported you?
Mor. Honest industry! I have heard talk of it indeed among the common people, but all great genius's are above it.
Poh. Have you no respect for virtue?
Mor. As a good phrase, Sir. But the practicers of it are so insignificant and poor, that they are seldom found in the best company.
Poh. Is not wisdom esteem'd among you?
Mor. Yes, Sir. But only as a step to riches and power; a step that raises ourselves, and trips up our neighbours.
Poh. Honour, and honesty, are not those distinguish'd?
Mor. As incapacities and follies. How ignorant are these *Indians!* But indeed I think honour is of some use; it serves to swear upon.
Poh. Have you no consciousness? Have you no shame?
Mor. Of being poor.
Poh. How can society subsist with avarice! Ye are but the forms of men. Beasts would thrust you out of their herd upon that account, and man should cast you out for your brutal dispositions.
Mor. Alexander the great was more successful. That's all.

Air LX (*The collier has a daughter*)
When right or wrong's decided
In war or civil causes,
We by success are guided
To blame or give applauses.
Thus men exalt ambition,
In power by all commended,
But when it falls from high condition,
Tyburn is well attended.

Poh. Let justice then take her course, I shall not interfere with her decrees. Mercy too obliges me to protect my country from such violences. Immediate death shall put a stop to your further mischiefs.
Mor. This sentence indeed is hard. Without the common forms of trial! Not so much as the counsel of a newgate attorney! Not

to be able to lay out my money in partiality and evidence! Not a
friend perjur'd for me! This is hard, very hard.
Poh. Let the sentence be put in execution. Lead him to death.
Let his accomplices be witnesses of it, and afterwards let them
be securely guarded till farther orders.

Air LXI (Mad Moll)

Mor.   All crimes are judg'd like fornication;
                    While rich we are honest no doubt.
                Fine ladies can keep reputation,
                    Poor lasses alone are found out.
                If justice had piercing eyes,
                    Like ourselves to look within,
                She'd find power and wealth a disguise
                    That shelter the worst of our kin. (pp. 584–585)

In this key dialogue, justice is for once justly decreed as the
symbols of virtue and vice finally confront each other in a
debate similar to that of Gulliver and his Houyhnhnm "Master" in Book IV of the *Travels*. In reality, it is the prosecution
of the town by the country, an idealistic fantasy realizable
only in the courtroom of an artist's or a beggar's mind. Detailed examination of this passage would be superfluous at
this point; it should be readily apparent that the questions of
Pohetohee voice the creed of country virtue, and the answers
of Macheath the code of town vice.

Macheath, on trial, puts the noose around his own neck by
asserting honestly, for once, the real principles upon which
urban or civilized society is based. The satire, implicit in the
actual voicing of a code which of course depends for its existence on one's secret acceptance of it, brings out how this
town viewpoint is based primarily on social injustices. The
shameful thing is to be poor, to lack the money which buys
out the virtues of taste, love, and justice. In reality, urban
society subsists only upon avarice. Yet, the wealth resulting
from this avarice destroys true taste in art by impoverishing

instead of rewarding the artist of merit. It destroys true love because it subordinates its essences of devotion and sacrifice to the debasing influences of faithlessness and self-advancement. And finally, it destroys justice because it provides the means of evading it. Wealth then can buy all, but above everything it can buy power, and success of this sort is the criterion by which town society judges its members. The natural goodness of these members degenerates under the attempt to be in vogue, to live up to the false standards set by the affluent, and thus they are corrupted by pride, vanity, and ambition so as to value their private good above that of the total welfare of the public. Kindness and friendship and honor are ignored because they interfere with the using of others for one's own selfish purposes. Wealth alone is certain good, because it enables its possessor to transcend the moral realm of good and evil. Such aberrations of man's reason upset the whole harmony of the natural order and cause poor taste in art, false distinctions among classes, and corrupt leadership in government. The return to the values of classical humanism and of rational theism, the furtherance of humanitarian sentiment, and a reorganization of British government are all means proposed by Gay in an effort to restore "piercing eyes" to justice and to alleviate the evils of urban civilization; but the chief recommendation which he advances is to flip over the pastoral coin and return to the simple but universal virtues which are basic to natural man.

Pohetohee may be, after all, only a sentimental figure from a primitive Golden Age, but this savage derives his nobility from the concepts which such an idealization embodies. In pain and distress, such a man maintains a stoic courage which enables him not only to reject the dishonest acquisition of wealth and the foibles it purchases, but also to endure the severest torture rather than barter his virtue. In happiness, he possesses a natural dignity, based on his respect for friendship, honesty, honor, and justice. This moral passion is based on a common-sense sort of reason which enables him to understand and follow nature, to comprehend the divinity of the eternal order that governs and preserves the welfare of the whole of society. This natural wisdom also enables him to know himself through the experience he has gained by living in a beautiful and healthful rural environment. He knows that his chief duty is to be functional and virtuous in the place which God has assigned to him. And though he may be poor from the viewpoint of those accustomed to needless luxuries, still he has the security, and even the prosperity, which comes to those who have labored faithfully and acquired by honest toil the basic necessities of life. With this sort of noble poverty comes true peace of mind, and whether this man be King, like Pohetohee, or shepherd, like Bumkinet, he lives in the natural state of man, a state which Gay, with the nostalgic memory of his Devonshire childhood prompting him on, declares to be one of happiness, goodness, and contentment.

Even the most competent critics of Gay [13] have yielded somewhat to the notion that Gay's real excellence lies only in his songs and descriptive powers with the concomitant implication that he was keen in his wit but superficial. Revivifying conventional patterns of expression through burlesque and satire as well as contributing many original patterns of his own, Gay did present a panorama of eighteenth-century life in all of its many fascinating aspects. But is this all that can be said for him? I think we must give Gay credit for being a more thoughtful man than he has been regarded hitherto. The chief error of most students of Gay is to accept to some extent the traditional view that he was a man who did not discriminate, a man who did not really care about his principles, a man who blurred issues. Even his distinguished biographer, W. H. Irving, maintains, "He [Gay] is the voice of beast and spirit if you like, of the fleshly and of the ideal, but he refuses to recognize any dichotomy." [14] The bulk of this study has been devoted to illustrating just how Gay did continually recognize the dichotomies of existence. It would seem that Gay has attempted many discriminations between the beast and the spirit; such discriminations form the very foundation of his view of life, and of his moral and social philosophy. Probably only in his songs, or in those passages of *Rural Sports* and *The Shepherd's Week* where the affinity of man's and animal's feelings are elucidated, does Gay ever fail to indicate the abyss between illusion and reality, the disparities of social existence, and the gap between supposed moral standards and actual immoral actions. Though Gay may have conformed outwardly in some instances to the way of the world, the sincerity of his moralizing cannot be doubted in the face of the substantial pattern of belief which the reiterated themes of his poetry and dramas construct. It is true that Gay was "amused by the absurdities, and sometimes saddened by the revelations" of man's existence; but hardly true that "he was never outraged by its perversities." [15] Even if we overlook the intimations of disapproval of certain aspects of society in *Trivia* and other early poems, how can we disclaim the social protest which lies behind the burlesque of *The Beggar's Opera* or of *Achilles*, how can we disregard the code of primitive benevolence which Gay, with equal parts of sentiment and satire, propounds in the social contrasts of *Polly*, how can we overlook the heavy traces of resentment and bitterness which so often color the tone of his satiric *Epistles* and his later *Fables?* Gay may not have been one of the great minds of the Augustan Age, but he did ponder the place of man in the milieu which man had evolved for himself, he asked the questions—to what purpose, to what end? Above all, he was not willing to accept life just as he found it. No true neoclassicist, no person capable of being a most intimate friend of Swift and Pope, could do that. It seems more accurate to say that Gay examined the role of man in society and was displeased and even depressed with what he saw. He recognized that his power of remedying such evils was negligible. But he did feel it his duty to live up to the satirist's calling by pointing out those vices that debase man and his society and to imply, whether through the direct portrayals of examples of nobler and simpler lives or through the negative assertion of moral values by the use of ironic contrasts, the existence of a moral code and a way of life much preferable to the one operative in his own day.

It is possible that the critical underemphasis of Gay's thinking powers lies in the traditional belief that Gay was more of the town than of the country, that he was the victim of a penchant to adjust too easily to his immediate surroundings. It would seem that the evidence to the contrary—the frequent satire on urban evils, which indicates that Gay could not wholly adjust to the environment of the town, and the nostalgic pictures and images used to depict rural and primitive life, which indicate that Gay could never really purge himself of his love for the country milieu of his youth and deepest inclinations—implies a capacity for thoughtful speculation. A mind in conflict, torn between issues and pulled in opposite directions by circumstance and desire, must necessarily weigh pros and cons, and in so doing, arrive at conclusions acceptable to the integrity of the man it belongs to, especially if the man is as "honest" as John Gay.

The conclusion of any task almost necessarily causes one to ask if it was worth the doing. Can a thorough study of the work of John Gay contribute any significant insights which might enable us to understand our contemporary society any more clearly? It would seem entirely possible. The one firm grasp which all classicism or neoclassicism maintains upon the human mind is its constant attempt to depict universals, universals of social and moral good which are still valid and can give us a substantiated ethic to live by, and universals of social and moral evil which we may be taught again to re-examine and reject. Shall we just ask ourselves momentarily the questions which John Gay asked himself about his own Augustan Age? Is justice available equally to the rich and the poor? Is the artist of merit fully appreciated, and are his criteria the bases of contemporary good taste? Do the wise and virtuous have any genuine influence in setting our moral standards? In a world of terror, what does each man truly desire; the love and peacefulness of a quiet, rational, existence, or the hatred and turbulence of a bestial struggle for wealth and power? Country and town, after all, are only symbols.

Appendix

As a genre, the Fable is supposedly another product of the pastoral Golden Age when the affinities between man and beast were more obviously recognizable. The possibilities of truth in such an assumption are evident in the use which Gay, the pastoral poet of town and country, has made of this genre to substantiate and reiterate the themes of his major works. Centering on the two primary motifs of political corruption and the man-beast problem, the *Fables*, as a method of formal verse satire, reinforce the attack on town vices. In this sense, they are similar to the allegorical pastorals of Virgil, Mantuan, Spenser, and Milton. At the same time the *Fables* depict the idealized lives of shepherd and beast when virtuous, indicating how their sharing of the harmony and beauty of the rural environment enables them also to share in its natural wisdom. Rather than risk repetition by overextensive analyses of the less important *Fables*, the following chart of fable themes has been prepared to guide the reader and to point out more completely the many instances where the *Fables* restate the chief themes of Gay's poems and dramas:

CHART OF FABLE THEMES
FIRST SERIES

    I. On the education of a prince to love and justice; man rules by power politics as much as the lion.

    II. On flattery.

    III. On human vanity.

    IV. On justice. The grass is greener in the next yard. Discontent is characteristic of man's "restless mind and proud ambition."

First Series (*Continued*)

V. Against violence and war, actions which hoist man by by his own petard.

VI. On money; its use and abuse. Man corrupts all things; gold is neither virtuous nor vicious in itself.

VII. On government exclusively for the benefit of one's own kind; what's good for foxes is bad for geese. Against flattery in the Walpole administration; no justice in an evil reign.

VIII. Yielding to flattery encourages improper advances, and thus disaster.

IX. The tutor (or environment) determines the nature of the child. He who lives by the sword, dies by it. Poetic justice invoked against butchery.

X. On brute reason as superior to human reason; killing for hunger as opposed to killing for pay. Beasts learn their vices from man, and not vice-versa.

XI. On envy; blemishes show up most on the beautiful peacock, who is compared to the city nymph.

XII. On avarice as a motive for marriage; the courtly love game with money or rank as the sole objective.

XIII. On familiarity breeding contempt.

XIV. On false education.

XV. On ingratitude. Condemnation of man as the worst of the beasts, because he uses and destroys others.

XVI. On ignorance, naïveté, and overhasty speech. Objects have value according to their function (in helping man?).

XVII. On false friendship versus open enmity. Against needless butchering of sheep. Also on the natural harmony of the great chain of being; "Whatever is, is right" because the weaker are created to satisfy the needs of the stronger, and thus apparent evil subserves the purpose of universal good.

XVIII. On flattering a superior's vanity; the painter and his problem of reality and illusion. Honesty versus intellectual dishonesty.

First Series (*Continued*)

XIX. On judging one's self by worthwhile criteria. The pride of unworthy leadership; worth must be based on merit.

XX. On restraint bringing on temptation.

XXI. On sharing wealth, cooperating, and being just. In a world of harmony, there is enough for all. Avoid the envy of kings, Idols, and squires.

XXII. On the singularity of fops, which makes them the jest of the society they live in. Eighteenth-century violation of decorums through vanity. Cf. the preface to *Joseph Andrews.*

XXIII. One is judged by the company he keeps. Also on superstition.

XXIV. On the false pride of *nouveau riches* disowning their backgrounds.

XXV. On slander being returned on the slanderer.

XXVI. On justice at court; satire on Walpole, his spies, his bribery, and his place-giving. Honesty and the dishonesty of lawyers.

XXVII. On greed; the sick man fails the test of generosity and so dies unrepentent in his soul. On the reality of the deed and the illusion of the good intention. Contains a catalogue of eighteenth-century social evils.

XXVIII. On scandal. True merit wins over envy's calumny. On the jealousy of critics' condemnations.

XXIX. On human frailty and false repentence; good counsel without action is ineffective.

XXX. On man corrupting beasts. Attack on the vices of court and town.

XXXI. On anxiety which destroys love, health, riches, and power, and even rural peace. Take care before you act, else Care will follow you.

XXXII. Pride in pedantry, exemplified by the illusory association with Greece of the two owls. Follow nature, advises the sparrow; be functional and catch mice.

First Series (*Continued*)

XXXIII. On the changeability of courtiers being greater than that of Proteus.

XXXIV. On the meddler mastiff, who loves to fight, being trounced by both sides.

XXXV. On false pride. The upstart barley-mow is rebuked by the dunghill who was its midwife.

XXXVI. Against man's butchery of animals (humanitarianism). Man is made by nature to help animals, not tyrannize over them. On justice.

XXXVII. Against superstition.

XXXVIII. On gluttony. On having a mote in one's eye.

XXXIX. On the knowledge of real good and evil according to virtuous standards. Not the having of talents, but the right use of them is important. Seek virtue, and let God take care of the rest. The father's prayers exalt outer show over inner reality.

XL. On the relativity of decorum. Monkeys think men imitate them.

XLI. On false pride. The stupid owl condemns man for preferring the nightingale to him. Few follow wisdom; there are many fools.

XLII. The skilled Juggler is defeated in a contest of magic by Vice and her symbolic tricks. We all embrace evil under the disguise of good. List of eighteenth-century social types.

XLIII. On the council of horses (cf. Swift). All of us are assigned by God to our own place where we must be functional and cooperate. The determinism of *An Essay on Man.*

XLIV. On ignorance and vanity.

XLV. Only man strives to seem better than he really is in the chain of being.

XLVI. On prating people deserving their punishment. On curs and coxcombs.

XLVII. On choosing Death's minister. Intemperance wins be-

First Series (*Continued*)

cause as a trusted guest he opens the door of the body
to all other diseases.

XLVIII. On choosing friends carefully. Against brutality and
stupidity.

XLIX. On the innate vanity of all things. The relativity of
worth is shown by the pride of the flea who thinks
man was created for him to feed upon.

L. On false friendship.

SECOND SERIES

I. On justice and true honesty as opposed to the decep-
tion of words and the connivery of the legal profession. Our own actions fix the caricature of the beast
we are compared to. On conscience.

II. On the vices necessary for success in the town. On
justice in government. A eulogy on the peace of mind
to be found in the country.

III. On flattering rank, wealth, or power. On dignity being
due to the place, not to the characteristics of the individual. Against war and the military.

IV. On offending the powerful. On financial dishonesty
in government. A plea for the survival of justice and
good government in England to be gained by electing
honest men to office. Against bribery and graft.

V. On knowing one's self, i.e., knowing one's own limitations. On the vanity of ambition.

VI. On the ideal monarch.

VII. On knowing one's self. Happiness can only be found
in peace of mind derived through honesty, justice, and
virtue.

VIII. On the mutual independence of everyone from king to
clown. Each should observe his place in the chain of
being. On functionalism. A rare eulogy on British
commerce.

Second Series (*Continued*)

IX. On justice in government. On having friends only when one is affluent.

X. On integrity. A contrast of the life of nonfunctional luxury with that of the life of honest toil. Evil exposes itself, and nature will see that good triumphs.

XI. True nobility must prove itself anew in every generation by its actions.

XII. On gambling.

XIII. On the correct use of time.

XIV. On training each child according to his own talents, and not according to the preconceptions of his parents. Against false learning and for education based on common sense. On trained men in government.

XV. On being content with one's place in the chain of being.

XVI. Beauty and wealth must come eventually to dust, therefore, rely on reason, virtue, and health to gain content. The carrion of man and beast is the same; the distinction can only be made on a basis of the virtue in man's soul.

Notes

Introduction

1. *John Gay: Favorite of the Wits*. For any biographical information on the facts of Gay's life this work is invaluable. See also Irving's *John Gay's London* for a comprehensive view of the Augustan social scene.

2. Although Swift queried jokingly whether "the farmers [have] found out that you cannot distinguish rye from barley, or an oak from a crab tree?" in his letter to Gay on May 4, 1732 (Ball, *The Correspondence of Jonathan Swift, D.D.*, IV, 294), we know that it is not necessary to be a farmer or a botanist to appreciate fully country life and nature. The multitude of precise images and the minuteness of detailed descriptions culled from the country environment prove without doubt that Gay knew and loved this environment intimately. For further corroboration, see C. E. DeHaas, *Nature and the Country in English Poetry of the First Half of the Eighteenth Century* (Amsterdam, 1928), pp. 62–77.

3. In his PROEME to *The Shepherd's Week*, his preface to *The What D'Ye Call It*, certain prologues and epilogues, and in explicit statements within his poems and plays, Gay himself makes essentially the same subdivisions.

4. See Bond, *English Burlesque Poetry, 1700–1750*, pp. 3–18.

5. An article of Wallace C. Brown's on "Gay's Mastery of the Heroic Couplet," *PMLA*, LXI (1946), 114–125 has applied to Gay the methods of Tillotson's *On the Poetry of Pope*.

6. Faber, *The Poetical Works of John Gay*, p. 291, ll. 142–146. All future page and line references to Gay's works in this study pertain to Faber's Oxford edition.

7. *Favorite of the Wits*, p. 308.

8. Elwin and Courthope, *The Complete Works of Alexander Pope*, VII, 435–436.

9. Ball, *The Correspondence of Jonathan Swift*, IV, 285.

CHAPTER I: *Implications of an Age of Innocence*

1. See Empson, *English Pastoral Poetry*, pp. 203ff., where the country clown becomes the hero of proletarian literature because of his innate common sense, his contact with nature, and his courageous stoicism.

2. See Gay to Pope (September 7, 1732, in Elwin and Courthope, *The Complete Works of Alexander Pope*, VII, 450); and Pope and Arbuthnot to Swift (December 5, 1732, in Ball, *The Correspondence of Jonathan Swift, D.D.*, IV, 365–366). This illness, which caused his death, had been recurrent for some years.

3. As symbols of the entire urban milieu, the pirates in *Polly* measure success in terms of wealth, love in terms of satisfied lust, and honor in terms of an effective token word with which to deceive the honest people who fall prey to their treachery and hypocrisy.

4. A strange irony is that Gay, who seems to know a phantom when he sees others pursuing it, himself pursued various ones such as money the greater part of his own life—but, unlike those he satirizes, at least not with hypocrisy and deceit.

5. See pp. 12 and 13 in this book.

6. Durling, *Georgic Tradition*, pp. 6–7.

7. *Ibid.*, p. 8.

8. "Essay on the Georgics," I, 136–137.

9. Virgil, *Georgics II*, 458–462 (Fairclough translation, p. 148). Dryden translates the passage:

> O happy, if he knew his happy state,
> The swain, who, free from bus'ness and debate,
> Receives his easy food from Nature's hand,
> And just returns of cultivated land!
> No palace, with a lofty gate, he wants,
> T'admit the Tides of early visitants.

10. As has often been pointed out, most of the components of Wordsworth's nature poetry were already developed and waiting for the finishing touches of his genius and his application of the associational psychology of Locke and Hartley.

11. Richard Payne Knight, *An Analytical Inquiry into the Principles of Taste*, 2d ed. (London, 1805).

12. "Lectures on the English Humanists," Thackeray's *Works*, XI, 248–249.

13. See Gay's letter to Swift (August 8, 1732, in Ball, IV, 341), in which he mentions having "shot nineteen brace of partridges."

14. Another example of affinity may be found in "Wednesday," where Sparabella's mood of sadness at the loss of her lover is reinforced by the forlornness of the dusk (ll. 19–23).

15. Lest any misconception arise, we must state that it would be entirely unfair to Gay, the neoclassicist, to impose on him any theory of associative intuitionalism whereby these nuances of experience suggest the seeds of sublime truths in a Wordsworthian manner.

16. His *Collected Poems*, published in that year, enabled him to invest in the South Sea Company scheme, through which he hoped to gain independence.

17.   Oh, could I thus consume each tedious day,
         And in sweet slumbers dream my life away.
                  (*Panthea*, ll. 65–66)

References to escape in sleep or "pleasing dreams" (usually occurring in a rural atmosphere) are frequent throughout Gay's works; for example, see *Araminta*, ll. 3–4; *Rural Sports*, l. 61; *A Contemplation on Night* (1714 and 1729 versions, ll. 34ff.); *A Thought on Eternity*, ll. 28–30; and various passages in *Dione* and *The Captives*.

18. See Lovejoy, "The Parallel of Deism and Classicism," in *Essays in the History of Ideas*, p. 85.

19. An "internal proof of the divine original of the law of nature," wrote Gay's friend Bolingbroke, "is the plainness and simplicity which renders it intelligible in all times and places, and proportions it to the meanest understanding. It has been made intricate by casuistry, that of lawyers and divines. . . . [But]

these principles want neither paraphrase nor commentary to be sufficiently understood" (in his "Fragments or Minutes of Essays," viii, *Works* [Dublin, 1793], V, 103–104).

CHAPTER II: *The Beggar's Milieu:* THE BEGGAR'S OPERA

1. Empson, *English Pastoral Poetry*, p. 17. See particularly the introduction and the entire chapter cn *The Beggar's Opera*. See also Bertrand Bronson, "The Beggar's Opera," *Studies in the Comic (Univ. of California Publications in English, 1941)*, pp. 197–231.

2. Joseph Spence, *Anecdotes, Observations and Characters of Books and Men* (London, 1858), p. 162. More recent scholarship and a closer examination of the biographical material on Gay seems to indicate that apart from his South Sea gamble, he was a good manager of his own and others' financial affairs. Spence is not always wholly reliable and when he is authentic we have no way of knowing how sincere or serious the person being quoted was at the time he spoke. The Duke of Queensberry thought enough of Gay's business ability to allow him to transact various financial dealings for him: Gay to Swift (March 31, 1730) in Ball, *The Correspondence of Jonathan Swift, D.D.*, IV, 138; Swift to Gay (March 13, 1731), in Ball, IV, 202; and Gay to Swift (July 18, 1731), Ball, IV, 240. Swift also had Gay act as his agent in London in the transaction of certain business matters: Gay to Swift (March 13, 1731–32), in Ball, IV, 285; and Gay to Swift (May 16, 1732), in Ball, IV, 301–302.

3. Gay's sisters received about £6000 at the settling of his estate.

4. The attack on money, because of its misuse by the Walpole group, was also a favorite topic of the Opposition Party writers; and, of course, the conflict between the desire for riches and the practice of virtue has always been a time-honored satiric theme.

5. See Shaftesbury's *Characteristics;* Steele's *Christian Hero, The Spectator;* and various clerical tracts of the period.

6. Gay is usually in full accord with the dictum presented by Pope in his *Moral Essay*, Epistle I, 149–150, that " 'Tis Education

forms the common mind,/Just as the Twig is bent, the Tree's inclined."

7. For stoic elements in Gay, see *Polly,* the second series of *Fables,* and the character of Sophernes in Gay's only tragedy, *The Captives.*

8. See Fables I: xlv, and I: xlix, for two of many explicit references.

9. Swift describes *The Beggar's Opera* as "a very severe satire upon the most pernicious villainies of mankind," despite its strong admixture of raillery; Swift to Charles Wogan (August 2, 1732), Ball, IV, 330.

10. Bredvold, "The Gloom of the Tory Satirists," in Clifford and Landa, eds., *Pope and His Contemporaries,* p. 19. Professor Bredvold finds this spirit entirely applicable to "the pastorals, fables, and ballad operas of Gay." See also Gay's Fable II: ix, as an example of this gloom veering toward a Hobbesian tone.

11. Similar ideas may be found in Pope's two *Moral Essays* on "Riches"; in Goldsmith's *Citizen of the World,* "Letters XI and LXXII," as well as in his *Tale* of *Asem;* and in the writings of Swift.

12. Macheath, as hero, also has a courageous concept of honor and he is willing to die stoically like Hotspur; "For death is a debt,/A debt on demand.—So take what I owe," (III, xi, Air LVII).

13. Compare Gay's presentation of the Ducats in Act I of *Polly* for further evidence of this attitude in the middle class.

14. Peachum amplifies these feelings at any opportunity throughout the play. In I, ix, p. 497, he says "The Lawyers are bitter enemies to those in our way. They don't care that any body should get a clandestine livelihood but themselves"; and in II, x, p. 511, he admits that "like great Statesmen, we encourage those who betray their friends."

15. Mr. Thrasher of Fielding's *Amelia* is a good example; he is described thus; . . . "the justice was never indifferent in a cause but when he could get nothing on either side."

CHAPTER III: *The Beggar's Milieu:* TRIVIA

1. James Heywood in his *Poems and Letters on several subjects* (1724), p. 17, eulogizes *Trivia* from this point of view; "thy useful Hints direct the rural 'Squire."

2. In Book I of *Trivia*, the list of necessary preparations, with an account of the most suitable shoes, coats, and canes for walking the streets, is matched in Book I of the *Georgics* by Virgil's description of the husbandman's preparations for planting and a list of the implements of his trade—the plough, the share, the mattock, the sledge, and the hammer. Gay's amplification of Swift's *Description of a City Shower* into the "Signs of Rainy Weather" is duplicated from Virgil's passage on the changes in the position of the moon or the shifts in the wind to mark out the approach of the rainy season (ll. 349–392). The perils of Parisian, Neapolitan, and Roman streets or the dangers of Venetian lagoons are to be contrasted with Virgil's fancied exotic excursions into China, India, or Ethiopia. Gay's counsel against superstition is a direct reflection of Virgil's list of omens in Rome at Caesar's decease—the filthy dogs and the ominous birds, the eruption of Etna, and the earthquakes in the Alps, the ghosts in the groves, and the speaking beasts. See also Durling, *Georgic Tradition*, pp. 40–41.

3. See *Trivia*, Book I, 189–202, for a comparison of the merits of functional and fashionable clothing.

4. See also "Tuesday," ll. 51–62.

5. Of course, *The Mohocks* is a farce and the brutal jokes perpetrated in the play are undoubtedly exaggerated. Actually, if Mohocks ever were a part of the Augustan scene, their bias was political; they were probably young Whigs given to baiting unfortunate Tories. Nevertheless, a basis for such specifically detailed incidents must have existed.

6. See Chapter VI, pp. 178–180.

7. It is possible that the rational theism of Gay might allow for connotations of an actual Scriptural heaven and hell; but if they

exist, the Augustan Gay feels that he should not state such views explicitly.

8. It is also expressed in Gay's *Epitaph*, in Fables II: xiii and xvi, and in *A Thought on Eternity*.

9. Unfortunately, because our records of Gay are so few, we do not have as much evidence of instances of practical benevolence on his part, as we do of his friends Pope, Swift, and Arbuthnot. However, all of these friends acknowledge Gay to be one of the kindest men they ever knew. It would seem logical to infer that men of such a reputation for honesty and benevolence would not bestow such an encomium lightly.

CHAPTER IV: *Wealth and Universal Darkness*

1. See M. Dacier, "An Essay upon Satyr," V, xii; and Dryden, "A Discourse Concerning the Original and Progress of Satire," II, 44–67.

2. Dacier, "Essay upon Satyr," xv.

3. See Mary Claire Randolph, "The Structural Design of the Formal Verse Satire," *PQ*, XXI (1942), 368–384.

4. Dacier, "Essay upon Satyr," xiv.

5. The lowest type would be represented by such amusing little verse notes as Gay's *A Receipt for Stewing Veal*, or Prior's *On a Fart, let in the House of Commons*.

6. Probably a barb directed against Dr. Woodward, the butt of so many witticisms of the Scriblerus Club.

7. Such a delightful passage also brings to mind echoes of Catullus as he was imitated by Jonson and Herrick as well as the delicacy of the Elizabethan lyric. Gay may well be termed the most "Elizabethan" of Augustan poets with regard to the lyric quality of certain of his lines.

8. Austin Dobson, *Miscellanies*, First Series (New York, 1898), p. 241.

9. See Caroline M. Goad, *Horace in the English Literature of the Eighteenth Century* (New Haven, 1918), pp. 11 and 380–387.

10. Pope translates this passage in his *Paraphrase* thus:

> Who thinks that Fortune cannot change her mind,
> Prepares a dreadful Jest for all mankind!
> And who stands safest, tell me? is it he
> That spreads and swells in puff'd prosperity,
> Or blest with little, whose preventing care
> In Peace provides fit arms against a War? (ll. 123–128)

See "Imitations of Horace," in John Butt, ed., *The Poems of Alexander Pope* (London, 1939), IV, 62–65.

11. See D. W. Roberts, *An Outline of the Economic History of England* (London, 1931), p. 142.

12. Gilbert Slater, *The Growth of Modern England* (Boston, 1933), p. 74.

13. A list of some of these "bubbles" may be found in Cobbett's *Parliamentary History of England* (London, 1806–20), VII, 656f.

14. See Irving, *Favorite of the Wits*, pp. 186–187.

15. A popular broadside ballad of the time jeered at the nobility, gentry, and others who had been victimized by crooked bankers like Mr. Snow:

> Five hundred millions, notes and bonds,
>   Our Stocks are worth in value;
> But neither lie in goods or lands,
>   Or money let me tell ye.
> Yet though our foreign trade is lost,
>   Of mighty wealth we vapour;
> When all the riches that we boast,
>   Consist in scraps of Paper.

16. Some of the papers on this topic (probably by Swift) in *The Examiner* may have influenced Gay.

17. The following lines (22–25) in this *Epistle* refer to Thomas, Earl of Coningsby (1656?–1729), who had many legal difficulties over his two manors of Leominster and Marden and probably attacked Lowndes for his support of the Land-Tax Bill. He was a rabid Whig whom Pope and Gay disliked because of his quarrels with their friend Harley.

18. Ball, *The Correspondence of Jonathan Swift, D.D.*, IV, 275.

19. *Ibid.*, 138.

20. Elwin and Courthope, *The Complete Works of Alexander Pope*, VII, 450, dated October 7, 1732. Pope had suggested (*Ibid.*, VII, 448–449) that Gay try to get back into court favor.

21. See also Fable II: iv, on the problems of patronage; and Fable II: ii, 37–38, which echoes the satiric line about virtue always being its own and only reward.

22. William Kent (1684–1748) was a painter, sculptor, architect, and landscape gardener. He and Burlington promoted the architectural style of Palladio and Inigo Jones. After his second visit to Rome in 1719, he acquired a reputation for skill in landscape gardening. Kent followed the principles laid down by Pope in his *Moral Essay*, Epistle IV, standards employed by Pope himself in the construction of Twickenham. He also designed some illustrations (all of which were poor), for Gay's *Fables*.

23. For an extended discussion of the problem of various artistic fashions and their merits in this period, see B. Sprague Allen, *Tides in English Taste* (Cambridge, Mass., 1937), Vol. II.

24. Examples are the colonnade of Burlington House by Burlington and Holkham Castle by Kent. Further examples of the designs of Kent and his patron may be found in the articles on these two men in the *Dictionary of National Biography* (Kent, XXXI, 25; Burlington under Boyle, VI, 118). See also Margaret Jourdain, *The Work of William Kent* (London, *Country Life*, 1948).

25. Cf. Pope's *Moral Essay*, Epistle IV, "To Burlington on the Use of Riches," especially lines 23–24, 65–69, 191–194.

26. The same phrase is used in *Trivia*, II, 498, to describe his reaction to the music of Handel. Anastatia is Anastatia Robinson, a friend of Pope and Gay, secretly married to the Earl of Peterborough.

27. Pope's *Moral Essay*, Epistle IV also emphasizes the functionalism of Burlington's architectural principles:

> Who then shall grace, or who improve the Soil?
> Who plants like BATHURST, or who builds like BOYLE.
> 'Tis Use alone that sanctifies Expense,
> And Splendour borrows all her rays from Sense.
>
> (ll. 177–180)

Contemporaries, such as Hogarth and Lord Hervey, however, accused Burlington of sacrificing the useful for the ornamental (*DNB*, VI, 117).

28. For Pope's attitude toward "Timon's Villa," see George Sherburn, "Timon's Villa and Cannons," *Huntington Library Bulletin*, No. 8 (1935), 131–152. In *Moral Essay*, Epistle IV, ll. 167–172, Pope shows that the "charitable Vanity" of a "hard Heart" (a heart unlike that of Pope's and Gay's friend Chandos) can contribute to the alleviation of poverty; see Chapter III.

29. It is interesting to note that Gay (whose four accepted classical masters are Homer, Virgil, Horace, and Ovid), in his *Epistle to Lintott*, considers the following authors also worthy of praise: Buckingham, Waller, Granville, Addison, and Garth. These poets were also eulogized by Pope in his early works.

30. Expressed chiefly in *The Sacred Theory of the Earth* (1684–90).

31. However, other deists did believe in the flood as a result of the geological discoveries of fossils in high spots in England at this time.

32. E. L. Tuveson, "Swift and the World-Makers," *JHI*, XI (1950), 54–74. See also R. F. Jones, "Background of the *Battle of the Books*," Washington University Studies, Humanistic Series II, VII.

CHAPTER V: *The Beggar's View of Augustan Courtly Love*

1. Quoted in note 1, pp. lxviii–lxix, of the introduction to his edition on Gay's poems. The anonymous poet goes on to name Gay's famous partisans: the Duchess of Marlborough, the banished Duchess of Queensberry, the Duchess of Bedford, and Lady Essex. In addition, the powerful Mrs. Howard, who was not mentioned in this poem, must certainly not be overlooked.

2. In Gregory G. Smith, ed., *The Spectator by Joseph Addison, Richard Steele, and Others*, I, 275–279.

3. In George Nettleton and Arthur E. Case, eds., *British*

Dramatists from Dryden to Sheridan (Boston, 1939), p. 151. The deviations from this norm, by age, class, wit, or beauty are the common topics satirized in the comic roles of Restoration comedy by dramatists who, unlike Wycherley, were the upholders of the decorum of the courtly love game.

4. To be black-listed by Peachum or Lockit was tantamount to an actual sentence of death, because their protection against the law was necessary for survival in this society.

5. Gay wrote in his dedicatory letter to Princess Caroline that its chief aim was to show virtue rewarded and distress relieved (Faber, p. 434). The conventional themes of love and war are expressed in a prosy blank verse, not in the usual couplets of Dryden's heroic dramas. Gay's tragedy, however, has its full share of the bombast characteristic of the earliest heroic plays.

6. Dr. John Harrington Smith's definition of exemplary comedy, in *The Gay Couple in Restoration Comedy* (Cambridge, Mass., 1948), p. 261, is fully as applicable to this type of late heroic drama. The definition is derived from two principles implicit in Jeremy Collier's criticism of the stage: ". . . that the code of human behavior expressed in comedy (or tragedy) ought to be better than the code in effect in life; and that comedy should devote itself to recommending these higher ideals by framing characters who should exemplify them and by punishing or chastening their opposites."

7. It is perhaps pertinent to note that there are certain signs of influence of Shakespeare upon Gay. He uses Shakespearean epithets in his descriptions; he often refers to Shakespearean characters; he employs dramatic situations which seem to be derived from Shakespearean drama; and, of course, his love for the country is similar to that of the rural Shakespeare of *As You Like It*. Undoubtedly his knowledge and appreciation were augmented by helping Pope in his editing of Shakespeare's plays.

8. Cf. Laetitia Snap in Fielding's *Jonathan Wild*.

9. Polly says of him: "The Coquets of both sexes are self-lovers, and that is a love no other whatever can dispossess" (p. 525).

10. This farce was produced in 1733, one year after Gay died.

According to Faber (p. 594), there were no really extensive revisions in the text after the author's death.

11. An example of this logic occurs in I, ix, when Ducat muses, "Family divisions, and matrimonial controversies are a kind of poor man's riches. The whole mode of keeping mistresses and maintaining separate households for estranged wives is held up to scorn in the conclusion of Ducat's soliloquy: "For the poor people [such as the contented and useful parents in *Rural Sports*, for example] are happy out of necessity, because they cannot afford to disagree."

12. Swift to Gay (June 29, 1731), Ball, *The Correspondence of Jonathan Swift, D.D.*, IV, 233–234.

13. Fable II: xvi, would seem to indicate that the Duchess was Gay's Laura, the lady of his few poetic eulogies, primarily because Gay in his tributes to Laura praises her moral virtues and reasoning ability, as well as her beauty—virtues which he has ascribed to the Duchess. See also George Sherburn, "The Duchess Replies to the King," *Harvard Library Bulletin*, VI (1952), 118–121.

14. In the British Museum (Add. MS. 4806).

15. In one of these joint letters (August 20, 1730, Melville, p. 120) to Mrs. Howard, Gay writes, "Now she says I must write you a long letter; but to be sure I cannot say what I would about her, because she is looking over me as I write. If I should tell any good of her, I know she would not like it, and I have said my worst of her already."

16. Mrs. Howard wrote of Gay two years after his death in a similar manner: ". . . it is a sort of pleasure to think over his good qualities: his loss was really great, but it is a satisfaction to have once known so good a man." (Quoted in Irving, *Favorite of the Wits*, p. 297.)

CHAPTER VI: *Lobbin Rapin*

1. Dr. R. T. Kerlin in his book *Theocritus in English Literature* (Lynchburg, Va., 1910), asserts that "Gay undoubtedly

knew Theocritus, but probably for the most part in translation"
(p. 58). Dr. Kerlin cites certain direct borrowings of Gay from
various Theocritan *Idyls* in *The Shepherd's Week, Dione,* and
Acis and Galatea. He notes also that the general influence of
Theocritus's *Fifteenth Idyl* is apparent in most of the town
eclogues of the period (pp. 58–60). Gay claims Theocritus as
his model in the PROEME to *The Shepherd's Week,* and he points
out some of his Theocritan "imitations" in his burlesque glosses
to the various poems. Goldsmith once said Gay resembled Theocritus more than any other English writer (*The Beauties of
English Poetry,* I, 133).

2. Gay follows the structure of the Virgilian eclogue very
closely at times, and there are many direct imitations of Virgilian
lines indicated by Gay himself in his glosses to *The Shepherd's
Week.* For a discussion of Gay's use of Virgil, see R. F. Jones,
"Eclogue Types in English Poetry of the Eighteenth Century,"
JEGP, XXIV (1925), 49, and note 23. Professor Jones maintains
that "the strictness with which the poems adhere to the Virgilian
type without any apparent artificiality makes them one of the
most successful attempts at putting new wine into old bottles
offered by the eighteenth century."

3. Greg, *Pastoral Poetry and Pastoral Drama,* p. 7.

4. Rapin, *Discourse,* pp. 24–25.

5. *Ibid.,* p. 25.

6. Pope adopts similar principles in his *Discourse on Pastoral
Poetry* (Sherburn, *Best of Pope,* p. 4).

7. Rapin, *Discourse,* p. 67.

8. *Ibid.,* p. 47.

9. Fontenelle's *Discourse on Pastorals,* a rationalist critique,
substantiates most of the tenets of the neoclassicist Rapin, emphasizing the carefulness which the writer of pastoral must exercise in pursuing a middle pathway between a too clownish and
a too elegant treatment of his theme. Such a course disallows
any realism in the poet's description of rural affairs; and when
Fontenelle also specified that the pastoral should really be an
imitation of an ancient shepherd's life, since the life of the modern
shepherd was too coarse and vulgar, he very effectively removed

any possible elements of emotional vitality from the eclogue. See Bernard le Bovier Fontenelle, *Poésies Pastorales, avec un traité sur la nature de l'églogue et une digression sur les anciens et les modernes* (Londres, 1707).

10. See Dryden, *Works of Virgil Translated*, Vol. I.

11. Jones, "Eclogue Types," p. 38.

12. Sherburn, *The Best of Pope*, pp. 4–5.

13. See Hoyt Trowbridge, "Pope, Gay, and *The Shepherd's Week*," *MLQ* (1944), 79–88. For Philips's views, see his "Preface to [his] Pastorals" in Anderson, ed., *British Poets* (1795), Vol. IX.

14. Sherburn, *Best of Pope*, pp. 6–7.

15. *Letters to a Young Lady on a Course of English Poetry* (quoted in Bond, *English Burlesque Poetry*, p. 114).

16. *Discourse*, p. 67.

17. It is interesting to note that these passages of titillation were not printed with (or added to?) the poem until 1720 after Gay had lived in the town for more than a decade.

18. See also the use of aphrodisiacs in "Thursday" (ll. 124–128), and in *An Epistle to a Young Lady, with some Lampreys*.

19. See chapters iii and vii of C. S. Lewis, *The Allegory of Love* (Oxford, 1938).

20. Cf. Captain Booth's eulogy of rural marriage in Book III, Chapter xii of Fielding's *Amelia*.

21. Or merely to describe town life in the case of Lady Mary.

22. See also *The Mad-Dog* (Faber, pp. 125–127, ll. 62–144), a very amusing tale of a Prude whose flesh is being constantly subdued despite her supposed opposition.

23. The contrast of ll. 71–72 and 79–80 with ll. 103–110 indicates that fear of social disapproval rather than any real moral devotion has prompted Sabina to don her widow's weeds.

24. The fact that Cloacina is a goddess enables her to make restitution for her abandonment of her son to an extent that would be impossible for a Moll Flanders.

25. Cf. *Joseph Andrews* and *Adam Bede*.

26. Cf. Pope's *Messiah, A Sacred Eclogue*.

27. Empson, *English Pastoral Poetry*, pp. 11–12.

28. *Ibid.*, p. 14.

CHAPTER VII: *Bob Booty and the Beast*

1. Professor Douglas Bush of Harvard University believes that the most likely nominees for these roles are Robert Cecil and his father, Lord Burleigh.

2. Robert Brice Harris, "The Beast in English Satire from Spenser to John Gay," Unpublished Ph.D. dissertation (Cambridge, Mass., 1930), p. 5.

3. "Preface" to his *Fables, Contes, et Nouvelles,* ed. by Edmond Pilon and René Groos, Pleiade edition (Paris, 1932). For translations of La Fontaine's *Fables,* see Elizur Wright, *Fables of La Fontaine,* 2 vols. (Boston, 1861). Reference should also be made to the excellent translations of Marianne Moore, whose capacity for realizing precise evocations of animal characteristics in poetry has seldom been equaled.

4. Max Plessow attempts to deduce specific sources in La Fontaine for many of Gay's *Fables,* but, although influences undoubtedly exist, it is more probable that La Fontaine and Gay share a common indebtedness to Aesop (*Geschichte der Fabeldichtung in England bis zu John Gay, 1726,* Berlin, 1906, pp. xciv–ciii). Gay was probably well aware of Sir Roger L'Estrange's *Fables of Aesop and Other Eminent Mythologists* (London, 1692), which had caused a fabling craze in London in the first quarter of the eighteenth century.

5. Wright, II, 201–204 (Book X, Fable vi).

6. Wright, II, 221–223 (Book X, Fable xiv); II, 158–159 (Book IX, Fable xii); and Faber, I: xlv; I: xlix; and II: xv.

7. Cf. works by Plessow, by Harris, and by Irving.

8. Plessow, *Geschichte der Fabeldichtung in England,* p. civ.

9. La Fontaine also employed this concept of the reasoning beast in his confutations of the "Bête machine" theory of Descartes.

10. See Arthur O. Lovejoy, " 'Pride' in Eighteenth-Century Thought," *MLN* (1921), 31–37.

11. May 16, 1732, Ball, *The Correspondence of Jonathan Swift, D.D.,* IV, 301.

12. Cf. Shakespeare, Spenser, and Jonson. Jonson and Gay possess many similarities; they were both neoclassical satirists devoted to the portrayal of "humours" or stock-type characters; their best work reflects a close knowledge of the city and its types, their worst, elements of the Arcadian pastoral; both distorted the traditional pastoral successfully by the inclusion of native English realism; both opposed the false worship of money and the misuse of wealth; each reflects the economic problems of his age; and finally, both employ beast satire to point out human vices.

13. David Worcester, *The Art of Satire* (Cambridge, Mass., 1940), p. 37.

14. Excerpts quoted from Bolingbroke, *Patriot King*, 111–204.

15. See Swift's defense of *The Beggar's Opera* and Gay in the *Intelligencer* (No. III) where he says this "is not the first of Mr. Gay's works, wherein he has been faulty with regard to courtiers and statesmen . . . he has been thought somewhat too bold upon the courtiers." See also, Swift's letter to Lady Elizabeth German (January 8, 1732–33, in Ball, IV, 373–377), for Swift's accusation that Walpole was directly responsible for Gay's failure to receive the patronage he deserved.

16. For the varying attitudes of the age toward Walpole, see Charles B. Realey, *The Early Opposition to Sir Robert Walpole, 1720–27* (Philadelphia, 1931).

17. As early as August 16, 1714, Gay refers to "Machiavelians" as the rulers of European politics (in a letter to Arbuthnot, Melville, p. 31). Other references to Machiavelli or the tactics advocated in *The Prince* with specific intent directed against Walpole, may be found in Fables I: i; I: iv; II: v; and in *The Beggar's Opera*.

18. Any reliable historical text will certainly give a much more accurate picture of Walpole than that drawn by Gay and his friends of the Opposition.

19. Dr. Harris notes pertinently (p. 315) that although the First Series of Gay's *Fables* were written expressly at the wish of Queen Caroline for Prince William, ". . . not once had Gay

paid a compliment to her, to her son, or to anyone connected with the court. On the contrary, he had ridiculed courts, censured ministers of state, and scorned the ways of preferment. Throughout the bitter days of disappointment, he retained his dignity and independence." The tone of these fables needs no other defense than Pope's comment, "one may write things to a child without being childish" (Pope to Swift, December 14, 1725, in Ball, III, 296).

20. Despite his love for sport, Gay recognizes that violence and butchery can lead only to the brutalizing of the human heart and mind.

21. See also Swift's "An Essay on Modern Education" in the *Intelligencer* (No. IX, 1728) for similar ideas voiced by Gay's friend and correspondent.

22. Pulteney (years after Gay's death) compromised his "patriotic" idealism by refusing to enter the ministry when Walpole fell and by accepting the title of Earl of Bath instead. See A. S. Turberville, *English Men and Manners in the Eighteenth Century* (Oxford, 1926), p. 220.

CHAPTER VIII: *The Double View*

1. See Chapter I for this usage in *Rural Sports* and *The Shepherd's Week;* variations on this relationship are reflected in *Trivia*, the city eclogues, and the airs of the operas as well as in the *Fables*. *Polly*, in fact, is a whole play on the man-beast problem.

2. Gay's theme is similar to that which King Lear expresses to Edgar: "Is man no more than this? Consider him well. Thou ow'st the worm no silk, the beast no hide, the sheep no wool, the cat no perfume. Ha! Here's three on's are sophisticated! Thou art the thing itself; unaccommodated man is no more but such a poor, bare, forked animal as thou art." Underneath the fop's and fine lady's fashionable clothes which keep them in vogue, or "sophisticated" is only a "poor, bare, forked animal."

3. See also Fables I: xv; and I: xvii.

4. Cf. Fables I: xxi; I: xxxv; and I: xli on this same theme where human pride is symbolized in the actions of beasts.

5. It must be remembered that to Gulliver the most horrible blow of all was the realization that the motives of these despicable Yahoos were just the same as those which governed the conduct of the "most civilized" men and nations.

6. Professor M. Ellwood Smith defines "A Fable [as] a short tale, obviously false, devised to impress by the symbolic representation of human types, lessons of expediency and morality." (*JEGP*, XIV [1915], 526).

7. This attitude is representative of an archetypal relationship. The habit among early civilizations of picturing beasts with human heads such as the winged bulls found at the palace of Ashurnasirpal II at Calah (885–860 B.C.) may be seen in the excavations on display at most art museums.

8. Gay sees both sides of the issue of superstition. See Fable I: xxxvii, for evidence of his rational eighteenth-century mind reacting against seventeenth-century fanaticism.

9. See Fables I: x; I: xv; I: xvii; I: xxi; I: xxx; I: xxxii; I: xxxvi; and I: xliii.

10. It is significant that this Fable is the last one he wrote. There would be grounds for regarding it as a summation of his thoughts on the reasons for man's existence.

11. See also Fable I: xl, about "The *two* Monkeys," which embodies the theme of relativity.

12. See also Appendix.

13. A book as judiciously and thoroughly written as the biography of Gay by Professor Irving deserves the highest praise for its definitive treatment of Gay's personality and reputation. One can also agree quite wholeheartedly with Professor Irving's final conclusions on Gay (*Favorite of the Wits*, pp. 313–316), but certain modifications must be made in the light of our thematic study.

14. *Ibid.*, p. 314.

15. *Ibid.*, p. 316.

Selected Bibliography

Works of John Gay

Volumes containing Gay's correspondence are entered in the second section of this Bibliography under the names of the editors. See Ball; Elwin and Courthope; Melville.

A collection of manuscripts, notebooks, and pamphlets collected and arranged by Ernest Lewis Gay is in the Harvard College Library.

Gay, John, The Poetical Works of John Gay; Including Polly, The Beggar's Opera; and Selections from the other Dramatic Work. Edited by Geoffrey Faber. Oxford edition. London, 1926. Unless otherwise specified, this is the edition referred to in all page and line references of the text and footnotes of this study.
—————— The Poetical Works of John Gay. Edited, with an introductory memoir, by John Underhill. 2 vols. London, 1893.
—————— Gay's Fables. Edited, with an original memoir, introduction, and annotations, by Octavius Freire Owen. London, 1854.
—————— Trivia. Edited, with introduction, by W. H. Williams. London, 1922.
—————— "The Present State of Wit." Critical Essays and Literary Fragments. Edited by John Churton Collins. Westminster, 1903.

Other Works

Ball, F. Elrington, ed., The Correspondence of Jonathan Swift, D.D. 6 vols. London, 1913.
Bate, Walter Jackson, From Classic to Romantic. Cambridge, Mass., 1946.
Bolingbroke, Henry St. John, Viscount, Letters on the Spirit of

Patriotism: On The Idea of a Patriot King. London, 1783.

Bond, Richmond P., English Burlesque Poetry, 1700–1750. Cambridge, Mass., 1932.

Bredvold, Louis I., "The Gloom of the Tory Satirists," in James L. Clifford and Louis A. Landa, eds., Pope and His Contemporaries; Essays Presented to George Sherburn. Oxford, 1949.

Cunningham, Peter, ed., The Works of Oliver Goldsmith. 10 vols. London, 1908.

Dacier, M., "An Essay upon Satyr," in Charles Gildon, ed., Miscellany Poems upon Several Occasions. London, 1692.

Durling, Dwight L., Georgic Tradition in English Poetry. New York, 1935.

Elwin, Whitwell, and William John Courthope, eds., The Complete Works of Alexander Pope. 10 vols. London, 1871–1889.

Empson, William, English Pastoral Poetry. New York, 1938.

Greg, Walter Wilson, Pastoral Poetry and Pastoral Drama. London, 1906.

Irving, William Henry, John Gay, Favorite of the Wits. Durham, N.C., 1940.

——— John Gay's London. Cambridge, Mass., 1928.

Johnson, Samuel, The Works of Samuel Johnson, LL.D. Oxford English Classics. 11 vols. London, 1825.

Lovejoy, Arthur O., Essays in the History of Ideas. Baltimore, 1948.

——— The Great Chain of Being. Cambridge, Mass., 1936.

Melville, Lewis [Lewis S. Benjamin], Life and Letters of John Gay. London, 1921.

Rapin, René, "Discourse of Pastorals," in The Idylliums of Theocritus with Rapin's Discourse of Pastorals Done Into English, translated by Thomas Creech. Oxford, 1684.

Sherburn, George, ed., The Best of Pope. New York, 1940.

——— The Early Career of Alexander Pope. Oxford, 1934.

Smith, Gregory G., ed., The Spectator by Joseph Addison, Richard Steele, and Others. 4 vols. London, 1907.

Sutherland, James, "John Gay," in James L. Clifford and Louis A. Landa, eds., Pope and His Contemporaries; Essays Presented to George Sherburn. Oxford, 1949.

Thackeray, William Makepeace, "Prior, Gay, and Pope," an essay in The English Humorists of the Eighteenth Century in the Works of William Makepeace Thackeray. The Centenary Biographical Edition. 26 vols. London, 1911.

Tillotson, Geoffrey, On the Poetry of Pope. Oxford, 1938.

Turberville, A. S., English Men and Manners in the Eighteenth Century. Oxford, 1926.

Virgil, [Works.] With an English Translation by H. Rushton Fairclough. New York, 1922. Vol. I. Loeb Classical Library, No. 63.

——— The Works of Virgil Translated into English Verse by John Dryden. With an introductory "Essay on the Georgics" by Joseph Addison. Edited by John Carey. 3 vols. London, 1819.

Willey, Basil. The Eighteenth Century Background. London, 1940.

Index

Gay, John *(Continued)*
39, 46, 54, 88, 89, 92, 93, 98, 133,
190, 205, 206, 207, 225, 241; debasement of, 137, 147-51, 169,
170, 176-80, 236; elements of
genuine, 133, 134, 139, 165-67,
182; humanitarianism, 35, 39, 53,
89, 92, 118, 182, 185, 190, 202,
203, 206, 215, 216, 223, 231, 251;
marriage, 129, 135-37, 139, 145-
46, 151, 165, 168, 170, 178, 229;
psychology of the feminine
mind, 128, 145-46, 166, 168, 169-
71; self love, 137, 138, 139, 140,
147; urban and rural relationships compared, 165-80
Religious and philosophical
views, 16-20, 52-55, 71, 208-15,
217-20; healthfulness, 9, 10, 29,
30, 41-42, 77, 85-86, 163, 182,
224, 233; man-beast relationship, 38-40, 209, 210, 212, 214,
215, 216, 217, 225, 228, 229, 230,
231, 233, 251, 252; neoclassical
humanism, 8-9, 20, 97, 98, 105,
126, 158, 182, 184, 185, 186, 187,
188, 190, 202, 203, 206, 208, 210,
217, 218, 219, 220, 223, 224, 225,
226, 227; primitivism, 2, 3, 9, 16,
17, 26, 31, 45, 46, 126, 136, 188,
208, 210, 211, 215, 220-24, 225,
226; religious position, 43-50,
94, 98, 223, 240-41; Stoicism, 12,
18, 20, 49, 54, 88, 182, 223, 236,
239; use of the great chain of
being, 54, 55, 57, 61, 63, 66, 67,
68 *(see also* Chain of being);
uses of reason, 29-30, 45, 53, 187,
188, 189, 200, 210, 211, 224, 229,
233, 252
Social views, 212; attributes of
the ideal ruler, 190-92, 198-207,
228, 232, 233; fashionable foibles
and vices, 2, 4, 5, 10, 11, 68, 69,
81, 100, 101, 103, 104, 105, 106,
107, 114-15, 124, 127, 130, 131,
132, 146, 147, 153, 167-71, 177,

190, 199, 209, 223, 229, 230, 240,
246, 251; functionalism, 10, 25,
27, 42, 56, 60, 81, 82, 83, 86, 94,
95, 103, 105, 163, 167, 179, 180,
186, 197, 224, 230, 232, 233, 240,
243; knowledge and love of
rural milieu, 9, 21, 26-27, 235;
knowledge of criminal practices, 69-71, 79, 83-85; ordering
and comparison of social classes,
57-62, 82, 131, 146-47, 150, 154,
171-76, 180, 181-82, 206, 239;
patronage, 4, 96, 110, 116, 118,
119, 120-23, 127, 195, 196, 243;
political beliefs, 190-207, 228,
229, 230, 232, 233; satire on the
professions, 62-69, 189, 232; social justice and injustice, 11-12,
51, 52, 55, 58, 61, 62, 64-67, 71,
73, 79-80, 89, 90, 91, 93, 94, 95,
150, 193, 194, 203, 205, 222, 223,
224, 227, 228, 229, 230, 231, 232,
245; town and country contrast,
2, 3, 4, 5, 6, 9, 10, 12, 15, 19, 27,
45, 46, 51, 55, 71, 75, 76-83, 85-
86, 89, 93, 95, 103, 104, 107, 155,
157, 162, 165, 166, 167, 169, 172,
173, 176, 179, 180, 182, 188, 189,
195, 197, 208, 212, 215, 216, 222,
226, 227, 228, 230, 232; urban
corruption, 2, 5, 9, 10, 11, 55, 69,
72, 75, 78, 81-85, 87-88, 96,
103, 107, 117, 125, 126, 135, 138,
140-42, 146-47, 150, 151, 169, 171,
173, 174, 177, 178, 179, 180, 182,
190, 193-95, 197, 200, 205, 208,
210, 211, 212, 216, 222, 223, 226,
228, 230, 232, 236
Works: *Achilles,* 4, 5, 142-46,
225; *Acis and Galatea,* 3, 124,
247; *Araminta,* 5, 237; *The Beggar's Opera,* 1, 4, 5, 21, 34, 51-71,
75, 83, 119, 124, 131, 132, 133,
142, 175, 176, 192, 211, 225, 238,
239, 250; *The Birth of the
Squire,* 4, 174-76; *The Captives,*
3, 52, 134-35, 237, 239; *A Con-*

Homer, 102, 111, 117, 244
Horace, 4, 9, 22, 23, 24, 73, 97, 98, 99, 101-3, 209, 213, 244; *Epistles,* 102; *Satires,* 73, 102, 103; Horatian satire, 73, 97, 114, 209
Howard, Mrs., 152, 244, 246

Intelligencer, The, 250, 251
Irony, 7, 8, 104, 105, 107, 110, 111, 116, 117, 118, 131, 141, 161, 162, 163, 169, 171, 179, 180, 192, 194, 209, 213, 226, 236
Irving, William Henry, 1, 11, 224, 225, 234, 235, 241, 242, 245, 246, 248, 249, 251, 252
Italian opera, 52

Jean de Meun, 165
John, St., The Gospel according to, 47-48
Johnson, Samuel, 48, 72, 73, 96, 110, 120, 183-84; *Life of Gay,* 183-84; *Rasselas,* 48
Jones, Inigo, 123, 243
Jones, R. F., 244, 247, 248
Jonson, Ben, 69, 84, 213, 241; *Bartholomew Fair,* 84; *Volpone,* 213; compared with Gay, 250
Jourdain, Margaret, 243
Juvenal, 7, 9, 97, 103; *Third Satire,* 73

Kent, William, 122-23, 243
Kerlin, R. T., 246, 247
King, William: *Art of Cookery,* 24
Knight, Richard Payne, 34, 237

La Fontaine, Jean de, 185-86, 188, 249
Landa, Louis A., 239
Land Tax Bill, 5
Langland, William, 184
Leibniz, Gottfried Wilhelm, 12
L'Estrange, Sir Roger, 249
Lewis, C. S., 248
Locke, John, 15, 39, 53, 187, 237
Longinus, 34

Lovejoy, Arthur O., 237, 249
Lowndes, William, 5, 7, 242
Lucilius, 97
Lucretius, 22, 157
Lydgate, John, 184

Machiavelli, Nicolo, 189, 193, 202, 250
Mandeville, Bernard, 53, 188, 217
Mantuan, 4, 155, 158, 162, 185, 228
Marie de France, 129
Marlborough, Duchess of, 244
Marlborough, Duke of, 203
Melville, Lewis [Lewis S. Benjamin], 246, 250
Methuen, Sir Paul, 5, 120, 127
Milton, John, 4, 6, 28, 29, 31, 38, 162, 228; *L'Allegro,* 28, 162; *Paradise Lost,* 38
Misuse of money, 55-56, 60, 62, 69, 87, 91, 94, 95, 96, 102, 103, 107-14, 117, 122, 127, 138, 146-47, 148, 175, 177, 178, 179, 190, 195, 196, 197, 200, 205, 219, 222, 223, 229, 230, 232, 233, 236, 238
Mock-heroic poetry, 118
Montagu, Lady Mary Wortley, 152, 169
Moore, Marianne, 249

Neoclassical imitation, 24, 73, 95
Nettleton, George, 244
Newcastle, Duke of, 200
Newgate, 71
Newton, Sir Isaac, 43, 44

Oglethorpe, James Edward, 89
Oldham, John, 73
Opposition Party, 116, 189, 190, 192, 194, 196, 199, 200, 201, 204, 205, 238, 250
Otway, Thomas: *Venice Preserved,* 87
Ovid, 22, 102, 215, 244; *Metamorphoses,* 215
Oxford, Robert Harley, Earl of, 242

7